THE LEGEND OF

NOBLE

DRILLING

THE LEGEND OF

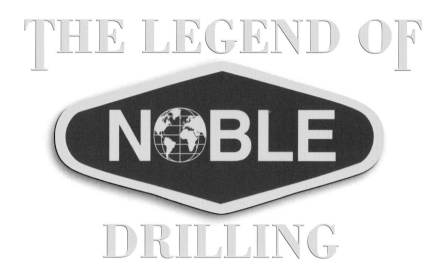

DRILLING

JEFFREY L. RODENGEN

Edited by Melody Maysonet
Design and layout by Dennis Shockley and Wendy Iverson

In loving memory of Peter Henkel,
whose talent was as boundless as his
passion for life

Write Stuff Enterprises, Inc.
1001 South Andrews Avenue, Second Floor
Fort Lauderdale, FL 33316
1-800-900-Book (1-800-900-2665)
(954) 462-6657
www.writestuffbooks.com

Publisher's Cataloging in Publication

Rodengen, Jeffrey L.
    The legend of Noble Drilling / Jeffrey L.
Rodengen. – 1st ed.
    p. cm.
    Includes bibliographical references and index.
    ISBN 0-945903-71-5

    1. Noble Drilling Corporation – History.
2. Petroleum industry and trade – United States –
History. 3. Oil well drilling – United States – History.
4. Offshore oil industry – United States – History.
I. Title.

HE9569.N63R63 2001   338.7'6223382
                         QBI00-701236

Library of Congress
Catalog Card Number 00-132158

ISBN 0-945903-71-5

Completely produced in the
United States of America
10 9 8 7 6 5 4 3 2 1

Also by Jeff Rodengen

The Legend of Chris-Craft

IRON FIST: The Lives of Carl Kiekhaefer

Evinrude-Johnson and The Legend of OMC

Serving the Silent Service: The Legend of Electric Boat

The Legend of Dr Pepper/Seven-Up

The Legend of Honeywell

The Legend of Briggs & Stratton

The Legend of Ingersoll-Rand

The Legend of Stanley: 150 Years of The Stanley Works

The MicroAge Way

The Legend of Halliburton

The Legend of York International

The Legend of Nucor Corporation

The Legend of Goodyear: The First 100 Years

The Legend of AMP

The Legend of Cessna

The Legend of VF Corporation

The Spirit of AMD

The Legend of Rowan

New Horizons: The Story of Ashland Inc.

The History of American Standard

The Legend of Mercury Marine

The Legend of Federal-Mogul

Against the Odds: Inter-Tel—The First 30 Years

The Legend of Pfizer

State of the Heart: The Practical Guide to Your Heart and Heart Surgery with Larry W. Stephenson, M.D.

The Legend of Worthington Industries

The Legend of Trinity Industries, Inc.

The Legend of IBP, Inc.

The Legend of Cornelius Vanderbilt Whitney

The Legend of Amdahl

The Legend of Litton Industries

The Legend of Gulfstream

The Legend of Bertram with David A. Patten

The Legend of Ritchie Bros. Auctioneers

The Legend of ALLTEL with David A. Patten

The Legend of Invacare Corporation with Anthony L. Wall

The Ship in the Balloon: The Story of Boston Scientific and the Development of Less-Invasive Medicine

The Legend of Day & Zimmermann

TABLE OF CONTENTS

INTRODUCTION

THE OIL DRILLING BUSINESS HAS always been uniquely focused on the future. In its infancy, the lure of instant riches and the romanticism of the hunt drew thousands of young men to the dusty plains of Oklahoma and Texas to drill for elusive crude. Always, they were thinking about and planning for the future, hoping to bring in the next big strike.

Noble Drilling, founded by Lloyd Noble and Art Olson in 1921, was created in the midst of these exciting times. Yet, run by Noble, a naturally careful man who made careful long-term decisions, Noble Drilling didn't get swept away by the vicissitudes of its industry.

While exploration companies came and went and instant millionaires squandered their wealth on far-fetched schemes, Noble Drilling quietly and patiently developed its expertise in the hard science of drilling. From its earliest days, Noble Drilling set records for the fastest and deepest holes in its industry.

Much has changed since those early days, yet most of the important things have remained the same. In 1985, Noble Drilling, which was then part of Noble Affiliates, was spun off as a stand-alone company and its stock listed on the Nasdaq exchange.

In conjunction with this move toward independence, another careful man, CEO Jim Day, was entrusted with leadership of the company. Like the company's founders, Day made long-term decisions and announced the company's commitment to flourish. But instead of plying the fields, tundras, and deserts of the globe, Noble Drilling evolved into one of the world's premier offshore drilling companies.

The story of this evolution is one of perseverance in a highly cyclical industry. Even with today's advanced exploration technology and harsh-environment rigs that can survive the worst pounding the North Sea has to offer, the oil industry remains a cyclical business. When the price of oil is high, exploration and drilling activity boom, with companies betting that the good times will last. Inevitably, though, the boom gives way to a market glut, and a suddenly overbuilt industry finds itself losing money.

Noble Drilling has not been immune to this boom-and-bust cycle, but it has ridden it out with expertise, loyalty, and plain old common sense. When the industry was strong in 1996, Day made the decision to sell off the last of Noble's land-based rigs. Noble secured a good price for this asset base and was able to use the capital to further its expertise in offshore drilling. Much of this was done through intelligent acquisitions—buying rigs at good prices.

Yet not all of Noble's growth was through acquisition. From the company's earliest days, innovation has been a hallmark of Noble's success. In the 1990s, as oil companies ventured into ever deeper water, there was growing demand for rigs that could drill at extreme depths. Yet deepwater rigs were among the most expensive to build, and the industry needed to consolidate, not build more rigs.

It didn't take long, however, for Noble Drilling to rise to the challenge. Day charged a group of engineers with developing a conversion protocol for existing Noble rigs. He wanted to take current assets and upgrade them to drill in depths of 5,000 or 6,000 feet. Thus was the EVA-4000™ design born.

EVA-4000™ rigs represented a risk, and many in the industry "thought Noble was crazy," according to one company vice president. But this skepticism didn't last. Before long, Noble proved that its EVA-4000™ rigs could drill in depths of up to 8,900 feet. Better yet, the conversion process costs less than half the price of a newbuild and takes less than half the time to complete.

Today, with sales just under $1 billion, Noble Drilling has emerged as one of the world's premier offshore drilling companies. Its fleet of 49 rigs is capable of drilling in water depths ranging from less than 100 feet to almost 10,000 feet. Equally important, Noble has won numerous awards for its commitment to environmental protection and safety. This, coupled with the company's intense devotion to its workers, has earned Noble Drilling decades of loyalty from its dedicated employees.

Operating in a business obsessed with the short-term future, Noble Drilling has built its success on a solid foundation of carefully considered investments, loyalty, and the wisdom gained over more than 80 years of experience.

ACKNOWLEDGMENTS

A GREAT NUMBER OF people assisted in the research, preparation, and publication of *The Legend of Noble Drilling.*

The initial research was conducted by Gary Clouser and Joan Thompson.

Special thanks are due to CEO Jim Day for the generous donation of his time and invaluable insight. Robert Campbell, president, also provided keen observations about Noble's operating culture and recent history.

Julie Robertson, senior vice president for administration and corporate secretary, was a tireless supporter whose depth of knowledge about Noble Drilling was a great asset. Similarly, Regina Allen, administrative assistant to Mr. Day, was an important element in the project's successful completion.

Many Noble Drilling executives, employees, retirees, and extended family greatly enriched the book by discussing their experiences at the company. The author extends particular gratitude to these men and women for their candid recollections and anecdotes: Danny Adkins, senior vice president of operations; Dave Beard, vice president of engineering; Lynda Bossler, retired manager of payroll; Mark Burns, district manager, United Kingdom and Norway; Michael Cadigan, manager of health, safety, environment, and quality; Michael Cawley, board member and president of the Samuel Roberts Noble Foundation; Charlie Copeland, retired vice president of administration and corporate secretary; Jay Courage, investment banker with Jeffries & Company; Hans Deul, director of deepwater drilling systems; Lewis Dugger, retired safety director of the Gulf Coast division; Alan Hay, contracts manager; William C. "Kurt" Hoffman, vice president of Western Hemisphere operations; Ed Holt, retired senior manager and former board member (deceased); Ronald Hoope, manager, commercial affairs for the Eastern Hemisphere; Bill Jennings, retired vice president of Western Hemisphere operations; Roger Lewis, manager, special projects; Steven Manz, vice president, strategic planning; Jon Murphy, manager/domestic marketing, Gulf of Mexico; Tom O'Rourke, director of administration; Larry Perras, general manager, Nigerian operations; Jitendra Prasad, vice president, technical; Jimmy Puckett, manager, Gulf Coast Marine division; Roy Rhodes, vice president of organizational development; Larry Richardson, manager, turnkey contracts; Bill Rose, vice president of Eastern Hemisphere operations; Eugene Rosser, retired district drilling superintendent and veteran of the Sherwood Forest project (deceased); John Rynd, vice president, investor relations; George Sauvageau, retired drilling superintendent; Leo Segerius, vice president, business development, Noble Brazil; Matt Simmons, CEO, Simmons & Company; John Snodgrass, director emeritus, Noble Drilling; Nick Swyka, vice chairman, Simmons & Company; Chuck Syring, retired Rocky Mountain division manager; Cees van Diemen, district manager, Netherlands-Denmark; and Bernie Wolford, division manager, Brazil.

As always, special thanks are extended to the dedicated staff at Write Stuff Enterprises. Proofreader Bonnie Freeman and transcriptionist Mary Aaron worked quickly and efficiently. Indexer Erica Orloff assembled the comprehensive index. Thanks are also extended to executive author Richard Hubbard and former executive authors David Patten and Anthony Wall for their assistance in compiling the oral history. Particular gratitude is also due to Melody Maysonet, senior associate editor; Jon VanZile, executive editor; Heather G. Cohn and Marie Etzler, former associate editors; Heather Deeley, associate editor; Sandy Cruz, senior art director; Rachelle Donley, Wendy Iverson, and Dennis Shockley, art directors; Bruce Borich, production manager; Gary Pulliam, former production manager; Grace Kurotori, sales and promotions manager; Sheryl Herdsman, director of marketing; Marianne Roberts, vice president of administration; Monica Kjeldgaard, executive assistant to the author; Amanda Fowler and Nancy Rackear, former executive assistants to the author; Nina Burrows, accounting assistant; Jennifer Walters, publisher's assistant; Rory Schmer, distribution supervisor; and Karine Rodengen, project coordinator.

The Noble Brothers Hardware store on East Main Street in Ardmore. Sam and Ed Noble were popular merchants in town.

CHAPTER ONE

PRAIRIE GOLD

THE BEGINNING–1929

*By 1921, the oil industry had struggled up through a trying infancy
and was flexing its adolescent muscles at the world. It was not a calling
for the faint of heart, but those willing to take a gamble found that the
excitement of the chase was unequaled. Drilling for oil was a roll of the
dice multiplied by infinity.*

—Imagination and Ability: The Life of Lloyd Noble

LOYD NOBLE WAS A BOOKISH AND reserved child. After he was grown and the oil-drilling company that bore his name had spread around the world, a friend remembered that he seemed to have been "born old."[1] Growing up, Lloyd kept best counsel with himself, rarely fraternizing with the other children and adolescents in his hometown of Ardmore, Oklahoma. Instead, he maintained a steady intellectual diet of books and probing questions. Yet sometime during these formative years on the dusty plains of Oklahoma, Lloyd Noble began the introspective process that would transform the intelligent and quiet young man into the founder of a global oil-drilling company.

Born in 1896 in Chickasaw Indian Territory three years after his family moved to Oklahoma, Lloyd Noble, it's almost safe to say, was destined to go into the oil industry. Although his father, Sam, and his Uncle Ed owned a hardware store, they lived in an era and a region at the epicenter of the exploding oil industry. To understand Lloyd Noble's place in the industry, it's important to understand the industry itself. In those days, oil exploration and drilling were still new, even to Texas. The first Texas wells had been opened in 1893 in Corsicana, where pioneers used a new drill called a rotary drill to remove about 2,300 barrels of oil per day.

With production like this, no one took the Texas oil business very seriously—at least not with wells in Pennsylvania and California producing tens of thousands of barrels every day, more than satisfying whatever demand for oil there was. But all that changed on New Year's Day 1901, when a wildcat drilling crew led by an Austrian named Anthony F. Lucas hit a gusher at a place called Spindletop. According to historians, a column of oil shot from the earth with a cannon-like roar and vaulted Spindletop and Texas into an oil craze that would last for decades. The first well, Lucas 1, produced at the then astonishing rate of 75,000 barrels per day.

With the gasoline-powered car beginning to catch on and the Standard Oil monopoly crumbling, the world had never been hungrier for oil, and there had never been greater opportunity for the independent oil producers and wildcatters who roamed the land. In a lot of ways, prospecting for oil was both better and crazier than prospecting for gold. A wildcat crew dragging its rig across the muddy plains could go from subsistence toolpushing to unbelievable wealth in a single explosive minute. Once a well had been found, a mad scramble for drilling rights ensued, with every kind of

A gusher in the Tonkawa field in Oklahoma. By 1906, Oklahoma was the top oil-producing state in the region. *(Photo courtesy Western History Collections, University of Oklahoma.)*

adventurer competing for the right to drill for the next big gusher. Leases could be secured for a couple thousand dollars, and if the field produced oil, the returns were astronomical.

This kind of wealth and instant opportunity cultivated its own vocabulary and popular image. At Spindletop, a lingo developed that would stick with the American oil industry into modern times. Helpers became known as "roughnecks" and well borers earned the name "drillers." The big strikes brought out hordes of treasure seekers vying for black gold. They were followed by merchants of every variety, some legitimate and some not, who erected hasty towns of clapboard and even cardboard to cater to the drillers' outsized appetites. In these early oil towns, killings and robbery were commonplace, and swindlers often made bigger fortunes than the men they preyed upon.

This wasn't the kind of atmosphere that a studious and bright young man like Lloyd Noble sought out. Rather it sought him out. From Spindletop, the oil industry began a steady northward and eastward march across Texas and into Oklahoma and Louisiana. Oil was found in Oklahoma in 1901. By 1906, it was the top-producing oil state in the region. In 1913, only five years after Oklahoma was granted statehood, oil was discovered in Carter County, where the Noble family lived. At the time, Lloyd Noble was 17 years old.

A Noble Beginning

By all accounts, Lloyd Noble had a good childhood. In his biography *Imagination and Ability: The Life of Lloyd Noble,* the authors remark that his home life was happy and satisfying. His father, Sam, and uncle, Ed Noble, although always on the ragged edge of financial ruin, had good reputations in Ardmore, where they were respected and well liked by the farmers they counted as customers. Sam and Ed had married sisters Hattie and Eva

Above: Lloyd Noble at one year of age. He was born in Chickasaw Indian Territory in 1896, shortly before Oklahoma's incorporation into the growing United States.

Right: The Noble family house at 621 B NW. Sam and Hattie Noble lived here with Lloyd, next door to Ed and Eva Noble. Although money was always tight, the families were known as good hosts and fair businesspeople.

Skinner. For a time, the families lived together in the same house, and the Nobles were remembered as gracious and unpretentious hosts who valued good company.

Although young Lloyd didn't befriend many children, he was well known among the town's adults. He learned early on that people will often answer direct questions, so he developed the habit of frequently quizzing people about their jobs. Besides developing a healthy respect for oral knowledge, he quickly learned that almost everybody had something to teach and something to offer. This lesson would serve him well after he went into business and employed a breed of men not known for their refinement and higher education, but whose commonsense approach to the hard work of oil drilling could make his company a success.

In 1913, the year oil was struck in Carter County, it's likely that Lloyd had only a passing interest in it. As the oil strike transformed his small town with paved streets and electricity, Lloyd prepared himself for an entirely different sort of profession. He dropped out of high school and decided to become a rancher on his family land. For the next year, he worked in near solitude, tending cattle and performing the all-consuming hard work of a cowboy. It turned out though that this life didn't suit Lloyd, and by 1914 he was enrolled in Southeastern Normal College in Durant, Oklahoma. Back home, oil money continued to flow into Ardmore, and new strikes were sought eagerly. The local Plains Development Company, which had opened the field in Healdton, Carter County, continued to prospect the land around Ardmore, and the rapidly growing city found itself with new hotels and storage yards.

During his first year of college, 1914–15, Lloyd Noble became a third-grade teacher at the Barrett Separate School. The following year, he taught at Cisco School, an eight-mile ride each way. Although these would be the only two years Noble spent as a teacher, his biographers wrote that he excelled at teaching.

Once again, however, the young man decided he had stepped down the wrong career path. In 1916, after wrapping up his year at Cisco, he enrolled at the University of Oklahoma and embarked on a course of general education classes designed to help him figure out what he wanted to choose as his career.

Things were happening at home, however, that would have a profound effect on Lloyd's life and his career. His father's health was deteriorating, and in the late summer of 1917, Lloyd made an important decision to drop out of school and stay home to care for his father. Sadly, Sam Noble died on November 2, 1917.

Oil derricks rise above the field at Healdton. As oil strikes crept nearer to the Noble family, a profound change came over the local economy. Oil strikes often brought instant riches and equally rapid bankruptcy for the hordes of speculators and wild roughnecks that roamed the prairies.

Sam Noble died in 1917 after fighting a protracted illness. Lloyd Noble had dropped out of school to stay home with his ailing father. After Sam's death, the family hardware store was sold and Lloyd enlisted in the U.S. Navy.

Oil Thirsty

After his father passed away, Noble Brothers Hardware was sold, meaning there was no family business for Lloyd to attend to, and he was once again free to do what he wanted. At that time, World War I still had Europe in its bloody grip and had finally provoked U.S. involvement. By the time Lloyd enlisted in the U.S. Navy as an ordinary seaman in the spring of 1918, the tide of the battle had shifted, and in November an armistice was signed. Lloyd Noble's enlistment was over less than six months after it had begun. Back home, the young man picked up where he had left off two years before and enrolled for the 1919 fall term at the University of Oklahoma.

By this time, the oil industry had already been transformed, mainly by the desperate need for oil during World War I, when mechanization and the internal combustion engine made their debuts to stunning effect. When World War I began, a steady supply of oil was not considered important to a successful military campaign. By the time the war ended, oil had become the single most important natural resource for any nation at war.

At the same time, the American oil industry had mushroomed. At the end of the war, America was producing about 335 million barrels of oil annually, about 67 percent of the world output.[2] This prodigious stream of oil flowed from wells throughout Texas, California, Pennsylvania, and Oklahoma.

Despite this output, however, the war ended with an oil shortage. War, after all, is a thirsty business for oil. But the shortage wouldn't last for long. Oil exploration in the United States boomed in the first years after the war. In 1920 alone, 34,000 new wells were drilled. In Oklahoma, the petroleum industry had become a big business, and Tulsa was its center. In 1919, Oklahoma fields yielded more than 18 million barrels of oil.[3]

The golden age of the automobile was beginning as well, increasing the need for oil. In 1916, still during the war years, only 3.4 million private cars were registered in the United States. By 1920, there were 23.1 million and demand was surging. New automobiles rolled off the assembly lines in Detroit, Michigan, in staggering numbers. In the 1920s, drive-in gasoline stations spread across the country, and towns and cities built better roads—all pointing to a need for more and more oil.

A Drilling Concern

In 1919, when Lloyd Noble was once again a college student, oil touched his life directly for the first time. On June 5, 1919, wildcatters brought in the No. 1 A. Denny well in the Hewitt field in Carter County, Oklahoma. Almost overnight, the area was besieged by lease hounds and other adventurers seeking a quick fortune. The Noble family was fortunate enough to have a stake in the field: Long before, when cotton farmers were going out of business, Sam Noble had sometimes accepted land in lieu of payment, including land in the Hewitt field.

Upon Sam's death, the rights to this land transferred to his widow, Hattie Noble.

With his mother enjoying her newfound financial security, Lloyd began learning about the oil industry, seeking out people who had firsthand experience. His sources included two classmates, Tom Holland and Earl Deacon. Both had worked summer jobs in the oil fields and could answer questions for the 24-year-old Lloyd Noble. It was from them that Lloyd began to pick up the lingo and the trade that would be his calling.

At this time, Lloyd still hadn't selected a course of study. Why, after being a teacher, a cowboy, and a sailor, he decided to give oil a try remains unknown. Perhaps it was his family's interest in oil-producing land. In his biography, the authors note that Lloyd harbored a secret ambition to secure leases on production land and develop his own proven oil reserves. Or perhaps it was the sense of limitless possibility surrounding the oil industry in those early days of exploration and instant riches. Whatever it was, in 1920, while still soaking up information from his friends, Lloyd Noble suggested to Deacon, "Why don't we go into the rotary drilling business?"[4]

The suggestion to go into drilling was fairly typical of Lloyd. In studying the oil industry, he recognized that a drilling contractor would have a stable, long-term profession. Wildcatting for oil was hard and often unrewarding work. And buying and selling leases could result in overnight bankruptcy just as easily as overnight riches. Choosing the conservative course, Lloyd proposed a business that would service a permanent need, no matter who owned the land or who profited from the oil. Over the years, the wisdom of this decision was borne out: the drilling company founded in 1921 outlasted many of the oil companies it worked for.

It didn't take Lloyd long to make good on his ambition. He was introduced in 1920 to Arthur O. Olson. Olson had some oil-field experience himself and owned part interest in a small steam-driven rotary rig that was being used to drill on land owned by the Noble family. During trips to see the rig, Olson and Noble struck up a lasting friendship. Before long, they began talking seriously about forming a drilling partnership.

When she first heard this, Lloyd's mother was none too pleased with her son's decision. There had been talk about Lloyd pursuing a career in law, which must have seemed respectable and stable when compared to the dirty squatter life of the oil wildcatters and the way they spent their fortunes. But Lloyd, a persuasive speaker, talked his mother into backing the idea. She used money from the oil leases on her own land and co-signed a $15,000 note to help Lloyd get established in business. Noble's biographers wrote vividly about the founding of the Noble Drilling Company on April 1, 1921.

When this picture was taken, the young Lloyd Noble had already formed a drilling company with Art Olson. Although he had limited oil-field experience, Lloyd Noble was a determined and indefatigable worker and quickly learned his chosen industry.

The crew of the company's first drilling rig, pictured in Carter County. From left to right are Art Simpson, floorman; Frank Bishop, fireman; Lief Olson, derrickman; Buck Fowler, floorman; and Art Olson, partner.

Olson, Noble, J. D. Patrick and Myrtle Moore, Lloyd Noble's first employee, met in the back of the Exchange National Bank of Ardmore to finalize the negotiation. Attorney R. L. Disney drew up the papers of partnership. Patrick's asking price for Rig No. 1 was $13,000; because all were jokingly superstitious on April Fool's day, they agreed to flip a coin to determine whether they paid him $12,999 or $13,001. Myrtle Moore provided and kept the dime. Patrick flipped and won the toss for $13,001. Thus the Noble Drilling Company was born.[5]

Noble Drilling Finds Its Legs

Noble Drilling Company was a partnership that drew from each of its founders. Olson, an experienced hand in the oil fields, was to run the drilling and field operations. Lloyd Noble was to handle the business end. Shortly after incorporating the business, Noble sold half of his concern to Deke Deacon, who also had valuable oil-field experience. Each of the three partners was to receive a monthly salary of $400.[6] (This partial ownership arrangement wouldn't last long: within a few years, Noble bought out Deacon's interest.)

While Deacon would remain involved in the company in various capacities over the years, the real strength behind Noble Drilling lay in the partnership between Olson and Noble. Recognizing

their complementary strengths, the two men had deep and abiding respect for one another. Olson, in an interview in *Horns and Wings*, a biography of Lloyd Noble, remarked that he liked Noble "from the very first. He was immensely ambitious and had something we needed. He helped me a lot."[7]

The brand-new company's first rig went to work for Max Westheimer in the Hewitt field with Olson acting as the foreman, leading a crew comprised of Art Simpson, Earl Deacon, Frank Bishop, Jake Iucker, and Jess Mullican. The crew dug a

hole to a depth of 1,800 feet. Throughout that year, the rig stayed in the Hewitt field. Accounts differ as to the success of Noble Drilling's first year. According to an annual report of later years, the company posted a $912.43 loss in its first year of operation.[8] In later interviews, however, Olson insisted that Noble Drilling was profitable from its first year of existence.[9]

The Man Matures

Standing on the threshold of a new decade at the helm of a newly founded company, Lloyd Noble must have been pleased, excited, and anxious all at once. These were the years that would set the tone for the rest of his life, the time when the once-shy young man from Ardmore would fully develop into the man people would remember.

Fortunately, they were good years, even the "busiest and happiest" of Lloyd Noble's life, according to his biographers.[10] In 1921, the same year he and Olson founded Noble Drilling, Lloyd met and began courting Vivian Bilby. Vivian was the granddaughter of John Sliker Bilby, reportedly one of the nation's largest landowners with about 1 million acres in 15 states. She was 19; Lloyd was 25.

They were married on May 24, 1924, in Vivian's hometown of Holdenville, Oklahoma. By all accounts, Vivian was a joy to Lloyd. They had three children: Samuel Russel (born August 12, 1925), Edward Everett (born March 19, 1928), and Ann Elizabeth (born March 29, 1930).

Above: In 1924, after a three-year courtship, Lloyd Noble married Vivian Bilby in Holdenville, Oklahoma. Friendly, gracious, and charming, Vivian became the mother of three children.

Right: The couple's first child, Samuel Russel Noble, was born on August 12, 1925. Sam would later become president of Samedan and Noble Affiliates, both companies that evolved from Noble Drilling and its various concerns.

From their very first days together, Vivian was an excellent influence in Lloyd Noble's life. Biographers called her a strong-willed and intelligent woman who could stand up to Lloyd perhaps better than any other person and knew how to temper his ambition. At the same time, she supported Lloyd's lifestyle completely, and Lloyd frequently credited his business success to tranquillity at home.

Noble Drilling Develops

Their domestic life unfolded against the backdrop of a growing and successful drilling concern. Not surprisingly for a business influenced by Lloyd's curious and insatiable mind, Noble Drilling quickly gained a reputation for innovation. Not only

Opposite: The Noble crew at Fox-Graham field in Carter County (clockwise from the back row left): Claude Martin, Sunshine Stewart, Art Simpson, George Kemnitz, Earl Deacon, and Jimmie McGee

Below: The Three Sands field near Tonkawa. Noble Drilling moved rigs into the field in 1922, prompting the company to buy a third drilling rig. *(Photo courtesy Western History Collections, University of Oklahoma.)*

was it a hard-working company; it was a smart company. Instead of draining Noble Drilling of capital for big salaries, Lloyd and Art made it a habit to reinvest their money in the business and continually pursue new opportunities.

In early 1922, Noble Drilling moved its rig to the Fox-Graham field to drill under contract for the Cameron Refining Company. Now that seven major fields circled Ardmore, oil had rapidly become the most important economic force in the area, and the city's growth reflected it. By then, Ardmore had a population of 20,000, two hospitals, and a wide selection of manufacturers and banks. Noble Drilling, with offices in the Bridgeman Building at 300 West Main, was but one of the 140 oil-field operators headquartered in the small town. The company's first office was a small affair. Myrtle Moore was the company's only office employee until Earl Sullivan joined in 1922 as the company accountant.

When Noble moved to the Graham field, it was busy enough that it leased a second rig. With two rigs operating, Olson and Noble were active indeed, and Olson even moved his family to the Graham field so he could be more involved.

From there, the company grew quickly. In only its second year of business, Noble was already receiving contracts to drill for the companies that would later become Texaco and Arco, and many of the legends and myths that would follow the

companies for decades were created in these early, dusty years. One of these concerned a man named Arthur Simpson, whom Noble's biographers remembered as "one of the most polite men to set foot on a drilling rig."[11] Simpson, who rose to toolpusher fairly quickly, had an unnerving tendency to disappear for long drinking binges.

In late 1922, Noble Drilling got a break in the Three Sands field near the infamous oil boomtown of Tonkawa, Oklahoma. Three Sands was a major field, and there was enough work that Noble bought a third rig. The company then had rigs under the supervision of Simpson, Jake Iucker, and an employee named Doc Kemnitz.

Three Sands was so busy that Noble existed peacefully with its competition and soon found that even three rigs weren't enough. In 1923, Noble added new rigs quickly, using the money the partners saved and borrowing against future contracts. All told, by the summer of 1923, the company had seven drilling rigs operating in Carter County and Tonkawa.[12] Rig number five was financed by Hattie Noble and put to work in the Graham field. Rig number six was used to drill for Governor Haskell.

In 1924, the Garber field was opened by the Sinclair Oil and Gas Company, and Noble Drilling

At the Tonkawa field, the frenzy to pump oil resulted in some spectacles. The men on the far right are unloading equipment to begin drilling on land owned by the Prairie View Church. Although the statewide church had sold drilling rights, local church members objected and threw the drilling contractor and his equipment over the fence. The driller obtained a restraining order, which was later upheld by the Oklahoma Supreme Court. *(Photo courtesy Western History Collections, University of Oklahoma.)*

once again found opportunity knocking. Moving into the field in 1925 for Royal Dutch/Shell, Noble crews had already heard that the geology in the area made for difficult and slow drilling. Much to their peers' surprise, however, Noble Drilling crews drilled about twice as fast as other companies did. Noble had chosen to use a coarse-cone bit produced by the Hughes Tool Company.

This feat more than any other earned Noble a lasting reputation for intelligent and innovative drilling. With its reputation growing, Noble was called upon in 1925 to help solve another problem that plagued drilling. In just a decade, the science of drilling had advanced rapidly. Holes were being drilled deeper than ever before to reach more distant oil supplies. By 1925, it had become apparent that some of these holes were deviating, or wandering, sometimes so far as to actually drill on a neighboring lease. That year, Noble got a contract to study hole deviation for a Royal Dutch/Shell subsidiary. The results of this study ushered in the modern era of oil-field technology as companies began to pay attention to the minutiae of drilling, including factors like steam pressure, pump strokes per minute, weight on the bit, and the revolutions per minute of the drill pipe.[13]

Innovation and Overproduction

With the science of drilling advancing, discussion persisted about America's oil reserves. No one knew exactly how much oil was in the ground, and many voices said the wells would soon tap out. In 1926, however, these skeptics were silenced when the Seminole field was discovered. Located in Noble's home state of Oklahoma, the Seminole field was one of the most rapid field developments in the history of the oil industry. During the mad scramble for leases, contract drillers like Noble had more work than they could handle, and Lloyd and Art virtually lived at the site.

By 1927, their enterprise growing robustly, Art and Lloyd decided it was time to incorporate. That year, they founded the Noble-Olson Drilling Company. At the time of its founding, Noble-Olson had a newly established office in Tulsa, Oklahoma, and was already transferring people from Ardmore to its new headquarters.

The Seminole field turned out to be both a blessing and a curse for the Oklahoma oil industry. One of the most prolific fields in the world, Seminole enabled young companies like Noble to expand rapidly and carve out a niche in the industry. But the discovery and removal of oil from the ground is a tricky business. Even with more cars on the road, big fields like Seminole could easily and rapidly flood the market with cheap oil, and it wouldn't take long before the price of oil began to drop.

A line of equipment in the Seminole field. This field opened in 1926 in Oklahoma as one of the most heavily producing oil fields in the world. The flood of oil quickly brought down the price of a barrel, and producers began to suffer under a glut. *(Photo courtesy The Fred Randolph Collection, University of Tulsa.)*

By 1928, Oklahoma was suffering from over-production, largely as a result of the tremendous production at the Seminole field. The problem was simple and part of a pattern that would repeat itself for decades to come. Too many companies were taking too much from the ground, and there was no coordinated authority to curtail production. That year, with the price of oil dropping and tax revenues suffering, the Oklahoma Corporation Commission tried to exert control over the industry. It set a statewide production limit of 700,000 barrels per day and limited the number of new wells that could be drilled.

But the decree had no teeth. There was no policing in the actual oil fields to make sure companies complied. Indeed, many companies increased their output to safeguard against the day when the government would curtail their production.[14] This move only drove the price of Oklahoma-produced oil lower, and more companies suffered.

Fortunately, Noble was prepared. In 1927, with the Seminole field gushers finally coming under control, Noble-Olson moved out of Oklahoma into neighboring Kansas, becoming the first company to use a modern rotary drill in that state. That same year, Noble-Olson crews moved into the Permian Basin in Texas, one of the most famous of the early oil fields.

The company further expanded with the 1928 construction of a drilling platform in the riverbed of the South Canadian River near the town of Sasakawa, Oklahoma. This feat was accomplished

Noble began using the Hughes Simplex rock bits in the middle 1920s and quickly earned a reputation as a technology leader that drilled faster and more efficiently than other drilling companies could. *(Photo courtesy Houston Metropolitan Research Center, Houston Public Library.)*

by building a derrick above the water, then running steam and water lines to the shore, where the mud pits, boilers, and pumps were located. This experience would prove valuable later in the Gulf Coast area. At the same time, Noble expanded into the Hobbs field in New Mexico.

Throughout this dizzying time, Lloyd Noble became more and more involved with the work of drilling, applying himself to learning everything there was to know about field work and running a larger business. Ed Holt, an early employee, remembered that Noble "went every place we drilled. He knew what it was like."[15] Moreover, Olson and Noble continued to grow as managers. They learned how to use rotating credit lines to keep rigs in operation and continually hired and trained new hands for the growing company. The company's philosophy was simple: hire good people and keep them. At a time when drilling was known for near-constant back-breaking labor, Noble offered its crews some perks. Laundry, for example, was done weekly for the crews, and hot meals—some of which were cooked by Noble himself—were provided whenever possible.

Innovation also continued to play an important part in Noble's success. In 1929, Noble-Olson introduced an improved cone-drilling bit that had been patented by Arthur Simpson. The new bit greatly improved the speed of drilling—so much so that the company set a new record, as reported by the *Wichita Beacon*: "A drilling record unequaled in the Kansas oil fields and unlikely to fall soon was set recently by the Noble-Olson Co., when that widely known company completed two wells below 2,800 feet within a single 30-day period for the Shell Oil Co."[16]

The Simpson bit sped up drilling by cleaning as it worked. Moreover, it reduced costs by 20 percent and required only half as many sets of cones as its predecessors. "Simpson applies the water pressure directly to the formation at the bottom of the hole, while other bits are so constructed that the force of the water is minimized by being first directed to the point where the cones mesh," the newspaper explained. "The stream thus strikes hot metal before hitting the formation. Simpson's method loses none of the pressure of 500 or 600 pounds."[17]

On the Horizon

By the end of the 1920s, the oil industry was already beginning to take on the global shape that would become its hallmark—and Noble-Olson wanted to be a part of it. In 1929, Art Olson negotiated a job that moved Noble-Olson rigs to the Turner Valley field in southern Alberta, Canada.

It was a challenging job. The Noble-Olson crew fought strange geology that caused hole deviation great enough to threaten to push the hole beyond the lease area.

This effort consumed most of the first half of 1929. At the time, Noble-Olson had 38 rigs operating in the American Southwest and into Canada. Riding the crest of a busy decade, Noble-Olson had grown quickly and gained an excellent reputation in the industry. But as spring moved into summer, there sprouted a feeling that great change was coming. Activity in the stock market was frenzied and unpredictable, and the worldwide economy seemed to be teetering on the edge of disaster. Undoubtedly, Noble and Olson felt an era drawing to its end—what kind of end, however, no one could predict.

A Samedan Oil Corporation pump jack. During the Depression, Lloyd Noble founded Samedan to hold leases he accepted as payment for drilling the wells. The company was named for his children.

CHAPTER TWO

MIRACLE OF THE DEPRESSION

1930–1939

Markets were difficult to find, and the producer lucky enough to sell his oil did so at a price which amounted to economic waste.

—Russell Brown, general counsel,
Independent Petroleum Association of America (IPAA), 1965

AT THE END OF THE 1920S, A chorus of pessimists predicted oil shortages. With all the new cars on the road, they reasoned, and all the material wealth sloshing about the country, it was only a matter of time before the oil supply dried up. At the same time, big oil companies (most of which were remnants of Standard Oil, which had been broken up by federal trustbusters in 1911) were arguing about federal or state regulation of the oil industry. No one really favored a government-regulated oil industry, but every oilman shuddered when he thought of the Seminole field, whose oil flowed so freely that the price of oil bottomed out.

These remained mostly academic arguments, however, as demand for oil seemed destined to rise forever. Some economists actually predicted that an era of "permanent growth" had begun, and speculative buying drove the price of stocks far beyond any rational value.

Lloyd Noble, ever the conservative businessman, watched these developments with a nervous eye. By 1929, many conventional economic indicators were already showing a downward trend. Housing starts and industrial production had slowed. Demand for cars (a very important barometer for an oil company) was softening, and unemployment was rising. Yet stock prices continued to climb. Finally, Noble decided he wanted no part of it. By the summer of 1929, Lloyd Noble had sold all but 200 shares of his family's stock on the chance that something catastrophic was coming.[1]

Noble was prescient. On September 4, stock prices dropped, but the drop was slow and the weakened bull market held on into October. Then on October 23, prices began to drop again—until word got out that leading bankers had agreed to stabilize prices. But by that time, the damage had been done and investors were nervous. Stock prices held shakily until Tuesday, October 29, when pandemonium broke loose and investors all over the country unloaded their portfolios. In one day, the stock market registered a 13 percent decline—its greatest so far.

Lloyd Noble had wisely protected his family from the falling stock market, which was only a harbinger of things to come. The crash, coupled with a severe drought in the United States and a worldwide depression, launched America into the Great Depression and a new decade.

In 1930, on the eve of the Great Depression, Lloyd Noble incorporated Noble Drilling Company in Tulsa after splitting with his partner, Art Olson.

Lloyd Noble, left, and Art Olson, right, split their 38 rigs evenly. After they went their separate ways, the two remained amicable for many years.

An Amicable Split

In early 1930, before the effects of the Depression came home to roost in Oklahoma, Lloyd Noble and his partner, Art Olson, were on the verge of another major decision. In 1921, the two had founded their partnership on mutual respect for each other's abilities. By 1930, however, the partners were anxious to strike out independently.

Historical accounts give varying reasons for the split. Some pointed to the Canadian contracts as the beginning of the end of their partnership. In a later interview, Olson remarked that Noble's growing involvement in state politics and his duties with the University of Oklahoma were distracting.[2] In *Imagination and Ability,* Lloyd Noble's biographers noted that each man had gained valuable experience in the nine years of their collaboration. Olson, who had once relied on Noble's business experience, had spent a lot of time in the office and had learned how to run the financial end of a business. Likewise, Noble, who had once relied on Olson's field experience, had received an education as thorough and tough as any roughneck's as he traveled around the country supervising company rigs.

Whatever the cause, the two men decided to end their partnership in 1930, a decision made without rancor or bitterness. "There wasn't an argument," Olson noted many years later.[3] On April 15, 1930, they gathered in Olson's home (Art couldn't leave the house due to a recent injury) and split the company's assets. At the time, Noble-Olson had 38 rigs. The two men agreed to divide the company's assets straight down the middle and took turns picking rigs. Noble, who had made loyalty a guiding tenet in his business, chose rigs whose crews he wanted to keep. Early employees who ended up going with Noble included Doc Kemnitz, Dewey Morris, Ed Holt, Cecil Forbes, and Myrtle Moore.

Years later, Lloyd's son Sam wrote of the agreement: "The equipment was equitably divided, and the employees were allowed to choose freely which of the succeeding companies they wished to work for. Lloyd Noble and Art Olson, although competitors for many years, retained a firm and lasting friendship."[4]

Once the partnership had been split, Lloyd Noble was free in May 1930 to incorporate his new company as Noble Drilling Company.

Already the new company had plenty to do. A new strike had just been announced in Oklahoma City, leading Noble to buy three new rigs to work in the field. Originally discovered in the 1920s, the field in Oklahoma City didn't begin producing heavily until March 1930, when the Indian Territory Illuminating Company hit a gusher that reportedly sent a fine spray of gas 11 miles downwind of the derrick.[5]

From that day on, production in the field would be heavy and by 1935 would cover 11,000 producing acres.[6] The Oklahoma City field was unique not only for its enormous size but also because it was located within a major city. "Never before . . . had a large metropolitan area undergone the excitement of a major oil boom," wrote oil historian Kenny Franks. "Because of the location of the oil pool (one well was directionally drilled beneath the state capitol and another on the grounds of the executive mansion), it received an unusual amount of attention."[7]

At this time, Noble rigs were active throughout Oklahoma, Wyoming, the Permian Basin (in both New Mexico and Texas), and Montana. The new company's headquarters moved in 1930 from

---

The Oklahoma City oil field was unique because of its size and location. Overall, the field would encompass 11,000 producing acres and provide sorely needed work for drilling companies mired in the Great Depression. *(Photo courtesy Phillips Petroleum Company.)*

Above: The newly incorporated Noble Drilling Company issued $60,000 in capital stock. This original stock certificate was issued for $10, the price of one share.

Below: The skyline of Tulsa, Oklahoma, in 1929. The city was already established as Oklahoma's undisputed oil capital when Noble Drilling relocated its headquarters there in 1930. *(Photo courtesy Western History Collections, University of Oklahoma.)*

Ardmore to Tulsa, for there was little doubt that Tulsa was the capital of the Oklahoma petroleum industry—a claim that was strengthened by the presence of the International Petroleum Exposition and Congress.

The Depression Hits Home

When Olson and Noble split their business in the spring of 1930, the Depression had yet to seriously affect Noble-Olson—partially because of the busy Oklahoma City field. Meanwhile, the science of oil exploration and drilling had continued to advance dramatically. Benefiting from progress in aviation as a result of World War I, exploration companies used aerial surveys to identify likely oil reserves. Noble and Olson even got into the habit of air travel in the 1920s, taking regular business flights to their remote sites.

Air travel wasn't the only advancing technology. Oil companies had also learned to study sediments removed from the ground to analyze reserves. Most importantly, though, the seismograph was rapidly becoming a major tool in oil exploration, allowing exploration companies to "see" underground by using shock waves to identify salt domes, rock, and underground structures. The science of drilling also rapidly improved. In the beginning of the 1920s, the deepest wells were about 6,000 feet. A decade later, wells were reaching 10,000 feet below the earth's surface.

So for a while at least, the oil industry didn't feel the effect of the declining economy, but its resilience wouldn't last long. Stock prices continued to crumble in 1930, farms failed in increasing numbers, and consumer demand lapsed as incomes quickly dropped. At first President Herbert Hoover had predicted a rapid recovery and called the slump a "market correction," but by the summer of 1930 it was clear that the bad times were

not going away. The first breadlines had already appeared in Oklahoma City.

Lloyd Noble did everything he could to protect his employees, but he couldn't reverse the cruel economies of the oil field. With oil still flowing from Seminole and now from Oklahoma City, the price of a barrel was all the way down to 20 cents—a disaster at a time when Americans had stopped using their cars, seeing them as expensive luxuries.[8] As summer deepened into fall, Noble continued searching for solutions. That year, he incorporated Vivian Oil Corporation for the purpose of buying leases, something that Noble Drilling had never done. Two years later, he incorporated Samedan (named for his three children, Sam, Ed, and Ann) for the same reason. These were but two of the various lease-holding companies he organized in the early 1930s.

A Noble Drilling crew assembled on the derrick floor of a company rig in 1932. This rig was one of the first to drill deep holes for the company, a feat made possible by steadily advancing drilling technology.

As *The International Directory of Company Histories* noted, "With these two companies—Noble Drilling and Samedan Oil Corp.—combined with the producing properties he had acquired, Lloyd Noble had created a small yet viable oil company, an independent in a market dominated by much larger oil concerns."[9]

But it wouldn't be enough to keep his workers employed. Throughout 1930, with producers losing money at every wellhead, Noble was forced to lay off workers and stack rigs. He tried to keep his

Above: Pictured in 1934, these Noble drillers are working on the floor of an electricity-driven rotary rig. Located in Howard County, this rig drilled 2,125 feet in 16 days for Shell.

Left: This steam rig was located in Elk Basin, Wyoming, where it drilled for natural gas to supply Billings, Montana. Noble's rigs had by this time followed strikes throughout the United States and even into Canada.

best and most loyal employees working, sometimes asking men to travel to three or four states in one year, and he maintained only a skeleton crew in his office. Nevertheless, by late 1930, Noble rigs were active only in the Permian Basin.

Joiner's Black Giant

While Noble was desperately trying to keep busy in the Permian, the future of the Texas oil industry was leading a ragged wildcat crew across the piney hills of East Texas. His name was Columbus "Dad" Joiner, a stoop-backed septuagenarian who had been promising oil riches to his investors for the past decade. Silver-tongued and barely educated,

Joiner often relied on the obituaries to locate his future investors, calling upon widows to fund oil schemes that seemed outlandish to industry experts. East Texas, where thousands of empty wells had already been dug by major oil producers, was one of these schemes. For his "scientific evidence" that oil existed in East Texas, Joiner had procured a map of the major oil wells in the United States and drawn "convergence lines" on it. Miraculously, all of these lines came together on the plains of East Texas.

Throughout 1930, operating with a collection of farm boys and less than a shoestring budget, Joiner's crew worked the East Texas ground with rusted and antiquated equipment. When he couldn't afford to pay his crew, he offered rights to the oil he was convinced they were going to find, but even then crew

members wandered on and off the operation at will. Operating in total obscurity on the fringes of the oil industry, Joiner escaped attention until September 1930, when something incredible happened: The Daisy Bradford No. 3 well tested positive for oil.

The buzz began to build in the surrounding countryside, attracting hordes of onlookers who wanted to see oil struck in their backyard. Finally, on October 3, 1930, their hopes were answered. With first a gurgle, then a roar, the Daisy Bradford No. 3 erupted in a jet of oil and water that sprayed the crowd and forever changed the American oil industry. At 45 miles long and 10 miles wide at its broadest point, the East Texas oil field dwarfed anything that had been seen before and touched off an oil boom and frenzy that made even the rush at Spindletop look sedate.

It wouldn't take long for Noble rigs to move into the area. The company had recently put several rigs back to work—in Worland, Wyoming, and Bridger, Montana—and was only too happy to join the frenzy in East Texas. Noble rigs were sent south from Oklahoma City, Hobbs, and Tulsa on a rail line that passed only three miles from the discovery wellhead.

The "skyline" of Kilgore, Texas, epicenter of the gigantic East Texas oil field. Dwarfing any previously discovered oil field, East Texas flooded the global market with cheap oil, causing prices to plummet. Oil was selling for a dime a barrel in many places. *(Photo courtesy Archive Center, National Museum of American History.)*

Crews that had been idled earlier that year were put to work drilling for Stanolind, Sinclair, Amerada, and F. W. Merrick.

The frenzy built up quickly. Because of the area's unique geology, wells were easily dug, and oil was found between 3,600 and 4,200 feet. Only eight months after Joiner's discovery, 1,000 wells had been completed and the field was producing 500,000 barrels per day. By August 1931, 1 million barrels were flowing every day.

Like other major strikes before it, the prodigious oil field became both a blessing and a curse. Producing 1 million barrels a day, East Texas alone could satisfy almost half of the nation's demand for oil. This output was magnified by rapidly advancing refinery techniques that enabled producers to get more gasoline from every gallon of pure crude. A flood of oil quickly overran the United States, and the bottom fell out of the market. In Texas, where oil had recently been selling for $1.35 a barrel, producers got only 10 cents. At the wellhead, distressed producers sometimes sold oil for as low as two cents a barrel. In Oklahoma, things weren't much better: a barrel of crude was selling for 15 cents.

Something had to be done, but no one knew what. The conversations about government regulation in the oil fields fell by the wayside, and desperate producers scrambled to sell their oil. Because most of the producers in East Texas were fiercely independent companies, they did not want to limit production and viewed such talk with open hostility.

Unchecked, prices stayed low, and it seemed that many oil producers—and not only small ones—would be driven from business. The industry publication *WildCatters: Texas Independent Oilmen* later described the collapse that set the stage for government intervention.

For American investors, the bleak years of national depression began on the New York Stock Exchange in October 1929. For American oilmen, catastrophe did not occur until a year later, with the discovery of the giant East Texas field. At that time, in October 1930 no one could have predicted to what dire straits the East Texas oil field would reduce the American oil industry in a matter of months. As a tidal wave of East Texas production swamped the national crude

market, prices fell to levels at which production would be unprofitable.[10]

At first, the Texas Railroad Commission, which despite its name was in charge of the oil fields, tried to intervene. It set a limit on oil production. In response, nervous independent oil producers only pumped more, and the daily flow actually increased. Finally, amid talk of dynamiting competitors' wells and pipelines, the governors of Oklahoma and Texas lost their patience.

Oklahoma acted first. Governor "Alfalfa Bill" Murray declared a state of emergency on August 4, 1931, and ordered the state militia to take control of the major oil fields. National Guard troops were placed 50 feet around the wells, including Noble's, and Murray decreed that the wells could not begin producing again until the price of oil hit $1 per barrel. Desperate to stay in business, many oil producers ignored the decree and shipped "hot oil" across the state line to Texas, where it might bring only 10 or 12 cents a barrel, yet even that was better than nothing at all.

This tack wouldn't last long, however, as Texas Governor Ross Sterling soon fell in behind Murray. On August 17, 1931, he announced that East Texas was in a "state of insurrection" and "open rebellion," and he sent in several thousand National Guard soldiers and the Texas Rangers to take control of the field. Almost overnight, the clang and hiss and open-engine roar of the world's biggest oil field settled into an eerie quiet.[11]

Sterling's strategy worked. By early 1932, the price of oil had risen to 98 cents per barrel. Although the road would be rocky, the way had been cleared for government proration of oil production in big fields. In 1933, newly appointed Secretary of the Interior Harold Ickes established the Oil Code, a historic measure and the true beginning of government intervention in oil production.

Peace at Last

With production finally coming under control and oil prices rising, exploration efforts resumed, and Noble continued pursuing drilling contracts. Small strikes at the Lucien and Crescent fields brought in some work in 1933. Later that year, a bigger strike outside Ada, Oklahoma, moved Noble

With East Texas causing an oil glut and the Seminole field still producing strongly in Oklahoma, the governors of the states took action. In Oklahoma, National Guardsmen were sent to take over the Seminole field and stood guard around producing wells. *(Photo copyright 1931, The Oklahoma Publishing Company.)*

rigs into the Fitts field for Stanolind, Carter Oil, Simpson, and Fell, and even for Noble's own Samedan. Noble employees in the field included Ed Holt, Paul Buckley, Irl Rhynes, and Bill Smith.

Around the same time, Noble rigs were sent south to the Gulf Coast of Texas to work in the Conroe field. The Gulf Coast, which included parts of Texas and Louisiana, was a thriving oil region that had been developed for at least a decade. The region's geology, however, complicated the task for drillers like Noble. Many of the wells had to be drilled through shale, which had the tendency to heave upward as the drillers bored down into high-pressure reservoirs. In some remarkable cases,

drillers would find their holes actually getting shallower as they worked. The region was prone to hurricanes and other deadly weather as well.

While working on the Gulf Coast had its share of challenges, savvy exploration companies also recognized it as a potential major source of oil. Exploration companies used the seismograph to confirm underwater oil reserves in the Gulf of Mexico. But drilling in any kind of water presented a whole new set of problems. In the South Canadian River, Noble Drilling had set up a successful rig in a riverbed, but that was a completely different challenge from drilling in coastal marshes and the open ocean.

Nevertheless, the challenge had been presented and solutions were sought. In 1931, the Texas Company used an early kind of submersible drilling barge that could operate in 15 feet of water. Noble Drilling first gained experience with this kind of rig in 1935, but over the next several years the company would have only limited experience with offshore drilling of any variety. It would be years before this kind of expensive and risky drilling

became financially viable and critically important to Noble Drilling.

Heartbreak in the Noble Home

Throughout these years, with rigs operating throughout Texas, Oklahoma, and New Mexico and even into Illinois and Wyoming, Noble Drilling considered itself lucky. Thanks to the big strike at East Texas, Noble had managed to stay financially viable through the greatest depression in American history.

Lloyd Noble's personal life, however, took a sad turn. During a summer vacation at the seashore in California, Vivian became ill. She underwent an emergency appendectomy in Long Beach, and though she returned home in seemingly improved health, in reality she was hiding from her husband how sick she really was. In April 1936, Vivian bid Lloyd goodbye as he departed on yet another business trip. Soon after he left, her condition began to dete-

A Noble crew in the 1930s. With booms in Seminole and East Texas, the company was busy again even during unstable times. By the late 1930s, the worst of the Depression and the oil glut had passed and Noble rigs were once again busy all over the United States.

riorate and she was taken to the hospital. There, on April 11, Vivian Noble died of pneumonia complicated by the fact that she was two months pregnant. She was 34 years old. Lloyd Noble wasn't able to reach his wife in time and was not at her bedside when she died.

Vivian's death was a blow to all who knew her kind spirit and generosity, but none was so affected as Lloyd.[12] "His absence at her bedside haunted him for the rest of his life," according to Odie and Laurie Faulk, Noble's biographers. "In the weeks following her death, he was so despondent that those close to him feared for his health."[13]

There was also the immediate problem of his three motherless children. With his travel schedule and the demands of Noble Drilling, Noble himself was in no position to take over as a full-time father. Fortunately, he was able to turn to family and friends. That summer, Nora Shaffer, the family's housekeeper, moved with the family to La Jolla, California, where Lloyd's three children were enrolled in a private school. In 1938, they returned home to Ardmore, where they were cared for by Shaffer, family friend Florence Revelle, and their grandmother Hattie Noble.

Throughout these hard years, Lloyd gradually adjusted to his loss, and in 1938 he met and married Eloise Joyce Millard. For a brief time the three children again had a mother figure, but the marriage wasn't destined to succeed. Lloyd spent too much time away from home to help Eloise get established in her new town, and the shadow cast by Vivian was simply too much to overcome. In 1939, Eloise moved back to Oklahoma City, and the couple divorced later that year. On October 11, just before the divorce, Eloise and Lloyd welcomed a son, Richard Lloyd Noble, who stayed with his mother. Richard and his father remained as close as possible although they were always separated by great distance.

By this time, Lloyd Noble was spending almost all of his time on the road, living in motels, traveling from office to office, and sleeping on friends' sofas. His wide circle of friends became accustomed to calls at any hour or to the sight of an exhausted Lloyd Noble showing up on their doorstep, perhaps hoping for an invitation to dine and a place to sleep. Accustomed to conducting business at any hour, he also satisfied his hunger for friendly conversation by placing many late-night phone calls.

Meanwhile, Noble Drilling continued moving through the American oil states, following strikes and drilling holes. In 1937, the company followed

This 1939 photo shows a drilling barge owned by the California Oil Company. Noble Drilling moved into barge drilling in the late 1930s, although it would be years before offshore drilling became a vital part of the company.

oil exploration northward into Illinois, where the Carter Oil Company contracted Noble to delve into the Lowden Pool. Because oil operations were so rare in Illinois, mobs of local people reportedly showed up to watch the well's progress. After drilling was established in Illinois, Noble rigs moved into Indiana and Kentucky.

Noble moved into the Cedar Lake field in the Permian Basin in 1939 and into Galveston in 1940. In DeRidder, Louisiana, Noble rigged up its first submersible barge for the California Oil Company.

The year 1939 was important to Lloyd for another, more personal reason: Sam Noble, his eldest son, left Ardmore, Oklahoma, for Saint John's Military Academy in Delafield, Wisconsin. Sam's younger brother Ed wouldn't be far behind.

This statue, called Oil Patch Warrior, commemorates the Sherwood Forest oil fields, where Noble crews worked during World War II.

CHAPTER THREE

WORKING FOR THE WAR EFFORT

1940–1944

I am sure that when the record of this project has finally been written, it will not only be a credit to the organization, but it will be one which you can look back to with a feeling of great satisfaction and pride at having had an opportunity to make a real contribution toward shortening this terrible conflict.

—Lloyd Noble, September 1943,
in a letter to the crew of the Sherwood Forest project

IN 1939, WITH PRESIDENT FRANKLIN Delano Roosevelt in office and the Depression still going strong, the world found itself teetering on the brink of another world war. After years of instability in Asia, where Japan had already occupied Manchuria, and following the rise of fascism in Germany and Italy, the powder keg finally exploded in September, ignited by the Nazis' mechanized and devastating blitzkrieg attack on Poland. No longer satisfied with Austria and Czechoslovakia, German chancellor Adolf Hitler unleashed his troops into Poland with the stated intention of expanding his Third Reich across Europe. Within days, France and Britain declared war on Germany.

The United States watched the unfolding scene with a wary eye but didn't want to get involved in another bloody European war. Yet participation seemed inevitable, and gradually the United States shed its cloak of neutrality and began supplying oil and equipment to Britain and its allies. Throughout 1940, Nazi troops raged across Europe, first taking Denmark, then moving south through Belgium and the Netherlands. At Dunkirk, the beach was littered with the bodies of French and English defenders, and the German war machine thundered onward. By June, Italy had joined Germany in attacking France. Later that month, the swastika flew over Paris, and Hitler moved on plans to take the British Isles. That summer, the Battle of Britain was fought

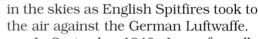

in the skies as English Spitfires took to the air against the German Luftwaffe.

In September 1940, Japan formally joined Germany and Italy in forming the Axis powers. Already in mainland China, the Japanese warlords saw ripe opportunity throughout the Pacific and Indochina for their "Greater East Asian Co-prosperity Sphere." Again the United States found itself backed into a corner. Hardly anxious to break off relations with Japan, the United States was nevertheless having a hard time working with an aggressor country that sought to subjugate its neighbors.

One theme suffusing these tragic years was the overriding importance of oil. World War I had ushered in the age of mechanized warfare, but it had only hinted at what would happen during World War II. By that time, aircraft had changed everything. No longer would troops be relegated to burrows and trenches. Instead, Hitler's nefariously brilliant military staff had devised a form of war that relied on strafing air attack followed by ground troops moving in armored columns of tanks and vehicles. It was a kind of war that had never been seen before, operating at an alarming

---

Lloyd Noble turned down profits from two wartime projects in the Arctic Circle and in Sherwood Forest. A deeply patriotic man, he considered the sacrifice his contribution.

British Spitfires, the planes responsible for winning the Battle of Britain. These planes used 100-octane fuel that made them more maneuverable and faster than the German planes. *(Photo courtesy* Air Force Magazine.*)*

speed that had never been approached, and for a time the strategy appeared invincible.

Yet when the British stopped the German advance in the air during the terrible summer of 1940, many historians credited the superiority of the Spitfire, which used advanced 100-octane aircraft fuel and was more maneuverable and faster than the German planes. For Japan, a country that relied on the United States for 80 percent of its oil, the primary strategic objective was to seize oil fields in Burma and Indonesia. In this modern era of war, oil was the single greatest strategic advantage.

Known at that time as the most oil-rich country in the world, the United States freely lent support to Britain and China during their darkest hours. But still America avoided joining the conflict. This policy changed abruptly on December 7, 1941. That morning, hoping to knock the United States out of commission in a single blow, the Japanese air force ambushed the main U.S. naval base of Pearl Harbor on Oahu, Hawaii. That same day, Japanese forces launched attacks throughout the Pacific on targets in Hong Kong, the Philippines, Wake Island, Guam, Thailand, and Malaya (now West Malaysia). It was designed to be the Japanese masterstroke.

The attack on Pearl Harbor was devastating. In two hours of heavy bombing, the Japanese killed about 2,400 American soldiers and civilians, sank or disabled 19 ships, and destroyed about 150 planes. Yet it fell short of a total military success for two reasons. First, the American aircraft carriers that would prove so crucial in later years were not at port, thereby escaping damage. Second, the Japanese ignored shore installations, including the critical oil supply. If the Japanese had blown up the oil tanks, every good ship left in the Pacific would have been immobilized for months until new fuel could be shipped in from California. Instead, the Japanese left a vulnerable 4.5-million-barrel reservoir untouched.

Assuming the United States to be weak in spirit, the Japanese had thought that one decisive and terrible defeat would crush the American will to fight, leaving Japan free to roam the Pacific unfettered. Yet nothing could have been further from the truth. Already tense because of the situation in Europe, America responded with instant and nearly unanimous outrage. On December 8, the United States declared war on Japan. Three days later, Germany and Italy declared war on the United States. With the mantle of isolationism thrown off for good, America began a determined effort to quickly build a fearsome military machine—one that would of course need a steady supply of oil.

Because of oil's obvious importance to the war effort, the U.S. government moved quickly toward unprecedented intervention in oil markets. In 1941 the War Production Board was created to regulate the economy so no vital defense industry would be compromised. The oil industry, of course, was one of these, but oil shortages were still common throughout the war years. On December 1, 1942, the government went a step further and initiated gasoline rationing, which would remain in effect until 1945.[1] Industrial users were encouraged to switch from oil to coal, and President Roosevelt pushed for development of natural gas.

Lloyd Noble, a former sailor, was a deeply patriotic man and was moved during World War II to assist in whatever ways he could. Primarily, that meant keeping oil flowing at home, working from proven fields under the strain of wartime shortages. During the war, Noble Drilling set records in the Wheeler field in Texas and also worked at Cape Hatteras on the first well that was drilled off the eastern coast of the United States.

But Noble also went two steps further to aid the war effort, first in Canada and later in England. Both times, Lloyd Noble eschewed profits and insisted that his company would be paid only for expenses. This would be Noble Drilling's contribution to the war effort.

The Canol Project

The need for oil was so great that governments leaped at any opportunity to find a secure supply. With Japanese advances in the Pacific threatening Alaska and German submarine wolf packs roaming the Atlantic, the Allies considered no safe supply of oil too remote or unimportant. Thus in 1942 Noble found itself working in the far north, near the Arctic Circle. There the company drilled in the Norman Wells field for a kind of oil that flowed at extremely cold temperatures.

Because of the field's extreme isolation, the United States and Canada agreed to build the Alaska-Canadian (ALCAN) highway to connect the United States mainland to Alaska. A north-south pipeline running along the highway would carry crude to refineries in the south, as well as in Alaska itself.

With this project under way, it wasn't long before engineers started seeing opportunity elsewhere along the freeway, especially in the Canadian province of Alberta. A project called Canol (Canadian Oil) was initiated to drill approximately 750 wells with the support of the United States government and in cooperation with Canada.

Noble Drilling received the contract to drill the oil wells along the Mackenzie River, which ran southeast of Norman Wells, a forbidding and challenging geography. An advertisement from Bechtel-Price-Callahan seeking construction

The Mackenzie River in Alaska (above). This river was a major transportation route to the isolated Norman Wells (map at right). Although these fields were remote and difficult to access, any source of oil was considered valuable during the war. *(Illustration by Sandy Cruz.)*

At right, Lloyd Noble is second from left in this 1943 photograph taken on the Mackenzie River in Alaska. Below, the oil camp at the Norman Wells site. The ambitious Canol project never resulted in any significant new oil supplies although it was a huge logistic and engineering feat.

LLOYD NOBLE SECOND FROM LEFT   1943 N.W.T ON THE MACKENZIE RIVER

workers emphasized the difficult working conditions in the region: "Temperatures will range from 90 degrees above zero to 70 degrees below zero. Men will have to fight swamps, rivers, ice, and cold. Mosquitoes, flies, and gnats will not only be annoying, but will cause bodily harm. If you are not prepared to work under these and similar conditions, DO NOT APPLY."[2]

Crews were assembled, and work began on the highway, pipeline, and oil fields. In February 1943 the *Tulsa Tribune* covered the project, declaring "World's biggest oil campaign gets under way; Tulsa drilling firm plays major part in U.S.-Canada program." The article proudly reported Noble Drilling's role in "the biggest wildcatting and drilling program ever carried out in the world. For months, Tulsa drillers, tool dressers, roughnecks and other skilled production men have been sent to Calgary to take part in the immense project."[3]

By April 1944, crude oil from Norman Wells flowed into Whitehorse, where the already completed tank farms and refinery were ready for operation. By some measures the project could be considered one of the greatest construction projects of all

time, but historians more frequently refer to the $134 million Canol project as a "colossal blunder" because the need for the oil field had ceased to exist by the time it was completed. Having taken only 20 months to build, it was shut down and abandoned in 1945, less than a year after it opened, because the Japanese invasion of Alaska never materialized. The story of the Canol project was retold on the occasion of the 25th anniversary of Noble Drilling:

This endeavor did not produce much if any oil. Our activities were suddenly stopped by the United States government, canceling the contract. This cancellation came about because of severe criticism of the government's acts on this CANOL project and other projects in the area. With all the criticism that had been advanced, there was not even a whisper of criticism of Noble Drilling Corp. or anyone associated with it. Mr. Noble and others in charge of this project dealt in such a way that no one could criticize their acts even though much of their efforts were with people that were severely criticized and censured.[4]

The Secret of Sherwood

Shortly after Lloyd Noble received the Canol contract, he was again summoned to a top-secret meeting in Washington, D.C., where he learned about an extraordinary oil field in the most unlikely of places: the legendary Sherwood Forest, home to Robin Hood, located almost in the exact center of war-torn England.

Right: Frank Porter, of the Fain-Porter Drilling Company, teamed up with Lloyd Noble and Noble Drilling to send crews into war-torn Britain to develop hidden oil fields in England. *(Photo courtesy Porter family.)*

Below: A book about this top secret project was written by Guy Woodward and Grace Woodward. *The Secret of Sherwood Forest* was published in 1973.

The Sherwood Forest oil reserve wasn't a huge producer, but it was a jealously guarded secret in England. Discovered in 1939, the fields produced only about 700 barrels a day. Under any other circumstances, almost no oil company would have gone to the great expense and effort needed to develop this middling field. But in 1942, the circumstances were anything but ordinary. Britain stood alone, protected only by its air force and desperately in need of oil. It was this need that compelled Lloyd Noble to attend a meeting in Washington to hear about a proposal to drill for oil in the leafy confines of Sherwood Forest. This project was later the subject of a book called *The Secret of Sherwood Forest*, by Guy H. Woodward and Grace Steele Woodward.

In September 1942, Lloyd Noble met with Charles Philip Southwell, the general manager of D'Arcy Exploration Company; Donald Knowlton, director of production in the Petroleum Administration for War; Frank Porter, from the Fain-Porter Drilling Company; and two drilling contractors from California. D'Arcy was a subsidiary of the Anglo-Iranian Oil Company (which would later become British Petroleum).

Southwell began his presentation to the group by revealing that there were producing oil wells in Great Britain. Until then, no one knew of their existence, and the news greatly surprised the drilling contractors. The Englishman went on to explain that about 50 producing wells had been completed at depths between 2,380 and 2,500 feet, yielding about 700 barrels a day. Moreover, he said, there was the possibility of greater production.[5]

Originally, Southwell had proposed that D'Arcy purchase equipment to drill 100 additional wells. To purchase this

equipment, however, D'Arcy would need the cooperation of the United States government through its Petroleum Administration for War and the Petroleum Industry War Council, the agencies responsible for furnishing America with its wartime requirement of petroleum.[6] Southwell's initial request was turned down because foreign corporations, governments, and individuals were prohibited from buying equipment.

The meeting with the drilling contractors represented Southwell's last-ditch attempt. If he could not buy the equipment, perhaps he could hire American drilling companies on contract to drill the wells. Knowlton agreed that this would be legal, especially considering that American companies were already drilling under contract in Canada.

But when Southwell appealed to the four drillers, he met with resistance. The Californians excused themselves immediately, saying they already had too many commitments and not enough equipment. Noble and Porter listened but ultimately came to the same conclusion: with equipment scarce, they could not afford to send any men or materials overseas.[7] Porter and Noble left the meeting under no commitment, and Noble returned to Oklahoma.

But Southwell would not give up so easily. He followed Noble to Oklahoma, where he appeared, exhausted, on Noble's doorstep the day after their meeting, determined to pitch his case again. Noble invited him in, and Southwell followed the oilman around as he shaved, showered, and dressed. Southwell was determined to convince Noble how crucial this project was to the war effort. Finally, Noble agreed to consider it again if Porter would partner on it with him. He went on to say that if he did take the contract, Noble Drilling would accept no profits.

Another meeting was arranged with Porter, Noble, the English driller, and attorneys. At this meeting, Noble and Porter agreed in principle to help. The contract that finally took shape committed the American companies to buying equipment on D'Arcy's account, hiring drilling crews and staff, and spending a year in England to drill approximately 100 wells. At first, Southwell wanted 10 rigs to be shipped over, but Noble vice president Ed Holt suggested that only four would be necessary for the job. To convince Southwell, Holt guided him through the producing fields in southern Illinois, where for the first time Southwell saw 87-foot jackknife-type rigs at work. Although not totally convinced the Americans could do the job with only four rigs, Southwell reluctantly agreed that only four would be purchased.

Recruiting Crewmen

Although Porter had agreed to participate, the management of the project would fall entirely to Noble Drilling, and all the crews would be employees of Noble for the duration of the project. Naturally, the first thing that was needed was a supervisor. For that, Noble turned to Eugene Preston Rosser, the new assistant to the general superintendent of the Rocky Mountain division of Noble Drilling. On November 9, 1942, Rosser was summoned to Tulsa and asked if he would be interested in taking on an important project located in the British Isles.

After asking Lloyd Noble if he would take the job (Noble said he would), Rosser agreed to buy the rigs, recruit the crews, and oversee the project. He was to personally make every hiring decision except for one: Porter had insisted that a man named Don Walker be included on the roster. Walker was a World War I veteran who was working for Consolidated Aircraft in San Diego. Although Walker didn't know anything about drilling, Porter assured Rosser that Walker was a good man who could help with the myriad regulations and challenges that would arise.

The recruitment began, and soon the drilling crews began to take shape. The men were interviewed and impressed with the secrecy of the operation. If they were suitable, military deferments were obtained and they were signed up.[8] Throughout these months of gearing up and negotiating contracts, the British grew increasingly impatient for work to begin. Even before arriving in England, the Noble crews were getting their first taste of the urgency of war's demands.

Good Fortune on Dangerous Seas

Finally, in February 1943, Rosser and Walker were ready to embark for England. The crews and rigs would follow while Rosser and Walker organized housing and set up the work site. Once again, the realities of war intruded. Rosser and Walker had originally planned to fly from Montreal to London, but because of the priority given to military personnel, they were bumped from their flight and journeyed by sea. On February 11, 1943, they

Eugene Preston Rosser was chosen by Lloyd Noble to lead the drilling crews working in England. Rosser was responsible for recruiting, training, and managing the crews as well as locating and shipping the four drilling rigs needed. *(Photo courtesy University of Oklahoma Press.)*

left the United States by boat, sailing aboard the British ship *Stirling Castle*.

Nine days into the trip, the plane on which Rosser and Walker had originally been booked crashed in Portugal, killing 15 passengers and seriously injuring 10 others. When he found out, Rosser reportedly slapped Walker's back and proclaimed, "Ole buddy, we don't have to be scared of anything now. 'The Big Man' upstairs has got his arm around us now! You can't ever tell me that he didn't have a hand in bumping us off that plane."[9]

Unknown to Rosser and Walker, their families had also gotten a first taste of wartime fear. A German broadcast on February 17 announced the sinking of a British vessel out of New York carrying a group of oil technicians.[10] Later, *Time* magazine reported that two U.S. passenger-cargo ships, crammed full of servicemen and civilians on war missions, had been sunk in the Atlantic.

A group of the oil field workers (above) in New York City before departing for London. The crews didn't know the location of the oil fields until they arrived in England. Donald Edward Walker (left) was hired to handle the staggering logistics of housing and feeding crews in war-ravaged Britain. Working closely with Rosser, he became an invaluable member of the team by keeping the men fed and healthy. *(Photos courtesy University of Oklahoma Press.)*

The incidents occurred four days apart and had a cumulative death toll of more than 850.

This threat of submarine wolf packs was very real. Rosser and Walker later learned that their boat had veered about 350 miles off course to avoid German subs, which followed it for several days. They speculated that their vessel had been spared because it was painted with large white crosses, proclaiming it an unarmed nonbelligerent vessel carrying medical supplies and hospital personnel.

On February 20, Rosser and Walker arrived in Britain and saw firsthand the devastating work of Nazi bombs. Walking through Liverpool, Rosser was amazed at the piles of rubble that once had been buildings. The same devastation was evident in London.

Roughnecks and Monks

The rest of the men wouldn't arrive until late March aboard the H.M.S. *Queen Elizabeth,* leaving Rosser and Walker time to find living quarters near the drilling site in Sherwood Forest in Nottinghamshire. Known as Duke's Wood, it was the same region made famous by the tale of Robin Hood and his merry band. In fact, the oil workers received their identification cards from the 1943 Sheriff of Nottingham.

Searching for places to live, Walker finally settled on an unusual location: an Anglican monastery near the village of Kelham. It seemed a strange

Left and below: The reality of the war hit home when Rosser, Walker, and the crews arrived in London. Nightly German air raids had reduced much of the beautiful city to rubble. The photo at left shows the view from Saint Paul's Cathedral while the photo below pictures Queen Victoria Street. *(Photos courtesy the City of London Police.)*

Bottom: Each member of the drilling crew received these cryptic departure instructions. Everything about the project was considered a matter of urgent national security since the Germans would quickly have destroyed any producing oil fields in England. *(Image courtesy Lewis Dugger.)*

choice for a group of young American oil-field workers, most of whom dressed like cowboys and were accustomed to a decidedly more nocturnal, boom-town environment. Before long, local punsters had dubbed the residents the "rogues and robes."[11]

But right from the beginning, Rosser was sure they had picked the right place. He guaranteed the monks that their young boarders wouldn't cause any trouble, and they didn't. The reality of war was too close, and there wasn't much alcohol or trouble to be found in England in those days. On their very first day, the group heard German bombers droning overhead, probably heading for Birmingham or Sheffield.[12]

Although they didn't mix much, a true feeling of comradeship eventually sprang up between the

CONFIDENTIAL

Report to the United States Army REGIONAL TRANSPORTATION OFFICE at EUSTON Station not later than 8:00 p.m. Thursday, March 30th. Baggage should be marked ONLY with the individual's NAME and the CODE which is "M 34". Proceed to the Station ALONE and tell NO ONE of the prospective journey. The approximate rail fare, first class, is £ 5 - 10. Destination will be given by the R T O at EUSTON.

sandaled monks and booted oil-field workers. Every week, the monks regularly posted notice of services in the chapel (although only Don Walker would attend every Sunday), and soon one of the monks, Father Edgar, got into the habit of greeting every shift of workers with jokes and riddles as they came home exhausted after 12-hour shifts, seven days a week.[13]

The Merry Band of Americans

Sherwood Forest had both advantages and disadvantages when it came to drilling for oil. First off, the geology of the area was not very complicated. Second, the towering trees hid the drilling rigs from probing German eyes. As a precaution, though, everything was painted green because the Germans would quickly have bombed any visible oil field.

Not surprisingly, most of the disadvantages were connected to the war. It took weeks to get equipment shipped over, and some was lost to German subs. Once equipment did arrive, it was always an adventure for Rosser and his men to retrieve it as British customs officials were justifiably concerned with any "secret" equipment coming into their country.

Worse even than the equipment shortage, however, was a persistent shortage of food. With the men working so hard, they required good food and a lot of it. But in wartime Britain, they were often reduced

A National 50 rig in Sherwood Forest in 1943. Originally the British had wanted ten rigs, but Noble vice president Ed Holt estimated that only four of the advanced National 50s could handle the task. *(Photo courtesy Lewis Dugger.)*

The "boys," as the drilling crews were frequently called, stayed in the Kelham Monastery for the year they spent in England. Relations between the monks and the exhausted drilling crews were excellent, with Father Edgar greeting crews with riddles and locals affectionately naming the strange mix the "rogues and robes." During the worst of the food shortages, crew members turned part of the monastery grounds into a vegetable garden. *(Postcard courtesy Lewis Dugger.)*

KELHAM.

to eating cold brussels sprouts or mash, and the lack of good food quickly began to affect their performance. Meat was a rarity, as were fresh vegetables. Throughout the year, Rosser's adventures in procuring good food became legendary, including the time he found himself in a shouting match with a U.S. general in the quartermaster's division as he tried to get his men food from the U.S. depot. This effort was finally successful, and the food problem was solved.

The environment posed another problem. That part of the English Midlands was prone to nasty weather and cold winds blowing in from the North Sea. The men worked in freezing rains and gales for much of the time and fought mud as they laid fuel and water lines. Worse yet, because of wartime restrictions, they could use only 20-watt bulbs to light the derricks at night.[14]

Because of the pressing concerns of running a drilling company during a war, Lloyd Noble was never able to visit the Sherwood Forest project. He later remarked that it was the only important project he didn't visit. He did help however he could, though, sending U.S. magazines and the local Tulsa newspaper for all the boys to read. He also wrote the crew letters, which Rosser read out loud, that reminded the men how important their work was and how grateful Noble felt personally.

Faster than a Speeding Bullet

Whatever challenges lay in the way, the crews from Noble didn't waste much time when it came to drilling oil wells. This was something they knew how to do, and their skill took their British counterparts by surprise. On the first 12-hour shift, the American drilling crew reported that 1,010 feet of hole had been drilled. When this figure was relayed back to D'Arcy, the British oilmen couldn't believe it and demanded that the figures be confirmed. They turned out to be accurate, and before long London was used to receiving astonishing drilling reports from the Americans.

There were many reasons the American crews moved so quickly. The new jackknife-type rigs were much easier to move around and didn't require a week to build. "We were ideally designed for that kind of drilling," remembered Lewis Dugger, who was one of Noble's drillers. "We had the jackknife masts. The English were used to

standard rigs. It'd take them about a week to build a derrick, and then they had primitive methods. It would take them about three months to drill a well, and it would take them three weeks to move a rig from one place to another."[15]

Also, the British had very strict rules about drilling. Bits, for example, had to be changed at 30-foot intervals regardless of their condition. When the Noble crew chief heard this, he could not believe it. Noble crews went through the time-consuming task of changing drill bits only when a particular bit had stopped making hole.

Although this was a small example, it pointed out an important distinction between American and British crews. Later, when Rosser was asked to give a talk to high-level executives of the Anglo-Iranian company about his crews' incredible efficiency, he pointed out that American drilling crews operated independently. Because every day and every situation varied, crew chiefs were allowed great latitude to make on-the-ground decisions. This approach stood in stark contrast to the more regulated British methodology.

In a month's time, with three rigs, seven wells had been completed and casing had been set in two more, with casing due to be set in the 10th well the next day. On average, Americans were completing one well per week, while their British counterparts' best time was one well every five to eight weeks.

A Funeral at Kelham

With the drilling going ahead and the crews settled into a routine of hard work while living in a historic monastery, the project in Sherwood Forest would be subject to only a single tragedy. On November 13, 1943, derrickman Herman Douthit was killed when he fell 55 feet from the double board of a drilling mast.[16] Rosser would later describe this accident as the worst day of his tour in England. Douthit was interred at a local cemetery, and the locals in Kelham raised money for his widow.

After the war, in accordance with the policy of the Veterans Administration, Douthit's body, along with the remains of American servicemen previously interred in cemeteries throughout Britain, was transferred to the American Military Cemetery and Memorial, located near Cambridge. Douthit is the only American civilian interred in that cemetery.

Above: On November 13, 1943, derrickman Herman Douthit was killed when he fell from a drilling mast. He was buried by his crew members at a cemetery in Kelham. This tragedy was the only fatality to occur during the project. *(Photo courtesy Lewis Dugger.)*

Right: In 1991, surviving members of the Sherwood Forest crew visited Douthit's grave. After the war, his body had been relocated to the American Military Cemetery and Memorial near Cambridge, where he remains the only American civilian.

A Welcome Return Home

Marred by this single tragedy, the Sherwood Forest project was otherwise a complete success. By the end of 1943, Sherwood Forest drilling had sent 2.28 million barrels of high-grade paraffin-based oil to refineries on the west coast of Britain and in the south of Scotland. From March 1943 to March 1944, under the cloak of secrecy, Noble Drilling, with a crew of 44 men, drilled 106 wells, 94 of which were producers, and England's oil production jumped from about 700 barrels a day to over 3,000 barrels a day.[17]

The project ended after a year, and shortly before the war ended, the weary crews returned home. But the Sherwood Forest drilling project would have far-reaching consequences. During the project, British drillers trained with the Americans and learned how Noble could move so quickly. These same methods were later applied in Saudi Arabia, where British Petroleum worked on the largest oil fields in the world.

Also, many of the men associated with the project won a place in their countrymen's hearts. In 1954, Queen Elizabeth knighted Sir Charles Philip Southwell for his contribution to the war effort. Southwell suggested that Walker and Rosser also be knighted, but the queen could bestow the honor only upon Englishmen.

Years later, Southwell wrote about the Sherwood Forest project. "The credit for that must lie with Lloyd Noble," he said. "It was extremely doubtful if anyone else would have tackled the job with the same interest and enthusiasm."[18]

The crews from Noble also reaffirmed the bonds that had formed during their experience. In 1987, 20 of them met for a reunion in Ardmore. It was the first time many of them had seen each other since their wartime adventures. Moreover, Rosser and Walker remained lifelong friends, and Walker would spend the rest of his career working at Noble Drilling.

In 1989, Energy Advocates, a group of independent petroleum executives, learned of the crew's heroics and raised $250,000 for a seven-foot statue to be placed as a memorial to the Americans who

Above: Sir Charles Philip Southwell, who was personally responsible for bringing American drilling crews into the project, was knighted in 1954. He is pictured here outside Buckingham Palace with his wife and son Richard immediately after the ceremony. *(Photo courtesy University of Oklahoma Press.)*

Below: In 1991, the surviving members of the American drilling crews traveled back to England—many of them for the first time since the war—to visit the Sherwood Forest site and dedicate the Oil Patch Warrior statue.

Jim Day and other industry executives listen as David Harding, CEO of British Petroleum Exploration Europe, dedicates the Oil Patch Warrior statue, which stands in Sherwood Forest, Nottinghamshire, England. The statue is a tribute to the men who aided the Allies' war effort.

contributed to the wartime effort.[19] Jay O'Melia, a Tulsa artist, was commissioned to produce a bronze sculpture, called "Oil Patch Warrior," that depicted a driller handling a Stillson wrench. (Reproductions of the statue adorn the reception areas at the Noble Drilling office in Houston and the Noble Foundation in Ardmore.)

Two years later, Noble Drilling financed an eight-day trip and sent the surviving 16 members of the crew to England for the dedication of the statue. David Harding, CEO of British Petroleum Exploration Europe, dedicated it at Duke's Wood, whose oil fields had been depleted and shut down in 1965.[20]

Unique in its place in oil industry history, the Sherwood Forest drilling project could have happened only at the behest of a patriot like Lloyd Noble, who was willing to forgo profits for the sake of his nation and send crews on a risky and daring adventure into a war zone. It was the only time in the company's history, and perhaps that of the whole industry, when a drilling project was commenced in the middle of a war.

With the end of the war in 1945, Noble stood on the threshold of a new era of economic growth and a nation thirsty for even more oil. As always, Noble Drilling would be there, following the flow of oil on its increasingly global journey.

Shown here in characteristically casual dress, Lloyd Noble was a hard-working man who expected the same of his employees.

CHAPTER FOUR

POSTWAR PROSPERITY AND A LIVING LEGACY

1945–1950

The obligation that rests squarely on the shoulders of each generation is not what they inherit, what they have handed to them, what they acquire from the standpoint of wealth or position, but what they do with the wealth and power they have in their hands. Because wealth and power, whether in the possession of an individual, community, or state, are merely tools that are placed in their hands.

—Lloyd Noble, 1943

AMERICA, WEARY OF RATIONING, emerged from the war primed for much-needed prosperity. One of the driving factors in the new economy—literally—was the country's renewed interest in the automobile. With fuel restrictions finally lifted, more and more Americans took to the road, pushing the fledgling oil industry to speed its switch from wartime production of high octane fuels to gasoline and home heating fuels. Black gold continued to seep its way into all aspects of American life, proving that, contrary to wartime fears, the supply was not yet running dry.

As peacetime ushered in the Age of the Automobile, the number of vehicles in the United States would more than double in less than five years, boosting sales of gasoline accordingly. Although the transition to the production of low-octane gasoline and home heating fuel proved a difficult one for the industry for a variety of reasons, the steady consumer demand held the promise of profit for those who endured changeover successfully. In 1945 alone, the price per barrel for oil rose from $1.64 in January to $2.44 by the end of the year.[1] Not surprisingly, this rapid increase led to more federal scrutiny and price control. Said author Kenny Franks in *The Oklahoma Petroleum Industry*, "[L]ower prices were not welcomed by an industry that had suffered the devastating economic blow of the Great

Depression, as well as the subsequent controlled rationing and price regulation during the war years."[2]

Yet despite its distaste for regulation, the industry, now freed from wartime constraints and better equipped to supply the country, was poised for growth: the market looked wide open. According to *Wildcatters: Texas Independent Oilmen*, a historical account,

Though wartime dislocation and regulation had created some formidable barriers to profit making, market conditions in 1945 were much better than in 1933. Wartime improvements in pipeline systems made it easier for producers to sell the oil they produced. All that seemed to stand in the way of a new era of prosperity was federal price regulation.[3]

As it did for much of America, the newfound post–World War II abundance created multiple opportunities for Noble Drilling to grow. The company augmented its equipment fleet, garnered new contracts nationwide, and continued to innovate by experimenting with creative techniques such as

In 1945, Noble Drilling contracted to drill within view of the historic Cape Hatteras lighthouse. *(Photo courtesy Lewis Dugger.)*

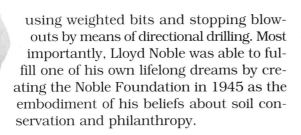

using weighted bits and stopping blow-outs by means of directional drilling. Most importantly, Lloyd Noble was able to fulfill one of his own lifelong dreams by creating the Noble Foundation in 1945 as the embodiment of his beliefs about soil conservation and philanthropy.

A Debt Paid

After observing how the eroded, depleted southern Oklahoma soil continued to diminish crop yield each year, Lloyd felt compelled to save not only the land but those who relied upon the land for their living. He named the Samuel Roberts Noble Foundation after his father, "to give recognition to the most charitable individual I ever knew," said Lloyd at the foundation's first meeting in October 1945.[4]

Although Lloyd was adamant that the foundation's first concern should be the conservation and improvement of the soil, the trust agreement creating it permitted work in science, literature, education, charity, and religion as well. Through this organization's work, Lloyd could assuage the sense of debt he felt toward his fellow man, whom he believed responsible, in part, for his own fortune.[5] As Lloyd himself envisioned it, the foundation would "assist mankind so that it might ultimately achieve full physical, intellectual, and moral development."[6]

Yet beyond Lloyd's sense of obligation, the Noble Foundation would correct what he perceived as flaws in the Vivian Bilby Noble Foundation, which he had created after the death of his beloved wife. This first foundation had, among other endeavors, supplemented the salaries of professors at the University of Oklahoma during Lloyd's tenure on

the university's board of regents. Nonetheless, Lloyd felt that he had more to give and vowed that he would create another trust able to take on loftier goals should he one day have the financial wherewithal to do so. By 1945, he had acquired the wealth that would enable him to more than "do his part" for his generation.

Exploration on the East Coast

In the mid-1940s, Noble Drilling was doing its part to increase business and further industry, although the risks were increasing by the foot as drillers were forced to seek greater and still greater depths in order to find oil. To mitigate the risk, companies like Noble began negotiating contracts that paid them on a per-day, rather than a per-foot, basis.[7] Following the war, Noble Drilling had more than 40 active rigs and contracts with Shell Oil, Standard of California, Standard of Indiana, Standard Oil of New Jersey, and Texaco.[8] Noble by this time had drilled in more than 25 states, both offshore and abroad.[9]

It was just after the war, in fact, that Noble contracted with Standard Oil of New Jersey to drill several East Coast wells, including one of the first exploratory wells in the Atlantic Ocean using one of the world's largest offshore barges to transport materials to the drilling site.[10] These wells included the 1 Maryland Esso, which was located three miles north of Ocean City at the extreme eastern point of Maryland. Work on that well began in late 1946 with plans to take it 5,000 feet deep. Noble Drilling would also drill an important well near the Cape Hatteras lighthouse on North Carolina's Outer Banks.

Above left: Lloyd realized a lifelong dream when he created the Samuel Roberts Noble Foundation in 1945.

Left: Noble Drilling's Cape Hatteras rig was located just 1,700 feet from the lighthouse. (The lighthouse has since been moved a short distance to avoid beach erosion.)

Opposite: Although the Cape Hatteras well yielded no oil, the data gathered during the project proved invaluable to geologists. Here, a roughneck rigs tackle. *(Photo courtesy Special Collections, University of Louisville.)*

With the historic lighthouse bearing silent witness, drilling of the Esso No. 1 commenced in December 1945 in Cape Hatteras, North Carolina.[11] Because the closest available railroad was more than 100 miles away in Elizabeth City and the nearest road ended halfway between that city and the barrier islands, getting materials to the site was a tricky proposition. To surmount these challenges, it was necessary to use barges in a six-foot-deep channel[12] dug in Pamlico Sound specifically to bring in the more than 1,000 tons of supplies needed to set up and operate the rig.[13] Once the supply-laden barges reached the end of their water trip, it was still necessary to drag equipment another two miles across sand to the project warehouse.

Although the East Coast lacked the western fields' promise of black gold, drilling there would serve a twofold purpose: In the event this well did, in fact, tap into a new oil reserve, the United States would have an easy means of supplying the East Coast without the use of tankers, which had

Above: The Esso No. 1 crew included (left to right) Lewis Dugger, J. L. "Fay" Waits, Louis Stephenson, V. D. "Spike" Miller, Cotton Dickson, and a Carter Oil Company geologist. *(Photo courtesy Lewis Dugger.)*

Right: Men at work: (left to right) Noble's Cotton Dickson, V. D. "Spike" Miller, an unidentified man, and J. L. "Fay" Waits.

proven to be dangerous targets during the war.[14] But even if the well yielded only data, this information would be invaluable to the study of coastal geology and the science of oil exploration as well. Noble was an important part of this exciting endeavor, and the company gained vital knowledge by solving the knotty logistics problems caused by the rig's barrier-island location.

Roughnecks were brought in to operate the Esso No. 1 from as far away as Oklahoma, Louisiana, and Texas, with islanders hired to replace those who could not endure the isolation. Spike Miller served as Noble's toolpusher and engineer for the job. Ray Miller, a Buxton, North Carolina, man interviewed by the *Island Breeze* in 1995, recalled the arduous 12-hour shifts: "I was pouring 100-pound bags of mud down a pipe for 12 hours a day. The first day after I started working, I wasn't sure I could get out of bed." Nonetheless, drilling continued 24 hours a day for more than half a year.[15]

Noble eventually drilled the Esso. No. 1 well to 10,054 feet but found no oil—as had been expected. Yet despite this seeming lack of success, Standard Oil would still call the Esso No. 1 "the most important wildcat venture in eastern America in 1945 and 1946."[16] It was critical but expensive work, costing Standard Oil stockholders more than $477,000.[17]

Noble drilled the Esso No. 2 well for Standard Oil in Pamlico Sound, North Carolina. The well was drilled from a large barge that was towed from the Gulf of Mexico. *(Photo courtesy Special Collections, University of Louisville.)*

At about the same time as it had contracted with Noble to drill in Maryland, Standard Oil chose a site for the Esso No. 2 in Pamlico Sound 32 miles north of the Esso No. 1 and 17 miles from Manteo, North Carolina. Until it could determine a precise location, Standard Oil pondered whether to drill the well from the "center of a 300-foot island to be built by dredging or from a huge drilling barge to be towed here from the Gulf of Mexico and anchored in the Sound."[18] This barge, which would have to be refurbished for the job, was 207 feet long and 45 feet wide. It would be partially sunk and then anchored with heavy piling.

Once it had fixed a location, on October 18, 1946, Standard Oil chose the barge plan. The depth of the water at the site, some three miles west of Barrier Beach, was about five feet. An *Oil and Gas Journal* article in October 1946 reported that drilling would begin "upon the arrival of a large sinkable barge now under construction in New Orleans."[19] Standard Oil saw this second North Carolina well as another long shot in tapping oil. However, it would be "the first overwater drilling

ever attempted along the Atlantic Coast."[20] The well proved to be kin to its Cape Hatteras predecessor. It was abandoned in 1947 at 6,410 feet with no oil or gas found.

Supply and Demand

The United States had provided around 90 percent of the oil used in the war effort—the "high-water mark for its role as supplier to the world."[21] By 1943, however, especially after the Middle East assessment of geologist and Petroleum Administration Deputy Everette Lee DeGolyer, it had become clear that the world's future oil supply would be found in the Persian Gulf.[22] In 1945 America was still producing some 4.7 million barrels of oil per day.[23] Even two years after the war had ended, the country had 110 major oil fields yielding prodigious amounts of oil.[24] By 1948, however, the telltale sign couldn't be denied: America was importing more oil than it was exporting as the sudden increase in demand quickly taxed domestic supplies.[25]

The end of the war—along with subsequent price changes—brought renewed attention to exploration and offshore drilling. Oklahoma-based independent Kerr-McGee, along with Phillips Petroleum Company and Stanolind Oil and Gas Company, drilled the world's first commercial well out of sight, completing it on November 14, 1947. This

GROWTH BEYOND IMAGINING

ED HOLT, A NOBLE VETERAN and friend of Lloyd Noble, once commented that of all the many projects that Lloyd Noble was involved with, the Samuel Roberts Noble Foundation "had a more human element" than any other. Lloyd, who was always looking for something "bigger and better," was interested in broadening his mind and finding ways to improve mankind.[1] Through the foundation, he could realize both these dreams.

As Lloyd Noble saw it, the ties that bound the oil and agricultural industries were not as tenuous as they might first have seemed. After all, both relied upon the earth's bounty for their success. And just as science had improved the oil extraction process, so too could it help heal the battered Oklahoma soil. Just as critical was education because it provided the means of transmitting these lessons and advancements from generation to generation.

As was Lloyd's desire, the Noble Foundation concentrated its early efforts on conservation and crop improvement. It also made several important philanthropic gifts.[2]

In 1952, the foundation broadened the reaches of its research by adding a biomedical division that focused primarily on cancer research until the division was relocated to the Oklahoma

Medical Research Foundation in Oklahoma City in 1993.

When Lloyd died in 1950, the vast majority of his multimillion-dollar estate was bequeathed to the foundation. Its original trustees were Lloyd Noble; his mother, Hattie Noble, who served until her death in 1953; and three officers of Noble Drilling: Cecil Forbes, P. G. Rawdon, and Jerome Westheimer, the first managing director of the Noble Foundation. Lloyd's son Sam was elected a trustee; two of Lloyd's other children, Ed and Ann, were elected in 1951.

Because Westheimer, a geologist with Samedan at the time of his appointment, felt he could not handle both roles, he resigned from his foundation duties in six months. He was replaced by Colonel Francis Wilson, a U.S. Army Corps of Engineers retiree. Colonel Wilson resigned in 1951 and was replaced as managing director by P. G. Rawdon. Rawdon had been employed in the tax department of Noble Drilling and, before that, by the Internal Revenue Service. He was succeeded by James Thompson, a former Noble Drilling attorney, in 1953. Upon Thompson's retirement in 1965, John March, a longtime Noble Affiliates/Samedan officer, took the reins as foundation president. Under his guidance, the foundation expanded significantly.

accomplishment not only cut the costs of drilling offshore but also helped to eliminate fears of dry holes. The well, located in just 18 feet of water some 10 miles from the nearest land off Louisiana, would yield gas and oil for years to come.

The discovery of oil at shallow drilling depths of about 1,700 feet prompted a race to obtain leases along the Gulf Coast, and by January 1948, 20 oil companies had rushed to sink wells along Louisiana's shoreline.[26] Noble Drilling had first drilled in Louisiana 12 years earlier.[27] Now, taking advantage of postwar supplies, the company would

purchase a number of Navy landing ship tanks, or LSTs, for use as service barges in its Gulf Coast drilling operations.[28] Johnnie Hoffman, retired vice president and general manager of the company's Gulf Coast division, recalled how the rough weather made working conditions even more difficult: "You worked 12 hours on a rig and then tried to rest 12 hours on that rolling LST in the rough Gulf waters. It could get miserable at times."[29] Conditions were just as taxing farther west, where Noble employees drilling in the Rocky Mountains contended with the hazards of snow and ice.[30]

The foundation's largest gift ever was a commitment of $7.5 million in 1996 for the construction of the Sam Noble Oklahoma Museum of Natural History. This was the largest donation ever received by the University of Oklahoma.[3] Later endeavors included a cattle development project called the Noble Line[4] and the addition of a Plant Biology Greenhouse in 1993. The foundation also donated $2.5 million to the National Cowboy Hall of Fame to build a multiuse hall in 1994. Today, it promotes research in cooperation with several Texas universities.

In 2000, the Noble Foundation celebrated its 55th anniversary. Presently it receives no federal or state funding and pays operating expenses and grants entirely with earnings from investments. In 1999, the market value of the foundation's total assets was $870.4 million.[5]

Mike Cawley, foundation president in 2000, said he felt certain that even though it had been more than 50 years since Lloyd started the foundation, it was still doing today exactly what he intended it to do. "Lloyd Noble planted a seed," said John March in a 1999 interview. "And it's grown way beyond what his imagination was."[6]

In the late 1980s, foundation trustees were (standing, from left) Dr. David Brown, husband of Ann Noble Brown; W. R. Goddard; Michael Cawley, executive vice president; Lloyd Noble II, advisory trustee; Vivian Noble DuBose; Dr. Randolph Brown Jr.; and John March; (seated, left to right) John F. Snodgrass, foundation president; Ed Noble, Lloyd's second son; Ann Noble Brown, sister of Ed and Sam; Sam Noble, Lloyd's oldest son, executive vice president of Noble Affiliates at the time; and Mary Jane Noble, Sam's wife.

Lloyd's 25th Anniversary

In 1946, Noble Drilling celebrated Lloyd's 25th year in the industry with a surprise party.[31] He was a firm—and sometimes intractable—but caring employer who had done much to look after his Noble family over the years, including starting one of the first profit-sharing plans in the oil industry. The scope of his benevolence extended much further than his employees, however; it was during the celebration that Lloyd announced his intention to use his own stock dividends to fund the Samuel

Roberts Noble Foundation, which he had first established on October 22, 1945.[32]

In the spring of 1948, just two years after celebrating his 25th anniversary in the industry, Lloyd Noble stepped down as the company's president. According to minutes from the April 1 board meeting, Lloyd "advised the directors that it had long been his desire to be relieved of responsibility as active executive head of the corporation."[33] His resignation came exactly 26 years after the April 1, 1921, birth of his limited partnership agreement with Art Olson. The board named Lloyd to a salaried position as chairman and elected Cecil Forbes to guide the company as president. Forbes, previously executive vice president, would continue in this role for the next five years.

Under the leadership of Forbes, Noble Drilling by mid-1948 had division offices in Tulsa, Fort Worth, Midland, Houston, New Orleans, and Casper, Wyoming. In the summer of 1948, in addition to its work in Alberta and other locations, Noble was preparing to operate two rigs from offshore platforms in the Gulf of Mexico. The lucrative Gulf Coast region had attracted many oil companies to search for oil or extend its known fields. In June 1948, more than 675 rigs, or a third of the nation's total, were drilling along that coast.[34] By the end of the year, Noble had won contracts from the California Company and Amerada Oil Corporation for Gulf wells ranging from 9,000 feet to 10,500 feet deep. Noble could brag that it already had drilled more than 150 wells below the 10,000-foot mark.[35]

At this prosperous time for the company, those at the Noble helm in addition to Lloyd Noble, now chairman of the board, and Forbes, president, included P. M. Johns, vice president and treasurer; George Kemnitz, vice president in charge of drilling; M. E. Tate, vice president and general superintendent for the Rocky Mountains; John Roring, vice president and general superintendent for Oklahoma and North Texas; Smith Spradling, vice president and general superintendent for West Texas and New Mexico; Ed Holt, vice president and general superintendent for Kansas; R. E. Favor, general superintendent for the Gulf Coast; and L. E. Stewart, district superintendent for West Texas and New Mexico. James Thurston was company secretary, and C. J. McCoy was chief engineer.

Lloyd may have stepped down from his position as Noble's president, but he remained active in both Noble and industry affairs, serving on the boards of directors of several associations, including the Drilling Contractors Committee of the Independent Petroleum Association of America and the Mid-Continent division of Production of the American Petroleum Institute in 1947, and the Mid-Continent division of the Oil and Gas Association in 1948. He was also a member of the Rocky Mountain Oil and Gas Association and petroleum clubs in Tulsa, Oklahoma City, and Dallas.

Political matters kept Lloyd busy as well, although he did not actively seek office. Persistent rumors in 1949 that he was being considered as a possible candidate for Oklahoma governor were dismissed by Lloyd himself in the January 31, 1950, edition of the *Tulsa Tribune*. Business commitments and the Noble Foundation kept him busy enough without the addition of politics to his schedule, he told the newspaper. In addition, Lloyd had lately confided to friends and family members that he had not been well.

A Well Runs Dry

After a business meeting on February 13, 1950, Lloyd Noble met long-time friends George Kemnitz, Dick Favor, and Ben Scott at the Lamar Hotel in Houston for a late-night game of cards. After being plagued all day by what he told friends was "indigestion," Lloyd, then 53, suffered a fatal coronary and died before the medics could reach him in the early morning hours of Valentine's Day.[36] At the time of his death, Lloyd Noble was president and chairman of the board of Samedan as well as Old Ocean Oil Company and J. S. Abercrombie Oil Company, both Houston companies.[37]

Ironically, Lloyd's death came not long after he had agreed to serve as chair for an Oklahoma Heart Association fundraiser. Questioned about his motivation for getting involved with the organization, Lloyd had responded: "Heart disease is your business and my business because your family and friends are among its potential victims. No one can say with any real assurance, 'This can't happen to me.'"[38] In retrospect, Lloyd's biographers questioned whether the timing of his chairmanship was prescient, but he was a man who was mysterious about many things, as Art Olson, his friend and first partner, would later say.[39] And, as an article in the *Daily Oklahoman* (headlined "Prophecy of Death? Did Noble Know Time Was Up?") suggested, "Perhaps, with his love for mystery and his tinge of mysticism, Lloyd Noble again knew many things he did not say."[40]

At the time of his death, Lloyd Noble was a multimillionaire. Although the exact value of his estate was unknown, estimates ranged from $10 million to $50 million. Little financial information about the company prior to 1950 is available because of

A LEGACY FOR MANAGEMENT

My hope is that when into other hands are placed the responsibility for the management of our mutually built enterprise, those in command will not lose sight of the fact that no individual builds anything worthwhile by his effort alone; that, though none of us can be totally fair, as we are human, our companies will continue down through the years to attempt to give to people associated with them an equitable portion of the fruits of their labor which, of course, bears with it the like responsibility on the part of the management to weed out those who do not want to make a sincere contribution, in order that room may made for those who do. It has been my further belief that it was the duty of management, and to that end my mind has been constantly surcharged, to so build the organization that when men evidenced capabilities to give them a part of my work and find other tasks to do which might result in increased benefits to the organization, or step aside; and on the other hand, should death intervene, to have matters so arranged that I would be missed personally, while the machinery continued to function smoothly.

—from the Will of Lloyd Noble

Through careful planning, instinctive hiring decisions, and his tough yet tender way with employees, Lloyd Noble (shown here at the Tulsa airport) helped ensure that his legacy would live on.

Lloyd's distaste for publicity: he believed his business was a private affair and that the details of his business arrangements were also a private matter. Area newspapers, reporting on Lloyd's death, estimated that Noble companies operated some 50 drilling rigs in 20 states and Canada.[41]

Noble Benefactor

At well-attended services at the First Presbyterian Church, Lloyd's Ardmore, Oklahoma, church home, he was "mourned by roughnecks and ranking statesmen, by all colors and creeds."[42] Hundreds stood outside the church's main auditorium; others found seats in the basement and in the adjoining Noble Memorial Chapel, which had been built by Eva Noble, Lloyd's aunt. Among those in attendance were former Governor William H. Murray; past and present members of the University of Oklahoma board of regents; University of Oklahoma President George Cross; and Lieutenant Governor James E. Berry. Lloyd Noble's pall bearers included employees Dick Favor and Howard "Red" McCarty.[43]

Lloyd Noble's will would further illustrate his unending generosity and dramatically change the management of Noble Drilling over the next two decades. The vast majority of his estate—which principally consisted of his oil-related companies, including Noble Drilling—was given to the Noble Foundation, with Cecil Forbes filling in for Lloyd at Noble Drilling and Lloyd's son Sam taking the reins at Samedan. In addition to the Noble Foundation, Lloyd's will named 106 other beneficiaries, including his housekeeper and some of his employees' children.

Most importantly, the will converted Noble Drilling, Samedan, and other oil-related properties and companies into subsidiaries of the Noble Foundation. With the producing companies eventually folded into Samedan, the arrangement took Noble Drilling out of the oil-producing business and restored it to its former position as exclusively an oil-drilling contractor, drilling wells for third parties. Noble Drilling and the other oil companies would operate with the Noble Foundation as "parent" until 1969, when tax changes governing the operation of nonprofit organizations prompted the Noble Foundation to sell the for-profit subsidiaries.

Although Lloyd's seemingly sudden death shocked the public, those closest to him had seen the signs of trouble brewing over the years through a series of "episodes" that clearly frightened Lloyd and left him seeking almost constant company.[44] Just prior to his heart attack, Lloyd seemed to know—at least viscerally—that the wellspring of his life would soon run dry. He began to tie up the loose ends of his professional and personal lives. The completion of his tenure as an Oklahoma University regent and the formation of the Noble Foundation served to cap his life's work: his years of giving would live on through the legacy of these organizations.

The Changing of the Guard

Lloyd's oldest son, Sam, was just 25 years old when his father passed away and he became the head of Samedan. The young man would also take his father's position as chairman of the board of Noble Drilling. His father's death, he would later say, "left a giant hole—not only in my personal life but in the organization as a whole. Noble Drilling was a well-organized and sizable drilling company for the time; however, Samedan was really just getting started."

Although the task was an arduous one for a young man forced into adulthood and obliged to wear the mantle of leadership upon his father's death, Sam Noble said he was compelled to accept the gauntlet laid before him:

One of the main reasons I stayed is that shortly after my dad died, we heard from several reliable sources that the industry experts were giving us from six months to two years to fold up. That was an insult to two good companies as well as a personal challenge for me. I was particularly fortunate, however, to have had several loyal old-timers

to lean on for advice and counsel. Their guidance was invaluable.[45]

One such "old-timer," Cecil Forbes, continued as president of Noble Drilling; another, Ed Holt, was brought back from retirement and became vice president to assist with the transition. Cecil Forbes, who is given much credit for the leadership transition and for coping with the Noble Foundation as the corporate parent of Noble Drilling, would serve as company president until his retirement in 1953. His friendship with Lloyd dated back to their college days, when the pair schemed to go into the clothing business. Specializing in administration and operation, Forbes was with the company when Lloyd and Art Olson dissolved their partnership in 1930 and was one of the key officials transferred from Ardmore to Tulsa when Noble Drilling moved its corporate headquarters.

In addition to the new Noble hierarchy and the management changes, the 1950s would present even more challenges as the face of the oil industry continued to change. In 1951, the Middle East would provide 80 percent of the world's oil. In order to stay afloat, drilling companies like Noble had to find a way to survive the cutbacks in contracts. But Noble Drilling had seen hard times before and—somehow—had always found a way to survive. Even after Lloyd Noble's death, this survival instinct would remain strong, allowing the company to continue to grow and prosper in the years ahead.

Restructuring at the end of the 1960s and into the early 1970s would prompt the company to split itself into four divisions. This land rig, *E-554,* is at work in the Bossier area of northern Louisiana. It operated for the Central division, which included Arkansas, Mississippi, Alabama, and parts of Oklahoma, Texas, and Louisiana.

CHAPTER FIVE
A TIME OF TRANSITION
1951–1969

*It has been my further belief that it was the duty of the management . . .
to so build the organization that when men evidenced capabilities to give
them a part of my work and find other tasks to do which might result in
increased benefits to the organization, or step aside; and, on the other hand,
should death intervene, to have matters so arranged that I would be missed
personally, while the machinery continued to function smoothly. As to the
degree I have succeeded[,] others can now pass judgment.*

—Lloyd Noble, from his last will and testament

THE YEARS FOLLOWING THE death of Lloyd Noble marked the beginning of a significant transition for Noble Drilling in more ways than one. For one thing, the politics of the industry as a whole changed dramatically as oil's epicenter continued its shift from the United States to the Middle East. Wartime fears of limited resources were soon replaced with new concerns as Middle Eastern oil began to glut the market, causing a price slump and depressing domestic exploration and drilling. In addition, the advent of the Korean War in 1950 and the specter of communism hovering over the Middle East gave both the U.S. government and the oil industry much cause for concern.

And just as the industry was undergoing a major transformation, the decisions at Noble would shift to new leaders in rapid succession in the wake of Lloyd Noble's death. These management changes, along with the changing face of the industry and the reorganization of the Noble companies, made for a tentative future. Not surprisingly, some industry insiders were quick to predict the company's imminent demise. But Noble Drilling, much like its founder, had always been something of a scrapper. It had survived troublesome times before and would do so yet again.

During this bumpy interval, the business of Noble Drilling shifted organizationally. Noble Drilling, Samedan, and other oil-related properties and companies became subsidiaries of the Samuel Roberts Noble Foundation.

Innovations and Leaders

Despite all of these concerns, Noble continued its long-standing history of pioneering new drilling techniques. In the early 1950s, it became the first company to drill in Bay Marchand, off the coast of Louisiana, using electrical power from shore. Previously, Noble had used self-contained electric rigs and took the next probable—though seemingly impossible—step of laying electric cable in the water. A man named C. J. McCoy came up with the idea and used Army surplus equipment to build several electric rigs in the Ardmore base hangar.[1] According to Lewis Dugger, retired safety manager for Noble, the company worked out a deal with Louisiana Power & Light to get shore-based power from a 13,000-volt submarine cable.[2] Though the endeavor was a dangerous one, it was an important step for offshore drilling, which would continue to become more vital over the next two decades.

Cecil Forbes would serve as president of Noble Drilling until his retirement in 1953.

Noble's management, meantime, was going through a number of rapid changes. From 1950 to 1967, Noble Drilling would have four different presidents. Immediately after Lloyd Noble's death in 1950, Cecil Forbes continued in his role as president of Noble Drilling, focusing his efforts on administrative duties. Ed Holt returned from retirement to help with operational concerns during several periods of leadership transition.

Holt recalled the aftermath of Lloyd's death.

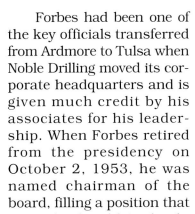

[Forbes] was really the next man on the list to run the whole Noble Foundation and all the other interests. I think all the rest of us pitched in and took a load off of his shoulders, and in the meantime, the Foundation was formed. So that just knitted this all together better. I think Mr. Noble had that in mind all the time anyway, to keep his family together, to keep his people together too.[3]

Forbes had been one of the key officials transferred from Ardmore to Tulsa when Noble Drilling moved its corporate headquarters and is given much credit by his associates for his leadership. When Forbes retired from the presidency on October 2, 1953, he was named chairman of the board, filling a position that had been vacant since Lloyd Noble's death. Percy M. Johns, vice president, replaced Forbes as president and would guide the company for the next decade. An Ardmore native, Johns had joined Noble in 1933.

Sam Noble, who upon his father's death had become a member of the board of directors of Samedan, would serve as Samedan's president from 1952 to 1965. In August 1954, both Sam and his younger brother Ed were named directors on Noble's board.

"Sam did a real good job with carrying on that oil company," said Eugene "Gene" Rosser, longtime Noble Drilling employee. "I think he had some static to start with, but by golly, who could come into

the shoes that he was supposed to fill and even come close to it?[4]

Hard Times

In the 1950s and 1960s, the number of active rotary drilling rigs in the United States began dropping dramatically and would continue to decrease through the early 1970s.[5] As industry writer John L. Kennedy noted, the price of oil and gas naturally affected the number of wells drilled. According to figures from the *Oil and Gas Journal*, the average number of working rigs in the United States peaked at 2,687 in 1955.[6] These figures would decline from 1956 until 1973, when the oil embargo and resulting price increases prompted an upswing.[7] "[F]rom the middle of the 1950s 'til the early 1970s, survival alone was the real achievement for most of the independents and small drilling contractors," said Sam Noble in Noble Affiliates' 1979 annual report.

Fortunately, Noble Drilling's decentralized management system, which gave its experienced field managers the freedom they needed to deal with local markets and issues, kept the company healthy during the hard times that followed.[8] Noble Drilling's continued belief in its employees' ability to do their jobs was exactly the kind of trust Lloyd Noble had counted on to keep the company running well long after his death. Sam Noble wrote that "because both Samedan and Noble Drilling had delegated much of the responsibility for field operations and exploration activities to highly competent division managers, with the authority to act quickly and autonomously, they many times had an advantage over our larger competitors."[9] He went on to say that since his father had left the companies' ownership to a charitable foundation and

Left: Longtime Noble employee Ed Holt would be summoned back from retirement to manage operational concerns following Lloyd's death.

Opposite: Despite uncertain economic and internal conditions, Noble Drilling continued to focus its efforts on finding new and better ways of drilling. Shown is a tender-assist platform rig from the early 1950s.

because the foundation "had enough other assets (which he had provided) to carry out its charitable purposes without calling on our organizations for funds, we were able to keep a nucleus of good people, do a modest amount of exploration, and maintain our equipment during these rough years."[10]

Indeed, the company still held firmly to its founder's beliefs with regard to personnel. And just as Noble Drilling had found creative ways to keep men working during the Depression, so did the company keep key personnel on the payroll during this downturn by "bumping" everyone back. "Drillers went to roughnecking, tool pushers went to drilling, and superintendents went to pushing tools," recalled longtime employee R. C. "Duke" Hinds. "It was a step backward for everybody, but we still had a job. Eventually, it paid off because

Noble had good people when the rig [activity] picked back up."[11]

The Williston Basin and Gulf Drilling

Despite the general slowdown in domestic drilling and exploration, North Dakota experienced a major boom in 1951 when the Amerada Oil Corporation discovered oil near Tioga in the northwestern part of the state. The site was located in the Williston Basin, which stretched into the neighboring states of Montana and South Dakota as well as parts of Canada. This discovery and another one in Montana caused a "frenzied race for oil leases."[12] By late 1955, North Dakota had more than 600 producing wells in the basin.

Exploration in coastal waters hadn't stopped completely during this time, and with technological improvements aiding the hunt for oil offshore, a legal battle called the Tidelands Controversy ensued between the federal government and the coastal states over where, exactly, a state's offshore borders were. The federal Submerged Lands Act of 1953 solved the debate by giving the states title to underwater lands within three miles of shore, although Texas and the west coast of Florida were given up to 10.4 miles offshore. Another piece of federal legislation in 1953 allowed the secretary of the interior to lease offshore lands through competitive bidding. The first Outer Continental Shelf lease sale took place in the Gulf off the coast of Louisiana in late 1954. By 1957, 101 offshore drilling rigs—96 off the coast of Louisiana alone— were at work in the United States.[13]

Despite the industry's enthusiasm, offshore drilling was disproportionately expensive, costing "as much as three times . . . similar operations on land."[14] While thirsting for the enormous oil and gas reserves believed to exist beneath the waters,

Above: Sam Noble (shown here in the early 1970s), son of Noble Drilling founder Lloyd Noble, took the reins of sister company Samedan at the tender age of 25. He later ran Noble Affiliates.

Opposite: Noble Drilling increased its offshore drilling efforts in the 1950s and 1960s. Shown is a K&N offshore double-structure rig working in Louisiana waters.

companies had to incorporate cost-saving measures wherever they could, all the while building barges capable of drilling to unheard-of depths. The California Company, or Calco, contracted with Noble Drilling in early 1954 and implemented a plan to drill multiple-directional wells using a uniquely designed derrick on an offshore platform about two miles off the Louisiana coast.

The Calco drilling site was located in 18 feet of water in the Main Pass Block 69 field, which had been discovered by Calco before the Tidelands Controversy. In an article titled "Cheaper by the Half Dozen," the *Oil and Gas Journal* reported that the rig was believed to be one of the first ever built for multiple drilling and could drill six wells without having to skid, or move, the rig.[15]

Lee C. Moore Inc., along with Calco engineers, designed the 140-foot-tall derrick for use on a platform built by Avondale Marine Ways. By using a specially designed movable crown block near the top of the derrick and by shifting the rotary table, the rig's crew could drill two rows of three wells each. The rows were spaced 10 feet apart, and the wells within the row were drilled seven feet from each other. The rig could drill up to 14,000 feet deep, although the wells at this site were to be drilled to only about 9,000 feet.[16]

Prior to its move into the Gulf, the six-well derrick had been erected on the Harvey Canal near New Orleans and its movable well-location equipment tested. Workers then partly dismantled the derrick and towed it by barge down the Mississippi River to

the drilling site. There the derrick and its decking were lifted onto the specially designed platform, supported by columns sunk 15 feet into the Gulf floor. An LST (landing ship tank), as a drilling tender, provided extra storage space and crew quarters.

As Noble's district superintendent in New Orleans, Dick Favor oversaw work on the Calco platform. According to a January 1954 article on the work, "Drilling crews have reported no special difficulties arising from the unique derrick arrange-

ment. Of course, a little time was required to become accustomed to the different relative position of the rotary table in respect to the draw works, but that has not slowed work in any way."[17]

The mid-1950s proved to be a time of continued innovation and exploration for Noble Drilling. In 1955, the company built its first mobile offshore "jackup" drilling rig. It also ventured outside the United States for exploratory drilling.[18] Associated Noble Corporation, one of the many temporary drilling companies created by Noble Drilling for specific jobs, had been formed in September 1948 to drill in Canada. In 1955, it sent workers to conduct exploratory drilling for Amoco in Jamaica, where it drilled three wells.[19] With the work for Amoco completed, the board of

In the mid-1950s, Noble Drilling drilled exploratory wells in South America and Jamaica. Here the company tows a rig to the drilling site on the island.

Beginning in the early 1950s, Louisiana and other Gulf Coast locations proved to be a hotbed of activity for Noble and other drilling companies. Employee Dick Fugler pulls lines in Golden Meadows, Louisiana.

directors of Noble Drilling dissolved Associated Noble in June. Noble Drilling also explored potential drilling sites in South America, sending Cecil Forbes, George Kemnitz, and James E. Thompson to Venezuela.[20]

B. F. Walker

B. F. Walker Inc., an oil-field trucking company, became a sister firm to Noble Drilling and Samedan in 1957. That year, the Noble Foundation, "in order to move some of [its] drilling and producing equipment more efficiently," bought an interest in Walker.[21] B. F. Walker had started the company in 1918. In 1960, he decided to retire and sold the remaining stock to the Noble Foundation.

Walker's company was one of the "big five" in the oil-field hauling business. According to a 1964 *Denver Post* article, B. F. Walker in just a year had pumped up its fleet of over-the-road tractors from 150 to 163 and its number of trailers from 175 to

222.[22] The company hauled not only rigs but also the drilling pipe. Indeed, according to the article, "Although fewer wells are being drilled these days, they are deeper and require more pipe footage. As a result, the oil field hauling business keeps getting bigger and bigger and B. F. Walker's gross revenue has doubled in the last six years."[23]

Price Checking

To protect U.S. producers from less-expensive imports, the federal government in 1959 placed mandatory quotas on foreign oil. In his Pulitzer Prize–winning book, *The Prize*, Daniel Yergin wrote that the quotas served as a catalyst to encourage more domestic investment in oil exploration. Yergin documented the effect of the quotas.

Indeed, domestically, the ten-year period following the introduction of the mandatory quotas was reminiscent of the price stability that followed the full implementation of prorationing in the 1930s. The average price of oil at the wellhead in the United States in 1959 was $2.90 a barrel; a decade later, in 1968, it was $2.94—stable, certainly, and also 60 to 70 percent above Middle Eastern crude in East Coast markets.[24]

In 1960, the Organization of Petroleum Exporting Countries (OPEC) was formed in direct response to price cuts made by U.S. oil companies. OPEC set production ceilings and indirectly dictated oil prices since OPEC's five founding members (Iran, Iraq, Kuwait, Saudi Arabia, and Venezuela) controlled more than 80 percent of the world's supply.[25]

Leadership Transition

Just as the international oil community was facing the changes that resulted from the formation of OPEC, Noble was facing changes of another kind.

Percy Johns was Noble Drilling's president from 1953 to 1963. He would then serve as vice chairman on the company's board until his retirement in 1969.

Percy Johns served as president of Noble Drilling through June 15, 1963, at which time he was named vice chairman, a position he would hold until his retirement in 1969. Upon Johns's retirement as president and his subsequent promotion, Howard "Red" McCarty, a 26-year veteran of the company, assumed the role of president.

McCarty, who had begun his Noble career as a roughneck and had been manager for the Oklahoma Panhandle division, first began working for the company during summers in the 1930s while he played football for the University of Oklahoma. His untimely death due to cancer at age 49, on March 1, 1965, just two years after he had been named company president, touched off yet another leadership transition.

For a time after McCarty's death, Noble Drilling continued to operate without a president. To help keep things running smoothly in the interim, Noble once again relied upon those men who had actually worked with Lloyd Noble. A little more than a year after McCarty's death, George

This philosophy was often cited as the reason Noble Drilling, like its sister and parent companies, could count so many loyal individuals among its employees. Like every family, Noble undoubtedly faced growing pains, but it had managed to survive because of its employees' unswerving dedication. "We just went on around the company and just [ran it as] it had always been run," said Holt. "I think we did a pretty good job."[27]

"[L]ike a family, the employees were genuinely interested in how and what each, as well as the company, was doing," said Sam Noble. "In the early days, we could pretty well keep up with each other by word of mouth."[28] All that changed as the companies grew. In 1967, Don Walker began putting out information about his fellow employees and the companies through the *Noble Newsletter.* This effort, said Sam, gave "our organization a sense of unity, which through the years has given the Noble companies a leg up on [the] competition."[29]

Drilling and Dedication

Noble would later describe its rig activity during the early 1960s as "fairly stable."[30] The company continued to pride itself on its ability to improve drilling techniques and in 1958 began air drilling, a method that involved the use of compressed air instead of drilling mud. Duke Hinds recalled that the company had also "drilled in New Mexico at 13,000 feet using air and soap. . . . We prided ourselves that nobody could outdrill us," he said.[31]

For a portion of the 1960s, Noble Drilling had three divisions covering the Gulf Coast, the

J. Matetich Sr. was named executive vice president. In early 1967, Noble's board named Matetich, then 44, president.

Matetich had joined Noble Drilling in 1953, having previously worked for a drilling company in Fort Worth, and would hold the title of president until his retirement in 1984. He earned a bachelor's degree in business and accounting in 1949 from Texas Christian University in Fort Worth. At Noble, he learned the values of founder Lloyd Noble under the tutelage of Ed Holt and Cecil Forbes. Matetich summed up their wisdom.

Their philosophy was that a company's strength is its people. You can have the finest equipment in the world, but it's the devoted and loyal people that make the organization prosper. Our people feel they belong. . . . Somebody cares. Somebody thinks about them. Somebody tells them they're doing a good job.[26]

Top: In 1963, Red McCarty, who had been with the company almost 30 years, was named president. He would serve in that role until 1965.

Center: In 1967, Matetich was promoted to president of Noble Drilling. He had joined the company in 1953.

Noble Drilling office employees and their spouses paying a visit to the Noble Foundation in Ardmore in 1963 included (1) Basil Wynn, (2) Charles Copeland, (3) Red McCarty, (4) Percy Johns, (5) Jim Thompson, (6) C. J. McCoy, and (7) Gene Rosser.

Oklahoma Panhandle, and the combined area of the Rocky Mountains, West Texas, and New Mexico. In 1967, it would add a research and development division headed by Eugene "Gene" Rosser, who had been managing Noble's West Texas operations. At the end of the decade, Hinds served as vice president and manager of operations, and Orval E. Ruth served as vice president. Don Walker, of Sherwood Forest fame, was the company's safety director.

The 1970s would bring continued innovation to Noble as the company experimented with an additional technique called "raise drilling," which enabled it to "dig vertical or angle shafts for the mining and construction industries; raise holes from the bottom to the surface; [and] drill large underground holes for use in ventilation shafts, ore passages, or personnel escape routes."[32] The raise drilling concept involved drilling a small hole downward to connect to a shaft, then attaching a large bit to the bottom of this small pipe and drilling back up to scrape out a larger hole. Noble used this particular drilling method to create ventilation shafts for mines in Alaska.[33]

A New Headquarters

Noble had kept its headquarters in the same 14-story downtown-Tulsa building for many years. The building had undergone several name changes: It was originally known as the Philcade Building and then as the Stanolind Building. In the late 1950s, it became the Pan American Building. In 1968, Noble left the Pan American Building for another downtown site, the 22nd floor of the Fourth National Bank Building. Noble would

remain headquartered there until the mid-1970s, when it moved to the Utica Bank Building, where it occupied two stories.

Noble Affiliates and the Tax Reform Act of 1969

In 1969, America watched mesmerized as NASA landed the first man on the moon. Hundreds of thousands of miles below, Noble Drilling was expanding its frontiers by drilling at unheard-of depths at sea. Soon it would have to dig into its own pockets as a result of tax changes. That year, the U.S. Congress passed a tax reform act that prohibited charitable foundations like the Noble Foundation from owning more than 20 percent of a company. Consequently, the foundation trustees had to either sell Noble Drilling, Samedan, and B. F. Walker or combine the trio and sell 80 percent of the consolidated company's stock to the public. In response to the new tax law, Noble Affiliates Inc. was created on December 29, 1969.

Noble Drilling was once again facing transition as it became a subsidiary under the umbrella of the newly formed Noble Affiliates. Noble Affiliates owned 80 percent of the three companies that the foundation

A typical Noble National 50 series land rig at work in the late 1950s. Noble Drilling would enjoy "fairly stable" drilling activity in the 1960s, followed by a boom in the 1970s.

had formerly owned completely. Now the foundation owned only 20 percent, as dictated by the tax act. "We thought it might be the end of the world, but it turned out to be a blessing in disguise," said John March, who worked for both Samedan and Noble Drilling.[34]

Divide and Conquer

By the early 1970s, Noble would once again be facing operational changes as it restructured into four divisions: the Central division, the Gulf Coast division, the New Mexico–West Texas division, and the Rocky Mountain division. The Central division, consisting of central Oklahoma, east Texas, Arkansas, northern Louisiana, Mississippi, and

Alabama, was managed by R. G. Fugler. Its main office was based in Shreveport, Louisiana. Dick Favor ran the Gulf Coast division, which had its main office in New Orleans. Earl Frederickson managed the New Mexico–West Texas division, which included work in the Permian Basin. Its main offices were located in Midland, Texas. R. C. "Chuck" Syring headed the Rocky Mountain division, which had offices in Denver and rig operations in Montana, Idaho, Utah, North and South Dakota, Wyoming, and Colorado.

With these new divisions in place, Noble Drilling, now under the umbrella company of Noble Affiliates, was ready to move forward and take on new challenges, including the company's first public offering.

John March joined Samedan in 1956 and went to work for the Noble Foundation in 1965. He was one of the key players in the foundation's decision to form Noble Affiliates.

The 1973 oil embargo prompted an increase in domestic exploration and drilling, particularly offshore drilling, which continued throughout the decade. Located offshore Corpus Christi, Texas, these rigs were operated by Samedan on its Northeast Chevron prospect in 1979.

CHAPTER SIX

COMING INTO ITS OWN

1970–1979

We at Noble have been in the oil business for more than half a century.
Thus, it is no accident that we have some of the most competent people
and the best equipment in the industry.

—Sam Noble, president, Noble Affiliates, 1973

I N THE EARLY 1970S, OIL CONCERNS would shift yet again as the Organization of Petroleum Exporting Countries (OPEC) tightened its grip on the world's oil supply to a stranglehold, sparking an unprecedented energy crisis. The politics of petroleum would weigh more and more heavily on Noble Drilling and the industry at large. Never before had the maxim "oil is power" rung so true.

At the beginning of the decade, control fell to OPEC, whose ability to determine international oil production and thus, indirectly, oil prices, had a profound effect on global affairs. OPEC could, simply by increasing or decreasing oil production, dictate the volatility of the industry. Other factors, such as the United States' support of Israel, further shifted the balance of power as major Arab oil producers, including Libya, Iran, and Iraq, became increasingly vocal in their opposition to American involvement and claims.

Back home, OPEC's control prompted much debate as President Nixon determined whether to abolish U.S. quotas. Although these quotas were meant to protect precious domestic supplies and to keep a surplus available in case of an emergency, the emergency had clearly arrived: America had developed an insatiable appetite for petroleum products but lacked the means to supply itself. With a demand much greater than its supply, the United States and much of the oil-consuming world had to turn to Middle Eastern and African suppliers.

Yet despite the gloomy global picture, this decade would prove to be an important one for Noble Affiliates and Noble Drilling as the United States, at a colossal impasse with its Arab suppliers, renewed its search for domestic deposits. With George Matetich firmly ensconced as president, Noble Drilling once again began to experience a level of stability that had been elusive in the years following Lloyd Noble's death. Now, despite unpredictable economic conditions in the oil industry, Noble Drilling was primed for a long-overdue growth spurt. This development would be fueled in part by the public offering of Noble Drilling's parent company, Noble Affiliates.

Growth Spurt

During this decade, Noble Affiliates' annual revenues would climb from $38 million to $214 million as each of its subsidiaries recorded dramatic growth in most years. To facilitate its monumental growth, the company would spend some $436 million for exploration and other expenditures. Noble Drilling would drill 1,865 wells and 21.1 million feet of hole and increase its number of rigs to 44 by the end of 1979.[1] Down from more

The Noble Affiliates logo in 1979 represented the "N" of Sam Noble's signature.

than 3,000 rigs in the 1950s to fewer than 1,000 rigs in the early 1970s, the country's total rig count would finally begin to increase once more.[2] Noble Drilling's sister companies would be active too: Samedan would make significant oil and gas discoveries, and B. F. Walker would purchase two trucking companies.

The 1970s would also bring continued innovation to Noble Drilling as it experimented with an additional technique called "raise drilling," which according to a company brochure enabled it to "dig vertical or angle shafts for the mining and construction industries; raise holes from the bottom to the surface; [and] drill large underground holes for use in ventilation shafts, ore passages, or personnel escape routes."[3]

Going Public

In 1972, Noble Affiliates and its subsidiaries were faring well—so well, in fact, that its income was up 36 percent from the previous year. As part of its decision to include Noble Drilling, Samedan, and B. F. Walker under the umbrella of Noble Affiliates (prompted by the Tax Reform Act of 1969), Noble Affiliates made its first public stock offering on October 17 on Nasdaq under the ticker symbol "NOBL."

"The main reason [Noble Affiliates] went public was to start liquidating below that 20 percent level of the foundation stock ownership," explained Mike Cawley, of the law firm Thompson and Cawley. In 1977, Cawley would take over legal duties for Noble Affiliates, the Noble Foundation, and the Noble family from Noble Affiliates general counsel James Thompson. Cawley would later become president of the Noble Foundation and a board member of Noble Drilling.[4] Over the next five years, the Samuel Roberts Noble Foundation would dispose of 2.5 million shares of its Noble Affiliates stock, which equaled 58 percent of its ownership in the company.

In 1972, Noble Affiliates general counsel James Thompson (shown here in a 1960s picture) helped to take the company public.

Spectacular Results

The Noble Drilling subsidiary in particular turned in "spectacular results" in 1972, according to Noble Affiliates' first annual report, with pretax earnings of more than $2 million—an incredible jump of 259 percent.[5] As his father had done before him, Sam Noble gave credit to the company's loyal and hard-working employees for their part in Noble Drilling's success: "Although high demand for drilling rigs contributed heavily to Noble's increased volume, top-level performance by its crews and the rigs they operated were responsible in large measure for the company's dramatically improved profitability."[6]

As U.S. oil companies were compelled by the Arab embargo to focus on domestic drilling and exploration, the company also reached 78 percent rig utilization in 1972, up 13 percent from the previous year. In addition, Noble Drilling put three new rigs capable of drilling at depths of 20,000 feet or greater into operation, including an inland and a shallow-water drilling barge.

Both Samedan and B. F. Walker experienced significant growth as well, with Samedan's earnings increasing 16 percent and Walker's jumping 67 percent. Samedan continued to explore worldwide, pursuing interests in the North Sea as well as in Canada, Louisiana, Texas, Oklahoma, and New Mexico. Walker underwent its own growth spurt, spending $750,000 to augment its fleet with 88 trucks and 80 trailers (both leased and bought).

The year also marked Sam Noble's implementation of an award-winning safety program, developed in response to the Occupational Safety and Health Act (OSHA), which was passed in 1970 to help decrease the overall rate of on-the-job accidents and deaths due to unsafe working conditions. Although Noble Affiliates, like many companies, disliked the government's interference, it also prided itself on safety. Claiming its safety program should be an industry model, Noble Drilling reduced its lost-time accident rate by approximately 75 percent during the 1970s.[7]

An Oil War

When Egypt and Syria took up arms against Israel on Yom Kippur, the Jewish Day of Atonement, in the fall of 1973, the attack prompted more than just an Arab-Israeli war. OPEC was clearly waging an oil war too by refusing to sell oil to countries like the United States that supported Israel during and after the Yom Kippur War. OPEC's ensuing embargoes and restrictions wreaked havoc upon the delicate balance of the world's industrialized economies, creating an energy crisis that was far more fearsome than any anticipated before, during, or after World War II.

Author Daniel Yergin drew a vivid picture in *The Prize.*

By 1973, oil had become the lifeblood of the world's industrial economies, and it was being pumped and circulated with very little to spare. Never before in the entire postwar period had the supply-demand equation been so tight, while the relationships between the oil-exporting countries and the oil companies continued to unravel. It was a situation in which any additional pressure could precipitate a crisis—in this case, one of global proportions.[8]

In the early 1970s, Noble Drilling enjoyed a high level of activity prompted by the oil crisis. Here Noble's *Barge No. 2* drills at Bay Jaque, Lafourche Parish, Louisiana, in 1972.

America became quickly and painfully aware of just how dependent it had grown on foreign oil as vehicles lined up in serpentine caravans at gas stations across the country. Headlines proclaimed "Energy Crisis!" But although the perception of the shortage was greater than the actual shortage, increasingly limited supplies did cause prices to skyrocket, magnifying the urgency of the situation. A barrel of oil that in 1973 cost about $4 would by the end of the decade cost nearly 10 times that. Natural gas prices were soaring as well after two decades of stability. Noble Affiliates had found little new gas in 1972 and 1973, and the issue of supply was further snarled by a paucity of drilling equipment and men to run it.[9]

Although the shift in oil production from the United States to the Middle East had in the 1960s caused a decrease in domestic drilling and exploration, the embargo in 1973 prompted a renewed search for domestic oil. Exploration, said Sam Noble, was a crucial weapon in the oil war. The discovery of untapped U.S. deposits would help the country "free itself from dependence on foreign oil and gas," he wrote in the company's 1973 annual report.

Accordingly, Samedan in 1973 increased the scope of its exploration both at home and abroad, participating in five wildcat ventures, including one in the Mediterranean Sea. Yet despite the increased activity, Samedan's oil production actually declined that year; its natural gas production, however, increased.

The Tulsa Tribune

Business—Oil

TULSA, OKLA., FRIDAY, AUGUST 31, 1973 — PAGE 1 B

Sam Noble likes Canada

By BILL SANSING—Oil & Finance Editor

ARDMORE — Soft-spoken Sam Noble, president of Noble Affiliates Inc., probably is the envy of many other executives in large cities who have to battle urban pressures.

Noble lives and works in this "All-America" city where the air is clean, the pace unhurried and the citizens friendly.

His company's primary operations are conducted by three major subsidiaries: Samedan Oil Corp., Noble Drilling Co., Tulsa, and B. F. Walker Trucking Co., a common carrier headquartered in Denver.

Although he presents an easy-going, relaxed manner, Noble obviously works hard at his job of directing the firm's worldwide operations. The financial reports attest to his ability and that of his officers and employes.

LAST YEAR the Noble Foundation sold one million shares of Noble Affiliates common stock to the public and mon stock to the public and this initial divestiture reduced the foundation's ownership to about 71 per cent.

The company, in its first annual report to shareholders, noted Noble Affiliates Inc.'s consolidated net income was up 36 per cent over 1971. Net earnings were $5.7 million or $1.67 per share compared with $4.2 million or $1.23 for 1971.

There were no extraordinary items last year, but the $1.23 per share in 1971 included an extraordinary gain of 27 cents per share.

THE TULSA drilling company turned in an increase of 259 per cent in pretax earnings to $2,066,000 compared with $575,000 in 1971.

Samedan was up 16 per cent to $3.2 million while B. F. Walker pre-tax earnings rose 67 per cent over the previous year to $560,000.

"This year," Noble said of the oil and gas operations, "our big money will be spent in the foothills area of Alberta."

The company spends $5 million to $7 million of its own money for exploration but is involved with others in expenditures of around $20 million, Noble explained.

Would $5 per barrel oil help your exploration effort? we asked. "You can bet it would," he replied without hesitation.

"We can't afford to pay Libya $4.90 per barrel with our dollars and at the same time let our production drop," he added.

"Millions of barrels of strip-per well oil could be recovered at $4.50 . . . or at least more than operators are getting now."

IN ADDITION TO the rising cost of foreign oil, he com-

See NOBLE page 3B

That same year, Noble Drilling experienced a 43 percent increase in earnings as it actively employed 83 percent of its 35 drilling rigs over the course of the year. As it had in 1972, the company purchased new equipment, this time a submersible drilling barge (Chevron's S-55) for use off the coast of Louisiana. This barge was capable of drilling to 25,000 feet— 5,000 feet deeper than drilling barges of the year before—and in up to 63 feet of water. Noble Drilling was assembling two land rigs that could each drill to depths of 30,000 feet.

The B. F. Walker subsidiary didn't fare as well, however, and saw earnings tumble substantially from $560,000 in 1972 to $186,000, due to government-implemented price controls.

Both Roy Butler, who was president of Samedan at the time, and George Matetich, who had become president of Noble Drilling in 1967, became directors on the Noble Affiliates board in 1973. The addition of Butler and Matetich brought the Noble Affiliates board to seven members, including Sam Noble, E. E. "Ed" Noble (Sam's brother), Ed Holt, James E. Thompson, and Dave J. Hess.

The Search Is On

When the embargo ended in May 1974, America renewed its sense of urgency about finding alternative energy sources. Energy conservation became the new catchphrase as the U.S. government encouraged the use of coal and nuclear power.[10] As oil imports decreased during the embargo and thereafter, domestic production continued to increase. As a result, Noble Drilling saw its earnings nearly double from 1973 to 1974. Demand peaked so much, in fact, that the company did not have enough rigs for the available work, despite having added three rigs and having a rig utilization

Left: In August 1973, the *Tulsa Tribune* featured a profile of Sam Noble and the extraordinary success—despite the energy crisis—of Noble Affiliates.

Opposite: In 1973 much of the company's drilling took place along the Gulf Coast using drilling barges such as *Barge No. 3,* working in Louisiana.

rate slightly more than 88 percent. Altogether the company had 38 rigs.

Among the three new rigs was the first offshore platform rig compatible with American Petroleum Institute (API) standards. Founded in 1919, the API is a national trade association whose equipment and operating standards are used worldwide. Because Noble Drilling's rig met these standards, it would require little or no modification when used on API platforms, thereby generating cost savings. In 1975, the company planned to add two additional API-approved offshore platform rigs, which it would use for drilling contracts it had tentatively obtained in the Gulf of Mexico.

Noble Drilling also explored options in Ecuador, where it joined forces with OKC Petroleum and Texas Pacific Oil (a subsidiary of Seagram Distillers of Montreal). This was a joint exploratory drilling project for two wildcat wells on 700,000 acres owned by OKC— a project that Samedan helped to finance. Noble Affiliates and Texas Pacific Oil purchased a 50 percent interest in OKC.[11]

Samedan was active in exploration as well, spending nearly $18.5 million in its search for new oil fields. To help mitigate the cost, especially as the company's actual oil production remained low, Samedan formed a joint venture with New England Energy. Together the two companies would spend up to $25 million over the next five years to find new deposits. For its part, B. F. Walker enjoyed a strong year of increased profits and expanded significantly.

The year 1974 marked significant management changes for Noble. Roy Butler, previously president of Samedan, was named executive vice president of Noble Affiliates, and George McLeod, who previously served as executive vice president for Samedan, took over presidential duties there. In addition, A. Marvin Dinges, president of B. F. Walker, was named to the Noble Affiliates board.

A Record Year

By 1975, Noble Drilling had reached a zenith. Although Noble Affiliates as a whole showed a combined revenue increase of 22 percent, Noble Drilling revenues climbed from $5.9 million in 1974 to $9.9 million—its highest figures ever. Moreover, these increases came in the face of changing tax laws and tax rates, the lack of a set energy policy, and a depressed economy.[12] Samedan also recorded exceptional figures for the year, earning more than $6.5 million. More importantly, it enjoyed a 65 percent success rate on wells drilled, and both subsidiaries found and developed sources of gas and oil.

With its two new API-approved platform rigs, Noble Drilling now operated a total of 40 rigs at a utilization rate of around 88 percent. Drilling activity that year was focused mainly in the Gulf, Utah, Texas, Louisiana, and Ecuador. Noble Drilling planned extensive rig maintenance for the next year, allotting more than $7 million for the task. It also focused its efforts on safety and recruitment, working with several colleges and vocational institutions to better train and retain valuable employees. Although B. F. Walker showed reduced earnings for the year, the decrease had been anticipated in 1974 and reflected depressed conditions in the trucking industry.

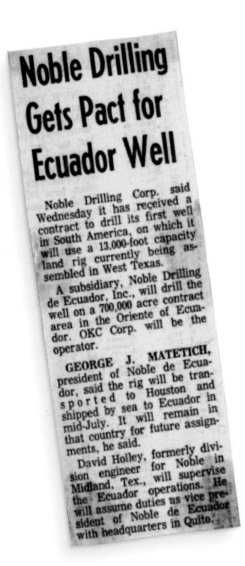

Noble Drilling Gets Pact for Ecuador Well

Noble Drilling Corp. said Wednesday it has received a contract to drill its first well in South America, on which it will use a 13,000-foot capacity land rig currently being assembled in West Texas.

A subsidiary, Noble Drilling de Ecuador, Inc., will drill the well on a 700,000 acre contract area in the Oriente of Ecuador. OKC Corp. will be the operator.

GEORGE J. MATETICH, president of Noble de Ecuador, said the rig will be transported to Houston and shipped by sea to Ecuador in mid-July. It will remain in that country for future assignments, he said.

David Holley, formerly division engineer for Noble in Midland, Tex., will supervise the Ecuador operations. He will assume duties as vice president of Noble de Ecuador with headquarters in Quito.

In board changes, Roy Butler was named president of Noble Affiliates, and Sam Noble was elected chairman.

A Lack of Energy

In 1976, the United States, which was importing about 40 percent of its oil supply and facing dwindling natural deposits, was still in the throes of an energy crisis.[13] "The continued absence of an effective national energy policy and the relaxed attitude of the American public toward the energy crisis are points of major concern to those of us in the natural resources business," said Sam Noble in his letter to shareholders in the Noble Affiliates 1976 annual report. As the search for domestic

With demand for oil at an all-time high, Noble's 1974 endeavors in Ecuador were of major importance, not only to the company but to the American economy. *(Clippings courtesy* Tulsa Daily World.*)*

resources continued, Noble Affiliates saw its earnings rise from more than $11.6 million in 1975 to more than $14.6 million in 1976.

Noble Drilling and Samedan saw increases as well. Samedan, which had increased its exploration expenditures by 72 percent, was particularly successful in locating gas deposits in the United States, Canada, and Tunisia. And although Noble's utilization rate for the company's 40 rigs was down 3 percent to around 85 percent, business continued to be steady, actually increasing by 13 percent. Noble Drilling drilled 201 wells and more than doubled the industry's average depth of around 5,000 feet, reaching 11,284 feet in 1976.

As had been planned the previous year, Noble Drilling spent nearly $12 million to refurbish existing equipment, including more than $4 million for the renovation of an offshore barge. The offshore drilling industry at this time was focusing on the Gulf of Mexico and offshore South America and the Middle East. Noble Drilling's efforts, however, were concentrated primarily in the United States,

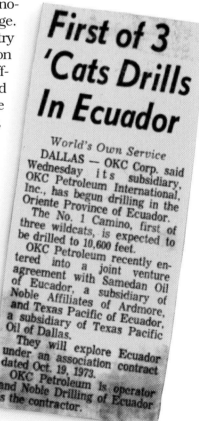

First of 3 'Cats Drills In Ecuador

World's Own Service
DALLAS — OKC Corp. said Wednesday its subsidiary, OKC Petroleum International, Inc., has begun drilling in the Oriente Province of Ecuador.

The No. 1 Camino, first of three wildcats, is expected to be drilled to 10,600 feet.

OKC Petroleum recently entered into a joint venture agreement with Samedan Oil of Eucador, a subsidiary of Noble Affiliates of Ardmore, and Texas Pacific of Ecuador, a subsidiary of Texas Pacific Oil of Dallas.

They will explore Ecuador under an association contract dated Oct. 19, 1973.

OKC Petroleum is operator and Noble Drilling of Ecuador is the contractor.

particularly in the Texas Panhandle, western Oklahoma, the Rocky Mountains, and the Gulf of Mexico. In addition, the company continued its focus on safety, training, and recruitment, reaping the benefits of its efforts with a decrease in lost-time accidents and an increase in promotable employees.

Although B. F. Walker saw its revenues increase, factors such as the general economy, operating costs, and government regulation continued to make profitability elusive for the trucking company.

Long Lines Again

When Jimmy Carter entered the White House in 1977, the energy crisis had reached a heightened frenzy as natural gas stores were depleted by a long, cold winter. Frustrated Americans once again had to wait to buy their gasoline as Carter and Congress battled to create a coherent energy policy. Noble Affiliates continued to decry the U.S. government's apparently fickle pricing structure, which it felt

SAM NOBLE   ROY BUTLER

Noble Affiliates Elevate Sam Noble, Roy Butler

penalized domestic producers with prices often half those offered for imports. It also criticized the expense of creating a Department of Energy, which it believed would "not produce one iota of energy."

The cost of creating the department "is equal to $3.43 for every barrel of domestic oil produced during 1976," said Sam Noble. "We believe it would be far more prudent to encourage the development of new oil and gas reserves by an industry which has proven its ability in the past to do the job."[14]

Marked by what Sam Noble called an "overdue" increase in gas and oil prices, 1977 proved to be a stellar year for drilling contractors nationwide, with more than 44,000 wells drilled by approximately 2,000 rigs.[15] Major oil companies shifted their funding from the international arena to the United States, Canada, and the North Sea. Because of these opportunities, which particularly benefited its Noble

TULSA DAILY WORLD
July 5, 1974

New Samedan President

George J. McLeod, left, has been elected president of Samedan Oil Corp., Ardmore, a subsidiary of Noble Affiliates, Inc. He assumes the position previously held by Roy Butler, right, who is now with the parent company. McLeod has been executive vice president of Samedan since July 1,

The *Tulsa Daily World* and other newspapers gave ample coverage of Noble's activities. At left, the paper announced George McLeod's ascension to president of Samedan while Roy Butler became vice president of Noble Affiliates. A few months later, Sam Noble's election to chairman of the board and Butler's rise to president of Noble Affiliates made headlines.

Drilling and Samedan subsidiaries, Noble Affiliates as a whole did well in the year following the country's bicentennial, showing an 18 percent increase in earnings. It also effected two stock splits and doubled the number of its authorized shares to 12 million.

Noble Drilling experienced its highest rig utilization rate yet at more than 97 percent—up from its slight 1976 slump—and a stock gain of 67 percent.[16] To keep pace, the company added three land rigs and a self-contained offshore drilling platform. Not surprisingly, Samedan also had an extremely profitable year as its exploration in the United States, Canada, and Tunisia yielded 21 discoveries. Even B. F. Walker, which had seen its profitability margin drop significantly in 1976, showed an increase in earnings.

Meanwhile, Noble Affiliates named George McLeod, president of Samedan, to its board. Another important appointment occurred in 1977 when Sam Noble and Roy Butler hired James C. Day to work in an administrative capacity for Noble Affiliates' human resources department. Day was charged with creating a consistent hiring, reward, and promotion policy during this unstable period for the oil industry. At the time he was hired, the company had a turnover rate of 300 percent on some of its rigs, making safe and consistent operation difficult. Day, who would later become chairman, president, and chief executive officer of Noble Drilling, began to analyze Noble Affiliates, creating policies and systems that would assist the company's operations as it grew.[17]

A Second Crisis

In early 1979, the Shah of Iran, with whom America had an amicable relationship, went into exile and was replaced by the Ayatollah Khomeini. In response, the Carter administration placed an embargo on Iran, a move which, along with OPEC price increases, served to highlight the United States' unresolved energy crisis. Coal appeared to be one possible solution, so Noble Affiliates involved itself in a joint endeavor to pursue reserves in the Appalachian Mountains.

Noble Affiliates' overall profits continued to rise, increasing 43 percent to more than $176 million. And despite the inability of most independent drilling contractors to keep pace with inflation, Noble Drilling's profits rose 25 percent to $26.6 million.[18] Independent drillers did better than their larger brethren, however, with 80 percent of the market share.[19] As always, Noble Drilling credited its dedicated employees for its success.

With four divisions and a home base in Tulsa, the company was operating a total of 47 land and marine rigs and maintaining a high utilization rate of more than 97 percent. In 1978, it added three new rigs, including *NN-1*, a newly designed 45-foot shallow-water jackup built specifically for a 50-50 joint venture with National Utilities and Industries. Noble Drilling's offshore efforts at this time were concentrated in the Gulf of Mexico. Other domestic activity focused on the area around the company's division offices in Oklahoma and Colorado.

Samedan, facing soft intrastate gas markets in Texas and Oklahoma and additional regulation,

In 1974, George McLeod (left) became president of Samedan Oil. McLeod is shown in 1976 with engineer Russell Talley.

Bethlehem Steel to build rig

Construction is scheduled to begin in April on a jack-up rig that will provide employment for about 140 persons at the Bethlehem Steel Corp. shipyard in Beaumont.

The multimillion-dollar rig will be built for Noble-National Joint Venture of Tulsa, Okla., using a design recently developed by Bethlehem. It is scheduled for completion in January 1979.

Barry F. Long, acting general manager of the Beaumont shipyard, said the rig will have the capacity to drill to a depth of 30,000 feet. The equipment can operate in inland waters of about 10 feet to offshore waters of up to 45 feet.

While the design is new, it is based on the mat-type jack-up rig Bethlehem has built here for years. The completed rig is expected to be used by Noble-National in the Gulf of Mexico.

The unit will consist of a buoyant platform hull 160 feet long and 72 feet wide, which will be supported by a mat foundation of the same dimensions. Four columns fixed to the mat and passing up through the platform will provide the means for the platform to be jacked above the water.

The contract with the Tulsa firm is the second multimillion-dollar contract signed by Bethlehem in 1978. Noble-National is a partnership between Noble Drilling Corp. of Tulsa and National Enerdrill Corp., a wholly owned subsidiary of National Utilities and Industries of Elizabeth, N.J.

Bethlehem Steel will begin construction soon on this jack-up oil rig for Noble-National Joint Venture of Tulsa, Oklahoma.

An artist's rendering of the *NN-1*, the jackup owned by a Noble joint venture, shows the rig's new design, which consisted of a buoyant platform hull supported by a mat foundation. The four columns allow the platform to be jacked up out of the water. (*Clipping from* Beaumont Enterprise, *March 21, 1978.*)

enjoyed increased oil production but decreased gas production for the year.[20] The company increased its activity in the Gulf of Mexico, where it had previously had trouble obtaining federal leases. Noble

Affiliates applauded the rise of gas and oil prices, which was necessary to fund an aggressive exploration campaign planned for Canada, the Gulf of Mexico, the Rocky Mountains, and Texas.

As it had during the previous year, B. F. Walker continued to have disappointing earnings despite restructuring and increased revenues.

In corporate housekeeping, Noble Affiliates offered its employees a stock ownership plan and moved its corporate headquarters to a new office at 333 West Main in Ardmore. It also budgeted $78 million for exploration and capital spending, a $24 million increase from the previous year.[21]

Despite the economic turmoil caused by the energy crisis, the 1970s was a golden decade for Noble Affiliates and particularly Noble Drilling. Rig *GD-2,* pictured, was one of 32 land rigs Noble Drilling operated in 1979. The company also had 12 marine rigs.

The End of an Era

The year 1979 marked more than just the end of an incredible decade of growth for Noble Affiliates and its subsidiaries. After 30 years of service, Sam Noble stepped down as chief executive officer of Noble Affiliates, passing the title to Roy Butler, who would also remain president. As an active member of the board, Sam Noble would continue to be involved in the company he had helped shape. He had started his career at Samedan at the tender age of 25, when he was thrust into the role of president upon his father's death in 1950. The guidance of his father's employees helped to see him—and the company—through the rough times.

Said Sam Noble in his last message to shareholders, "I would like to remind our present employees and stockholders that we are deeply indebted to the company's founder, Lloyd Noble, and to his

After Sam Noble retired in 1979, Roy Butler became Noble Affiliates' chief executive officer. Butler already served as the company's president.

numerous loyal and competent early associates for providing the proper combination of exceptional people, good equipment and financial stability that our generation could build upon."[22]

As the decade ended, Noble Drilling enjoyed an almost perfect rig utilization rate of 98 percent. Operations during 1979 included the contribution from the 50-50 joint venture between Noble Drilling and a subsidiary of National Utilities and Industries of Elizabeth, New Jersey. Noble Drilling, as the operator, used the newly designed shallow-water jackup drilling rig. During the year, that rig was employed 100 percent, mostly in the offshore waters of Louisiana.

Company crews drilled a total of 2.48 million feet of hole in 1979. Wells drilled on a footage basis accounted for $10.7 million, or 11 percent of gross revenues, while dayrate contracts accounted for $87.1 million.

By the end of the decade, Noble Drilling was flirting for the first time with total revenues of $100 million. The figure was all the more impressive when compared to the company's 1971 revenues of $17.3 million.[23]

Although Noble Affiliates and its subsidiaries had enjoyed remarkable growth during the crisis-filled 1970s, the coming decade would prove more challenging still. Amid the continuing economic turmoil in the oil industry, Noble Drilling would by the middle of the next decade discontinue its association with Noble Affiliates and begin to explore its own path as an independent company.

Working in the Gulf of Mexico, Noble's Rig 31 offshore platform rig could drill down 20,000 feet in as much as 650 feet of water.

CHAPTER SEVEN

GET OUT OF THE WAY

1980–1985

Those organizations not capable or unwilling to address the very key issues that Noble Drilling has undertaken will quite simply fail. . . . Our mettle has and will be tested during this time, but through our efforts Noble Drilling will continue to be a strong and aggressive drilling company.

—Jim Day, 1985

FOR THE FIRST FEW YEARS OF the 1980s, the horizon looked rosy for Noble Affiliates and its subsidiary companies. In 1980, the parent company debuted on the New York Stock Exchange under the symbol NOBL and was able to issue a three-for-two stock split. Gas production rose to a record level in January 1980, and contract drilling had already reached record levels in the United States.[1]

That year, Noble Drilling's revenues passed the $100 million mark for the first time. "Obviously we are convinced that the contract drilling industry has a bright future," wrote Roy Butler, president and CEO of Noble Affiliates, in his 1980 letter to shareholders. Butler wasn't alone in his optimism. Numerous industry analysts agreed with his forecast.[2]

Governmental Decontrol

The optimism was partially due to the decontrol of oil prices, which the Reagan administration implemented on January 28, 1981. The shrinking involvement of the federal government in setting oil prices immediately resulted in a higher price per barrel of oil and subsequent higher oil revenues.

Underscoring its directive to minimize government control, the Reagan administration created a $17 billion federal corporation, Synthetic Fuels Corporation, to provide seed money for con-

struction of synfuel plants.[3] Edward E. Noble, the second son of Lloyd Noble and himself a free-market advocate, was chosen as the company's chief executive. He was expected to implement a newly trimmed synfuels funding policy, offering loan guarantees and price supports rather than equity participation and grants, which the Carter administration had planned to use to get smaller companies into the synfuel arena.[4] Ed Noble resigned from Noble Affiliates' board in 1981 to accept the position.

Studies concluded that the decontrol of oil and gas prices would produce enough revenues to sustain a national rig fleet twice the size of 1979's 2,200 rigs.[5] Indeed, rig demand was high in 1980, and Noble's rigs had an average utilization rate of 99 percent, compared to 92 percent for the previous year. Throughout 1980, Noble drilled more than 2.5 million feet, mostly on low-risk dayrate contracts.[6] The upward trend continued through 1981, with Noble drilling more than 2.6 million feet of hole and boring 94 percent of its wells on dayrate contracts.[7]

In 1981, Ed Noble was chosen to be CEO of the Reagan administration's Synthetic Fuels Corporation, created as part of the government's plan to limit its role in setting oil prices.

A Bigger Fleet

With the decontrol of oil and gas prices, Noble Drilling was looking forward to more good years, so it made sense for the company to expand and upgrade its fleet. In 1981, seeking to replace assets that were 30 years old, the organization committed $145 million, more than it ever had before, to purchase new rigs, predicting that large rigs in particular would be in heavy demand.[8] Indeed, Noble's entire fleet was capable of drilling to more than 12,000 feet, and more than half the fleet was rated at 20,000 feet or more. In 1980, the industry's average depth of wells drilled was 4,594 feet, while Noble's average, 11,765 feet, more than doubled that figure.[9]

In December 1980, Noble Drilling took delivery of platform *Rig 31*, the first in a series of new rigs the company would add in the early years of the decade. The rig immediately began work for Arco Oil & Gas in Mississippi Canyon Block 148 off Louisiana. As an offshore platform rig, it was positioned on drilling platforms owned by other com-

The *OW-862*, a three-engine rig that could drill to 18,000 feet, at work on its first location in Evanston, Wyoming, in the summer of 1981

panies. The rig could drill as deep as 20,000 feet and could work in 650 feet of water.[10]

In March 1981, Noble added the *OW-862* three-engine rig to its Rocky Mountain division, which was headquartered in Denver. Rated at 18,000 feet, the rig began working in the Overthrust Belt shortly after delivery. A few months later, in December, the company added three deep-drilling land rigs to its Mid-Continent fleet. (A well was considered "deep" if it was drilled to at least 12,000 feet.) One of the new land rigs could drill to 20,000 feet, and two could drill to 30,000 feet.

Also in 1981, Noble added two units to its Gulf Coast division: the *PB-2*, a posted barge that could drill to 30,000 feet, and the *Ed Holt* cantilevered jackup rig, capable of drilling to 25,000 feet in 300 feet of water.[11] The *Ed Holt* was particularly important to Noble because it allowed the company to enter the deep offshore drilling market, a sector that would prove highly valuable to Noble in coming years. After delivery, the *Ed Holt* was sent to the Gulf of Mexico under contract with Chevron.[12] Ed Holt, the manager, was, like his namesake rig, of key importance to Noble Drilling.

In 1982, the *PB-3*, a posted barge rated at 30,000 feet, took its place among the Gulf Coast division's fleet, as did the *Sam Noble* offshore cantilever jackup drilling vessel. With 414-foot-long legs, the *Sam Noble* was capable of drilling to 25,000 feet in up to 300 feet of water and could withstand winds of 109 knots and seas of 50 feet. Its design, essentially identical to the *Ed Holt*'s (both were Levingston Class III-C rigs), gave Noble advantages in drilling efficiency, supply, maintenance, and crew training, but Noble's engineers made

minor changes to the *Sam Noble*'s blueprints that made it ideal for working in international and remote locations. Called the "Cadillac" of rigs by Noble's management, the *Sam Noble* had quarters

Right: The *Ed Holt* cantilevered jackup rig could drill up to 25,000 feet and launched Noble into deep offshore drilling. It is shown working in the Gulf of Mexico in the mid-1980s.

Below: Betty Holt breaks a bottle of champagne on her husband's namesake rig at the christening ceremony on December 29, 1981. *(Photo courtesy Lewis Dugger.)*

for 80 crew members, whereas the *Ed Holt* could accommodate only 54, and the *Sam Noble* had more storage room after spud can recesses were eliminated and engine mufflers were moved.[13] With such an immense storage capacity for spare parts, equipment failures could be fixed immediately with as little downtime as possible.[14] "While this drilling rig is basically an exploration tool, the design provides versatility," said Fred Adlam, Noble Drilling's vice president of engineering. "We can drill the wildcat wells, and we can perform work-overs and drilling on sites not completed. It is even designed to drill in near-freezing temperatures."[15] The addition of the *Sam Noble* brought Noble's number of offshore rigs to 15.

A Procession of Leaders

In the meantime, the management of Noble Drilling's divisions was shifting. In August 1980, R. G. (Dick) Fugler, formerly division manager for Noble Drilling's Central division in Shreveport, Louisiana, moved to the Tulsa headquarters

to become vice president of marketing. Lanny Bretches, who had been chief engineer in Tulsa, took Fugler's place as manager of the Central division.[16] The following year, Sam Noble retired as an employee of the company but stayed on as chairman of the board, while Amos Runner became manager for the Mid-Continent division in Oklahoma City.[17]

In April 1982, Merrick M. Harmon was elected a senior vice president of Noble Drilling. Harmon had joined the company as a roughneck in 1941 and had risen to vice president and manager of Noble Drilling's operations. That same month, R. C. "Chuck" Syring, who joined Noble in 1948 and was division manager of the Rocky Mountain division, was named a vice president of Noble Drilling, as was Johnnie W. Hoffman, who had been with the company since 1947 and was division manager of the Gulf Coast division in New Orleans.[18] Also in 1982, Eddie Paul, a 29-year veteran, kkdivision following his stint as assistant division manager.[19] In March 1982, John Snodgrass was named president of the Samuel Roberts Noble Foundation, a position he would hold until his retirement in 1992.

The Downturn Begins

The 1980 industry surveys that predicted continuing favorable performance for contract drilling were correct—for a while at least. The upward trend continued throughout 1981, when Noble Drilling reached record revenues once again. The following

Above: In March 1982, John Snodgrass was named president of the Samuel Roberts Noble Foundation. Later, he became director emeritus of Noble Drilling.

Left: The *Sam Noble* was a sister rig to the *Ed Holt,* but the *Sam Noble*'s design had been modified for drilling in more remote locations. Here it is shown drilling in the Gulf of Mexico in the early 1980s.

On December 7, 1982, Sam Noble had the honor of christening his namesake rig. The *Sam Noble* would prove to be a very lucrative asset for the company.

year, however, introduced a recession that was "the most severe of the postwar period," according to *Forbes* magazine.[20]

The boom in domestic drilling and production came to an abrupt halt. As interest rates soared and OPEC flooded the market with cheaply priced oil, the United States responded by cutting back its own production. And as the price of oil and gas see-sawed up and down, oil companies were forced to guess how much oil and gas they would need and were reluctant to enter into drilling contracts if there was no guarantee that the oil would bring a reasonable price. The contracts that were awarded tended to be footage and turnkey rather than dayrate, which paid a contractor a specified amount per day, no matter how long it took to drill the well. Footage contracts, on the other hand, paid a fixed amount for every foot drilled, while turnkey contracts paid a fixed amount once the well was completed. Both of these types presented higher risk for the drilling company because it would bear the expense of any mechanical malfunctions, equipment shortages, or other problems. To make matters worse, rig building had surged of late, and with the intense competition for available drilling contracts, many rigs sat idle, costing the drilling companies thousands of dollars a day in maintenance alone.

During the last six months of 1982, demand for domestic land drilling was virtually nonexistent, and because Noble Drilling's operations were mostly land based, the company's average rig utilization rate dropped to less than 60 percent. Its profits for 1982 were down 29 percent from the previous year.[21] Despite the gruesome market conditions, Noble Drilling managed to finish the year in the black, mainly due to the *Ed Holt* and the company's other offshore rigs, which had a higher utilization rate than land rigs. The company wasn't as fortunate the following year, however. At the end of 1983, Noble reported its first operating loss in the modern era, with a 42 percent decline in revenues.[22] The downward spiral continued through 1984, when several dayrate contracts for Noble's fixed-platform rigs were

terminated. That year, Noble recorded an operating loss of $24.8 million on revenues of $81.6 million.[23]

Investing in the Future

But it was these very challenges that presented Noble Drilling with new opportunities to invest in its future, increasing its operating efficiency while containing costs. In May 1982 Noble opened a central maintenance facility in Oklahoma City where the company's rigs could get major overhauls and repairs.[24] The 43,000-square-foot building included a shop, a warehouse, and a sophisticated oil analysis lab that could detect metal particles in lubricating oils. Twice a month toolpushers mailed samples of oil from their rigs' major parts for analysis. If a certain level of metal was found in the oil, the staff at the central maintenance facility knew the part was worn and would send out a replacement. In this way, Noble was able to anticipate potential equipment failures before they happened, saving the company time and money.[25]

Moreover, the unsettled domestic and land-drilling conditions drove Noble to expand its offshore fleet and begin pursuing international opportunities —both of which would become prime directives in Noble's future. Though Noble's land operations were severely depressed throughout 1983, its Gulf Coast division, made up of offshore rigs, remained profitable, with above-average utilization rates.[26]

Noble employees proudly accept the IADC Safety Achievement Award, presented to Noble Drilling for 1981. Pictured are (back row, from left) George McLeod, Lewis Dugger, Roy Butler, George Matetich, Sam Noble, Vernon (Hoss) Ramke (IADC Accident Prevention Convention chairman), Norvel Tomlinson, Merrick Harmon, Howard Harlson, Harold Hopkins, Jim Conner, Chuck Syring, Max Smith, Dick Fugler, (front row, from left) Bob Williams, Don Rankin, Jon Murphy, Dan Moore, Larry Richardson, Lanny Bretches, Amos Runner, and Eddie Paul.

Noble proceeded to upgrade its fleet so that it could offer newer equipment and a variety of drilling services. In 1983, the company retired two of its older rigs, rebuilt a platform rig, and purchased a land rig that could drill up to 20,000 feet.[27] The following year, Noble continued with upgrades and bought two land rigs, the *OW-501* and *OW-502*. As shallow- to medium-depth rigs, they could be more competitive because they were easier to move, could drill on smaller locations, and required less fuel. The addition of the two rigs brought Noble's total fleet to 36 land units and 15 offshore units.

The trend of a few years before that favored deep-drilling rigs had effectively reversed itself. "Shallow wells are where most of the drilling is today," explained Amos Runner. "Most companies are drilling for oil in a range of 10,000 feet or less. Our deep rigs can't be competitive in shallow drilling."[28]

Passing the Reins

The year 1984 was a transitional period for the management of both Noble Affiliates and Noble Drilling as the planned order of succession moved the companies' most valued leaders in and out of key roles. In June, Roy Butler retired at age 57 as president and CEO of Noble Affiliates, though he would stay on as a director. Butler began as an engineer with Samedan Oil in 1955 and was elected the subsidiary's president in 1965. He became president of Noble Affiliates in 1975. Butler was an impor-

tant driver in the organization's growth and helped set the stage for the company spin-off. He was succeeded by George J. McLeod, who had served the company for 23 years, most recently as president of Samedan Oil, a position he had held since 1974. McLeod had started his career as a geologist in Canada.

At Noble Drilling, George J. Matetich retired as president as of January 1984 and as chairman of the board at the end of the year. Jim Day had been promoted to executive vice president and elected to the board of directors in 1983. He took up the reins as president and CEO in 1984. Day had joined Noble Affiliates in 1977. He had earned a B.S. degree in business administration at Phillips University.

Safety and Training

During this difficult period, Noble Drilling's management team proved highly capable, for not only did it maintain the company's positive cash flow, but through aggressive bids it also kept Noble's rigs working, thus helping to retain the company's pool of well-trained and experienced personnel. Noble's experienced workforce gave it a competitive advantage, especially considering that the contracts the company was able to secure tended to be footage. The higher risk that these contracts meant for the drilling company made it more important than ever that the operating

personnel have extensive training and experience.

Noble understood the critical role of safety and training in an industry that was inherently subject to many hazards, including blowouts, cratering, fires, and adverse weather conditions such as hurricanes. Thus each division of Noble employed a full-time safety and training coordinator. Furthermore, Noble extended the in-house training program that it had begun in 1976. On their first workday, new employees were given a tour that pointed out possible drilling hazards. Then they observed the more experienced employees before taking on tasks themselves. Workers also went through a year-long home study, reinforcing the on-the-job training with lessons designed by the International Association of Drilling Contractors (IADC).

In addition, the company conducted a performance appraisal program and a management training program, both spearheaded by Dr. Roy Rhodes. A psychotherapist, Rhodes also carried a business degree and had been trained in business counseling.[29] His efforts went a long way toward building Noble's excellent reputation in safety and training. Not only was the company able to retain highly capable employees, but its accident ratio remained dramatically lower than the industry average, which in turn lowered its insurance premiums as well as costs involved with accidents. "Our philosophy is that if we can extend the life of equipment or prevent an accident, we can pay for an awful lot of tests and books," said Joe Hurt, Noble's training director. "The money is minor when compared to the cost of an accident."[30]

Throughout the 1980s, Noble's safety and training program was recognized by IADC, which, year after year, awarded Noble top honors in safety. In 1980, Noble won awards in both onshore and offshore drilling categories, and the following year it won a second-place Class A award for offshore drilling.[31] In 1982, Noble Drilling won Class A first-place awards from IADC for both onshore and offshore operations, making it the only company to win the prestigious award twice in the same year. In 1983, its land operations received the first-place award while offshore operations got second place. And by 1984, its safety record improved by nearly 30 percent after it once again won two first-place awards.[32]

The Spin-Off

Though Noble Drilling's endurance through the cyclical downturn was commendable, the subsidiary's unavoidably poor operating results got Noble Affiliates thinking about how different Samedan's business of gas and oil exploration was from Noble Drilling's contract drilling business. Beginning in 1984, the parent organization began discussing the idea of separating Noble Drilling from Samedan. (By that time, Noble Affiliates had sold off B. F. Walker, its trucking subsidiary, to private investors.)

Above: In 1984, James Day took up the reins as president and CEO of Noble Drilling. Under Day's leadership, Noble would separate from its parent company in 1985 and would eventually become one of the world's leading offshore drillers.

Right: Noble Drilling's safety and training program earned numerous kudos throughout the industry, and year after year Noble was recognized as one of the safest drillers.

Opposite: Noble Drilling continually expanded and upgraded its fleet, and in 1984 the *OW-501* and *OW-502* land rigs joined the Noble family. This photo shows the *OW-501* drilling southwest of Oklahoma City.

Noble Affiliates' board believed that the exploration and production business of Samedan and the contract drilling business of Noble Drilling were dissimilar enough that their financial performance and prospects should not be combined. They further believed that investors in these two divergent industries would have different investment strategies and profiles.

Noble Affiliates' shareholders agreed, and in the fall of 1985, they voted for a tax-free spin-off of Noble Drilling. Shareholders of Noble Affiliates received one share of Noble Drilling common stock for every four shares of Noble Affiliates common stock they held.[33]

While both companies eventually benefited from the separation, the advantages to Noble Affiliates were more immediately obvious since the contract drilling industry had been so volatile. The goals of the spin-off were to improve shareholder value by giving stockholders a clear investment choice between the two businesses; to allow Noble Drilling's management to focus on its own specialized business; and to let Noble Drilling take advantage of optimal market conditions for financing as they came up, giving greater access to capital markets. Also, Noble Drilling could develop employee benefit and compensation programs more appropriate for its unique operations and financial situations. Noble Affiliates, on the other hand, wanted to rid itself of an operation that was perceived as volatile and a drag on earnings.[34]

Thus on September 23, 1985, Noble Drilling's stock, under the symbol NDCO, became listed on Nasdaq. The company retained all of its assets, including its corporate headquarters in Tulsa, Oklahoma, and various division offices. Noble Drilling's new board of directors consisted of Jim Day, who also served as the company's president and chief executive officer; Johnnie Hoffman, who served as vice president and division manager—offshore; Sam Noble, chairman of Noble Affiliates; John Snodgrass, president and a trustee of the Noble Foundation; Michael Cawley, president of the law firm of Thompson and Cawley; and Ed Holt, former vice president of Noble Drilling, who was designated an emeritus member.

After the spin-off, Noble Affiliates contributed approximately $17 million in capital to the company. Noble Drilling was obligated to repay $25 mil-

On September 23, 1985, Noble Drilling became a publicly traded company on Nasdaq and was proud to advertise its new status.

lion over the next five years with a variable interest rate.[35] "It was a challenging ticket for separation, the toll, if you will," explained Bob Campbell, who served as outside legal counsel for Noble Affiliates during the spin-off and would become president of Noble Drilling in 1999.[36]

An Enduring Presence

Though the board and management knew the restructuring was in the best interests of shareholders and would prove beneficial in the long term, they also realized that the company's operations and their leadership skills would be put to the test during the industry slump, which showed no signs of abating. Clearly it was a difficult time to separate.

On the other hand, even with the difficult market, the company had a lot going for it. Its crews were well trained, and its leadership was strong. It had also retained a strong customer base, which, at the time of the spin-off, represented a mix of independent oil operators and major oil companies. Because Noble was able to form lasting relationships with oil giants such as Amoco, Shell, Exxon, Chevron, Texaco, and Gulf—many of them dating back more than 50 years—Noble was in a good position to gain a greater share of the market.

Communicating and maintaining a stable financial sheet were also key to the company's future. All over the organization, from operations personnel to the engineering group, Noble's people pulled together to batten down the hatches and wait for the proverbial storm to blow itself out. As Jim Day noted, "We will not succeed by a few individuals' efforts, but only if we all continue to work together."[37]

Indeed, there were a number of key management members during this transitional period: Ed Holt, former vice president of the company, was in his mid-seventies when he acted as an advisor and mentor of the management team.

These three veterans of Noble Drilling played key roles in the transitional period of the 1980s. Charles Copeland (left) began his Noble career in 1957 as an accountant; Johnnie Hoffman (center) joined as a roughneck in 1947; and Ed Holt began his Noble career in 1930 as an engineer.

Johnnie Hoffman was a prime leader and moving force in the reconfigured company. Chuck Syring provided great experience. And Charlie Copeland was an important organizer and cheerleader. These individuals and others would lead the company to success.

Perhaps most important of all to the company's eminent success was its "Noble Way" culture—the doctrine that people were the company's most important asset and that the entire organization should operate like one big family. Those beliefs, combined with strong leadership, savvy business decisions, and dedicated, experienced personnel, would go a long way toward helping Noble Drilling emerge from the downturn as one of the strongest drilling contractors in the country.

In 1988, Noble Drilling purchased Peter Bawden Drilling as part of its strategy to evolve into an international offshore drilling contractor. While carrying *Rig 43* and *Rig 44*, this Bawden platform rig, called the Marathon Brae "A" platform, flares natural gas in the harsh environment of the North Sea.

CHAPTER EIGHT

A STRATEGIC COURSE

1985–1988

While we are encouraged about the future for the industry, the near-term prospects will continue to be difficult.

—Jim Day, 1988

A FTER BECOMING AN INDEPENDENT, publicly traded company, Noble was faced with a depressed oil and natural gas market. Though the company had spun off from Noble Affiliates as a major domestic drilling contractor, with 15 marine rigs and 36 land rigs, it—like the rest of the energy-providing industry—had only a hard road ahead as OPEC continued to flood the market with cheaply priced oil. For the 12-month period ending December 1985, Noble Drilling had an operating loss of $16.5 million on revenues of $71.6 million.[1] Clearly this less-than-spectacular performance was due to the weak and highly competitive domestic contract drilling industry. Oil prices fluctuated wildly, and within this uncertain market, oil producers were careful about contracting drilling operations; thus rig utilization was down and consolidation within the industry was becoming quite prevalent. To add to the overall unrest in the industry, OPEC seemed unwilling to curb its overproduction. As Jim Day pointed out in his 1985 letter to company shareholders, "Noble Drilling became a public company . . . in the midst of the worst industry conditions in the past half century."[2]

Still, it seemed that the main problem for drillers wasn't the sinking price of oil but the fluctuation of the price. Day told a Tulsa newspaper in 1988 that "if the price were set . . . it would create a more stable market. Producers would know what they

could count on and then proceed with plans to drill."[3]

Traditionally a financially conservative drilling contractor, Noble Drilling, despite the oil crisis, was able to maintain most of its equipment and retain enough positive funds to operate. Unlike many of its competitors, Noble Drilling had a reasonable financial base before the oil crisis began.

Day, along with management and the board, had been positioning the company while it was still a subsidiary of Noble Affiliates, and those efforts continued after the spin-off.

Recognizing that he was less experienced than many in the drilling industry, Day sought out the leaders of some of the industry's main offshore players. Those competitors graciously shared their respective views on the industry's direction. "I came away from those discussions and felt that the sector was evenly divided between those who thought the market was going to return to the way it had been in the late seventies/early eighties and those who were prepared for a rough road ahead," Day said. With

After a gas discovery in December 1985, Stephens No. 1 well, in Carter County, Oklahoma, the company's birthplace, became the first operated well of Noble Exploration and Development (a subsidiary of Noble Drilling Corporation).

Noble Drilling received the IADC Safety Excellence Award for the second time in 1985. Pictured from left are Eric Krueger, Johnnie Hoffman, George McLeod, Jim Conner, Jim Day, Howard Harlson, Joe Hurt, Charlie Copeland, and Merrick Harmon.

that dynamic to deal with, he also had to decide which assets would be important and where the company needed to be to weather the downturn. "I took all that information, came back, distilled it, and basically came up with a plan," Day said.[4]

In essence, Day's plan called for Noble Drilling to reinvent itself, to evolve from a mainly land-based domestic contractor to principally an international and offshore drilling contractor. Specifically, Day's strategy involved improving operating efficiency, increasing international activities, expanding the rig and offshore fleets, and redeveloping its production base, which it had lost after the spin-off, when it was no longer affiliated with Samedan Oil.[5] (However, as Noble Drilling expanded its contract drilling operations, the production area of the company would dip in importance so that in 1992, the company would sell its oil and gas exploration and production operations.[6])

The gradual metamorphosis from a mainly land-based drilling contractor to an international offshore contractor was difficult at first, particularly for Noble's operational staff. After all, working offshore in a foreign country meant a huge disruption in their lives. "The company's roots were in land drilling," Day said. "But we could see that land drilling was, at least from our perspective, a fragmented business. Anyone could get in it. There was too much capacity, too many people involved, and the prospects, at least over the next several years, did not look good."[7] Offshore drilling, on the other hand, required more capital and technical expertise and therefore involved less competition. Moreover, the cost of finding foreign oil was much lower than that of domestic exploration, and international drilling contracts, particularly offshore, tended to be for longer terms than domestic contracts, which would promote stability.

Once Day set down the company's strategies, there wasn't, as he described it, a "unanimous 'That's right, Jim. You're absolutely right. We're going to go with you. No problem.'" Instead, Day recalled, "There was a lot of evangelical work by senior personnel to convince people action was needed. I told them that if we don't do this, the company will go broke. Now either we make these decisions and you come on board, or this company won't exist in the next four to five years." That argument worked for most of Noble's people, and they willingly came on board. "We all started rowing together," said Day. "I had everybody bailing water out of the boat, not into it, and we started making progress."[8]

Laying the Groundwork

Even with all of Noble's employees rowing together, the boat still needed strong leaders to steer it in the right direction. The company had traditionally taken a decentralized management approach, giving its managers and division officers the responsibility of

responding quickly to opportunities and problems or, as Day described it, having "one foot on the gas and the other firmly planted on the brake so we can react to market changes."[9] Such autonomous management made it extremely important that the company select the kind of leaders who could guide it through one of the industry's most tumultuous periods.

In July 1986, Johnnie Hoffman, vice president and division manager—offshore, retired after 38 years of service. Other notable retirements occurring during 1986 included Eddie Paul, Rocky Mountain division manager, after 34 years of service; Gus Androes, division drilling superintendent, after 38 years of service; and Frank Reiger, drilling superintendent, with 31 years of service. Also retiring during that time were John Sandifer and Joe Alford, both long-time rig managers (known at that time as toolpushers), with 26

and 32 years of service, respectively. All of these men were later honored by having rigs named after them.

One month later, Richard Patterson was named vice president—International to help meet Noble's long-term goal of increasing its international business. Terry Livingston was elected controller, and Byron Welliver, formerly controller, was promoted to vice president—Finance and treasurer. Welliver was later promoted to senior vice president and CFO. Amos Runner, operations manager in Tulsa; Charlie Yester, division manager in Oklahoma City; Roger Lewis, division engineer in Oklahoma City; Clemens Reiger, division manager in Denver; and Chuck Syring were also important members of Noble's management team.

With its management in place, Noble Drilling set in motion the strategies it had put forth. Given

Noble Drilling's board of directors in 1986 consisted of (clockwise from top) James Day, John Snodgrass, Michael Cawley, Johnnie Hoffman, Sam Noble, and Ed Holt.

its bone-dry cash reserves, the company had to initiate cost containment efforts that would ensure it could grow and survive without burying itself in debt. Management assessed the company's rig fleet and determined that a significant number of assets were noncompetitive. For starters, Noble mothballed seven deep land-drilling units in 1985 and retired a submersible offshore drilling rig and a platform rig in 1986. That brought the total number of drilling rigs to 51 (13 marine and 38 land). The number of employees fell as well, from 1,240 in 1984 to only 455 by the end of 1986.[10] Lynda Bossler,

who had worked for Noble since 1972 in various positions, remembered that the number of employees in the corporate office decreased from about 67 to perhaps 19 or 20. "It was pretty drastic," she said. "The people who were left behind took on two and three extra jobs, but the industry was slow, so that wasn't really much of a burden."[11]

Though the downsizing was necessary, many experienced people were lost to the industry forever, for by the time the energy economy would improve, they had pursued other careers.

In 1986, to reduce costs Noble Drilling left its suburban location and returned to the more economical downtown area, moving into the historic building at 624 South Boston. As an anchor tenant, Noble had the top three floors of the 10-story Noble Drilling Building. The brick and limestone structure, listed on the National Register of Historic Places, had been built in the late 1920s as the corporate headquarters for Oklahoma Natural Gas. It had nine-foot ceilings except for the top floor, which, according to *Tulsa World,* had an "'old money' feel, with 12-foot ceilings, original marble work, wood paneling and crown moldings."[12] Noble Drilling's residence there was short-lived, however. Noble Properties, a division of Noble Drilling, bought the building in 1988 and then sold it after the company relocated its headquarters to Houston in 1989.

One very critical step in its cost-containment efforts to reduce its debt was Noble's issuing of over five million shares to Noble Affiliates in June 1987 to pay its outstanding debt to its former parent company. At the end of 1987, Noble's debt constituted only 7 percent of shareholders' equity compared to 39 percent in 1986.[13] Ridding itself of the cumbersome debt, which Day described as a "big stone around our neck, dragging us down," was an important move toward Noble's future success. With a clean balance sheet, Noble had more negotiating power for future deals because its equity was worth more.[14]

Also in 1987, Day instituted companywide salary cuts for management, slashing his own salary more than any other's. To help soften the blow, rig managers were given stock options, a first in the industry. Many of them did not know what stock options were or why they might be significant. As it turned out, the options in many cases proved far more valuable than the salary difference.[15]

Consolidation and Expansion

The board, led by Sam Noble, was expanded in the late 1980s with the addition of Tommy C. Craighead of T. C. Craighead Company. A longtime associate of Noble, Craighead brought an independent view to the board. Two of the board's main priorities in the late 1980s and early 1990s were decreasing Noble's reliance on the weak domestic oil market

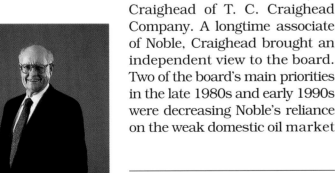

Tommy Craighead, president of T. C. Craighead & Company, joined the Noble board of directors in the late 1980s.

and pursuing international and offshore contracts. At the same time, it sought to increase the rig fleet by acquiring more specialized rigs, which would make it more attractive to oil companies. Consolidation was necessary throughout the industry because excess capacity was harming the chance that the price of oil would improve. "As consolidation occurs, equipment is taken out of the marketplace and you don't have the overhang that continues to depress prices," Day told the *Tulsa Business Chronicle* in August 1989. "There needs to be more consolidation in our business for things to improve—both onshore and offshore."[16]

Noble Drilling did its fair share to help consolidate the industry. But as a small, market-cap company with only 15 offshore rigs, the majority of which were not competitive, it was difficult. Day knew he needed to start by looking at smaller acquisitions and build the company's portfolio from there.[17]

After a significant search, Noble found the drilling assets of General Electric Capital Corporation (GECC), which GECC had acquired when two drilling companies it financed—R. C. Chapman Drilling Company and Temple Marine Drilling—went out of business. GECC did not sell the drilling assets immediately, in hopes that the oil economy would improve enough for the companies to thrive. Ultimately, GECC's executive vice president, James H. Ozanne, concluded that the oil market would remain depressed and that it was in GECC's best interest to dispose of its drilling assets.[18]

To help finance the acquisition, Noble retained Simmons & Company International, a Houston-based investment banking firm that would prove instrumental in Noble's future success. Matthew Simmons, chairman of Simmons & Company, remembered his first meeting with Jim Day in 1987:

There was such a total state of confusion in the industry at that time, and we were dealing with companies that were mortally wounded. I had never laid eyes on Jim Day when I got a call one day saying he was going to be in Houston and wanted to come in to talk with me. Well, he came in and, in pure Jim Day style, basically proceeded to interview me. It was really a fun interview. He asked thought-provoking questions, and we spent about an hour together. Then he thanked me and left.[19]

The board and management wanted to use Noble's leverage as a debt-free publicly traded company to help consolidate the drilling industry. But to make that happen, they needed competent financial advice. Simmons and his partner, vice chairman Nicholas Swyka, were asked to come to Ardmore, Oklahoma, to be interviewed by Noble Drilling's board. In anticipation of concluding an acquisition, the board centered its discussion on acquisition opportunities and the state of the industry.

"I've been very impressed with the way you've addressed all our questions," Day told Simmons. "That's the good news."

"What's the bad news?" Simmons asked.

"The bad news is our stock sells for $2 a share and we basically have no cash."

"Sounds great to us," said Simmons. "Sign us up as your advisors, and let's get to work on it."[20]

Thus began a long relationship between Noble Drilling and Simmons & Company.

Almost a year later, Simmons & Company and Noble secured the deal with GECC. The negotiations were protracted, and the deal had been all but finalized when Black Monday sent stock prices tumbling. The terms had to be negotiated all over again. At last the two sides came to an agreement. The transaction was valued at $30 million to $40 million, with GECC receiving equity securities in Noble Drilling. "GE really had to be convinced to take equity in Noble," said Nick Swyka. "Noble had to make the absolute best of its limited resources. We had to make a number of presentations to get GE to consider taking Noble equity, but it turned out to be an outstanding move for GE."[21]

In February 1988, Noble Drilling bought Temple Marine and R. C. Chapman, gaining 20 land rigs and five marine rigs. Three of the rigs were jackups, and two were posted barges. Not only did the acquisition increase Noble's offshore potential, but it allowed the company to upgrade its land fleet with

newer equipment, giving Noble one of the newest fleets in the industry. Having newer equipment meant that Noble's fleet was more diverse and therefore in higher demand, which in turn improved operating efficiency.

Noble also received $1.5 million in working capital and a 15-acre storage and maintenance facility in Harris County, Texas, along with a $15 million line of credit. Ozanne was named a Noble Drilling board member, and with his entrepreneurial attitude and fresh approach to business, he added to the company's success.[22]

Bawden Drilling

This important strategic step set the stage for future acquisitions. In November 1988, Noble Drilling bought Houston-based Peter Bawden Drilling Ltd., which, faced with the chaotic drilling market, was looking to sell. "Noble had a willingness to take some fairly significant risks," said Swyka. "Noble typically acquired during down cycles in the industry, but it had confidence that the industry would turn around."[23]

Owned by the Royal Bank of Canada, Peter Bawden Drilling was a Canadian operation that traced its roots back to 1952 and a lively entrepreneur named Peter Bawden. The company had been drilling internationally since it ventured into Australia in 1962, and it was this international presence that made it most appealing to Noble, for the acquisition effectively returned Noble to international operations without expensive start-up costs.

Not only were Bawden's crews accustomed to the harsh cold of Canada and the Arctic Circle; they were also well adjusted to the harsh desert climate of Australia and to the continent's offshore domain, where Bawden had owned the first self-contained platform rigs. Bawden was also the first company to operate slant rigs in the Middle East and had rigs in New Guinea, Algeria, and Indonesia. By 1976, it had become the largest development contractor in the U.K. sector of the North Sea. When Noble acquired it, Bawden had a Canadian division office in Calgary and an office in Singapore.

Above: James H. Ozanne, executive vice president of GECC, joined Noble Drilling's board of directors after Noble purchased GECC's Temple Marine and R. C. Chapman companies.

Opposite: When Noble acquired it, Peter Bawden Drilling had rigs operating all over the world, including *Rig 5* in Guatemala.

Analysts and investors heartily approved of Noble acquiring Peter Bawden Drilling. Upon announcing its letter of intent, Noble saw its stock jump 20 percent.[24] As with the GECC acquisition, Simmons & Company was involved in the deal. When the $28 million swap of equity was complete, Noble had acquired 25 land rigs, 13 labor contracts, a jackup management contract, and engineering and logistics expertise. Bawden provided drilling contracts in Canada, the United States, Latin America, the United Kingdom, the North Sea, Africa, and the Far East. In fact, all but one of the acquired rigs were located in the international market, which suited Noble just fine, for as Day astutely observed, "It appears the foreign drilling markets hold greater opportunity for recovery near term."[25] Noble's fleet now totaled 97 rigs.

Charlie Copeland, who then served as vice president of administration and corporate secretary, described how valuable Bawden's insights into the international market proved to be. "We learned from Bawden about bidding, working, and traveling internationally," he said. "In the United States, we pretty much knew how things operated, but there are different procedures and methods for drilling internationally, and we learned a lot from the Bawden people and integrated it into our business so we had the best of both cultures."[26]

Some valuable people with international experience came from Bawden to Noble, including Julie Robertson, who had worked in benefits and risk management and later became corporate secretary and senior vice president of administration; Tom O'Rourke, who had worked in accounting and information technology; Mark Burns, who later became Noble's operations manager for the United Kingdom and Norway; Larry Perras, who later became area manager of Noble Drilling West Africa; and Alan Hay, contracts manager. Hay called the deal a lifeline for Bawden because of the financial difficulties that

Left: Bawden was the first drilling company to operate a slant rig, which drilled at an angle to avoid natural obstacles such as rock formations.

Opposite: Peter Bawden Drilling had begun operations in the Far East as early as 1968.

Bawden was experiencing, and Noble had a strong board, strong management, and financial discipline. "The whole world became Noble's oyster," Hay said. "Bawden had contracts all over the world, which gave Noble the international foothold that Bawden had established over its life."[27]

Where the Action Is

By the end of 1988, Noble Drilling was on more solid ground thanks to the strategies introduced only a few years earlier. Annual revenues had improved by 58 percent from 1987 to 1988, and the company's net loss had decreased dramatically.[28] Moreover, after acquiring the assets from GECC and Peter Bawden Drilling, Noble had emerged as a stronger, larger company with strong board management, financial discipline, and a broader base of operations.[29]

Still, drilling activity in the United States remained depressed, and Noble Drilling made an important decision that would more closely link it to offshore and international drilling contracts. In May 1989, the company announced it would consolidate its headquarters, moving from Tulsa, Oklahoma, where it had resided since 1930, to Houston, considered the hub of offshore and international oil and gas operations. Though it was a difficult decision, the move was very

Bawden specialized in operating in harsh environments, such as the Arctic Circle of Canada, where drilling teams used dogsleds for transit.

necessary in the changing world market. The relocation was expected to save the company about $1.2 million a year.[30] "We're moving to where we're making our money," Day said in a press conference. "Seventy percent of our business is in the international arena and offshore. Those contracts are awarded in Houston. We're going to where our customers are located."[31] The move was completed in the fall of 1989.

Charlie Copeland retired after the move to Houston, though he kept his affiliation with the company as a Noble Drilling consultant. He described how Noble stepped up its marketing efforts to deal with the down cycle. "Even after Noble moved to Houston to have a closer proximity to operators, it was still pretty difficult to find work. But we developed a marketing department that was out searching for contracts and calling on customers full time. It was a very innovative time. And because management was very organized and had specific goals, our marketing people—everybody who worked for Noble—knew what their objectives were, and there was a lot of follow-up to make sure everybody was working toward the company's goals."[32]

The *Charles Copeland,* built in 1979, was an independent-leg cantilevered offshore rig that could drill down 20,000 feet in water depths up to 250 feet.

"When I first met Jim Day, the thing that most impressed me was his focus and vision," said Bill Jennings, who had come to Noble in 1988 after working for GECC and retired as vice president of Western Hemisphere Operations in 1999. "Jim's dedication and the commitment of the Noble people are really amazing."[33]

Those not within the Noble circle also praised Day's management. "Jim was totally committed to working his way out of a terrible time for the industry," said Matt Simmons.[34]

Indeed, the board and all of Noble's management had charted a path that would gradually lead the company away from domestic land-based drilling to the mobile offshore and international markets, and Nobleites all over the organization worked in unison to keep the company on course. Though Noble was confident that it would come out of the down cycle stronger than ever, it still had to weather the storm—and it was one of the longest, harshest storms the industry had ever seen.

The *Max Smith* submersible could drill down 25,000 feet in water depths of up to 108 feet. In the early 1990s, it was active in the U.S. Gulf of Mexico.

CHAPTER NINE

NO ALTERNATIVE BUT TO WORK OUR WAY OUT

1990–1993

While others have continued to bemoan the hand that was dealt our industry, our organization has taken advantage of the environment to strengthen our operation, to expand the organization into worldwide markets, and to prepare us financially for further opportunities.

—Jim Day, 1990

FINALLY, IN THE SPRING OF 1990, the price of oil began a slow upward crawl. This, according to management, was "not because we see a raging oil market before us, but rather because there are many more encouraging signs pointing to a recovering market than we've seen in many years."[1] Worldwide markets were experiencing an increasingly strong demand for energy, and domestic supplies had begun to decline, making it more likely that oil companies would be signing long-term drilling contracts. Moreover, oil prices had been stabilizing—all of which meant that equity investors were now becoming more interested in the oil sector.[2]

But just when it looked as though the oil industry was on its way to permanent recovery, on August 2, 1990, 100,000 Iraqi troops and tanks roared into Kuwait, seizing oil fields and refineries. The tiny country was quickly overrun, suddenly putting Iraq in control of more oil than any other single nation, including Saudi Arabia. From August to January, as the United States underwent the largest military deployment since the Vietnam War, the dramatic conflict was characterized mainly by rhetoric and tense waiting. Life went on, but for the U.S. oil industry, which still relied heavily on foreign oil, business was anything but usual.

Again, the nation's energy policy—or lack thereof—came under fire. Domestic reserves had decreased sharply while oil imports were on the rise, and the only way to fix the problem was to increase production of domestic oil. In September 1990, President George H. W. Bush told Congress that it "should, this month, enact measures to increase domestic energy production and energy conservation in order to reduce dependence on foreign oil. . . . This year, before the Iraq invasion, U.S. imports had risen to nearly eight million barrels per day, and we've moved in the wrong direction, and now we must act to correct that trend."[3]

Jim Day, who as president of the International Association of Drilling Contractors was interviewed by CBS News in September 1990, underscored the need for a reasonable energy policy. "This industry is on its knees," he said. "It's been on its knees since 1986. We are suffering from benign neglect, and we are slowly dying."[4]

Then, on January 16, 1991, the United States unleashed the initial air strike of Operation Desert Storm, and thousands of tons of munitions systematically pounded the Iraqi armed forces.

On September 21, 1992, Sam Noble, Noble Drilling's chairman of the board and son of the company's founder, died at age 67.

George Bush and his advisors had promised that Iraq's aggression would not stand, but a defiant Saddam Hussein unleashed his own weapons and swore that he would set Kuwaiti oil wells on fire.

Six weeks of continuous bombardment, blockade, and propaganda by coalition forces largely destroyed Iraq's military capability. When the ground war began in February, hundreds of thousands of coalition troops attacked and flanked the Iraqi army, whose troops began to surrender to anyone from the West. As the Iraqis retreated, they blew up more than 700 Kuwaiti oil wells, which made it more important than ever for the United States to step up its oil production.

But domestic production slumped ever lower. The only thing Noble Drilling could do was persevere, which it did admirably, proceeding with its international and offshore expansion to fill the gap left by so few domestic contracts.

Into Africa

In 1990, Noble Drilling got a big boost to its international presence when Shell Petroleum Development Company of Nigeria Ltd. (Shell Nigeria) hired four Noble offshore rigs for work in the high-pressure, shallow-water areas of southern Nigeria. Nigeria's petroleum and natural gas reserves accounted for approximately one-third of Africa's total reserves, so the drilling contracts were a particular coup for Noble, which subsequently formed a new division, Noble Bawden Drilling (West Africa), headquartered in Port Harcourt, Nigeria, with additional offices in Warri.[5]

The four rigs to be used in the Shell Nigeria contracts were the *Gene Rosser*, the *Chuck Syring*, the *Lewis Dugger*—all posted barges— and the 45-foot, mat-supported slot jackup *NN-1*, which Noble owned in partnership. Noble modified the rigs to handle the high pressure, widening barge holes and keyways on all the posted barges and raising the floor of the *Lewis Dugger* by 16 feet to accommodate the 15,000-psi-rated blowout preventers and wellhead equipment. When the refurbishments were complete, the rigs set out from Mississippi to Nigeria on a 21-day journey.

But Noble ran into a major snag during the refurbishment of the posted barges when the ship-

After several delays during refurbishment, the *Lewis Dugger* and *Chuck Syring* posted barges were finally on their way to Nigeria. *(Photo courtesy Lewis Dugger.)*

yard that was reconstructing them got into financial trouble and couldn't pay its subcontractors, who then put a lien on Noble's equipment, preventing the company from moving it. The situation was remedied after Day became actively involved in the shipyard's management, hiring a new team headed by Bernie Wolford, Dave Beard, and Leonard Jones.

"We were able to execute an agreement to allow us to move the rigs out and get them on the way to Nigeria," said Day. "But there was a penalty if the rigs weren't in Nigeria by a specified date. Shell Nigeria understood that the problems were not problems we created. They were problems created by the shipyard."[6] Although quite painful, this situation was an outstanding learning experience that proved useful in future projections.

After the crews were trained to Noble's standards of safety and quality assurance, the rigs were put to work. The *Gene Rosser* and *NN-1* were under two-year contracts, and the *Lewis Dugger* and *Chuck Syring* had signed up for three-year terms. By the end of 1991, the four rigs in Nigeria had contributed $6.3 million to Noble Drilling's operating income.[7]

Bill Rose, who was general manager in Lagos, Nigeria, from 1995 to 1997, described the unique

The *Gene Rosser* posted barge, shown here in the marshlands near Warri, Nigeria, in the early 1990s, was capable of drilling 25,000 feet.

Left: The *Lewis Dugger* posted barge, like the other rigs drilling in Nigeria, had been outfitted with state-of-the-art drilling technology and equipment. It was capable of drilling to 30,000 feet.

Below: The *Mighty Servant* heavy-lift vessel at Ingalls Shipbuilding on the Pascagoula River in Mississippi tows the *Gene Rosser* and the *NN-1* before their transport to Nigeria.

challenges presented by the differences between Nigerian and U.S. culture. "Nigeria is a very interesting place. It's a good place, but there were a lot of challenges. There are over 200 tribal languages in Nigeria, and people are quite territorial. We tried to keep a good balance of people representing the demographics, but we had to be mindful of the host community's need to make money from our presence, so we had to keep that balance too."[8]

A Win-Win Deal

Continuing its offshore expansion, Noble acquired the majority of assets of Transworld Drilling Company from Kerr-McGee Corporation in January 1991, gaining 12 more Gulf of Mexico offshore rigs (five jackups and seven submersibles).

As with its other recent acquisitions, Noble was short of cash, especially because the negotiations for the acquisition took place at the same time as the modifications to the rigs headed for Nigeria. "The cash requirements for the rig reconstruction were significant, and there was very little cash in the bank," said Byron Welliver. "In fact, in the June 1990 form 10-Q [quarterly report], Noble's cash balance was zero."[9]

Still, Noble managed to secure the deal because Kerr-McGee agreed to finance the acquisition on its own. The seller financing was later replaced with public financing.

In October 1993, Noble bought nine offshore jackups, including these two, from the Western Company. The acquisition strengthened Noble's worldwide presence.

When finished, the $75 million deal nearly doubled Noble's offshore fleet and greatly increased its diversity by enhancing its operating, engineering, and marketing expertise. The seven submersible rigs were particularly useful because they could operate in environmentally sensitive areas and on deep wells. Two of the submersibles had zero discharge, making them especially suit-

able for the growing number of environmentally sensitive areas, and four had state-of-the-art mud-handling equipment.

The largest of the five jackup rigs was an independent leg with 52-foot cantilever capability, top drive, zero discharge, and cascade mud system.[10] Independent-leg jackups employed newer technology than mat-supported jackups. The top drive, too, was a relatively new technology. Top drives replaced the conventional kelly-and-rotary system by using powered swivels that rotated the drill stem and bit. A top-drive system made it easier and safer for crew members to trim pipe, and it improved efficiency by allowing the crew to save time by adding pipe three joints at a time. "Top drives became the great-est thing out there and would give you additional premium on your rates," said Roger Lewis, vice president—special projects, who began at Noble as a construction engineer in 1980. "The top drive has been one of the most significant technological changes in the industry. If you don't have one these days, you're not going to be able to work the rig."[11]

One of the provisions of the Transworld deal called for Noble to retain Transworld Drilling's people for at least one year to give them a tran-sition period. Because Transworld had such a good reputation in the industry and its employ-ees were so well respected, Noble was happy to comply. Dave Beard, in fact, became Noble's vice president of project engineering and would prove essential in the coming years as the com-pany moved into deep-water drilling. Likewise, Bill Rose, who had been general manager for Transworld in the Gulf of Mexico, would become general man-ager for Noble's Gulf Coast Marine division after Max Smith's 1992 retirement. Eventually Rose would become vice president of Eastern Hemisphere Operations.

One of the most remarkable aspects of the Transworld deal wouldn't be fully realized for another few years. This time, Simmons & Company was on the other side of the bar-gaining table from Noble Drilling. As represen-tatives of Kerr-McGee, Matt Simmons and his cadre had been helping the company divest itself of the contract drilling business. Simmons had

One of two offshore submersible rigs Noble purchased from Portal Rig Corporation in October 1993. Both were stationed in the Gulf of Mexico.

been quite successful in selling most of Kerr-McGee's contract drilling assets for a good price but was now down to the component nobody seemed to want—the submersibles. Simmons had tried to sell the rigs to another independent drilling contractor but had been promptly lectured about what a bad reputation submersibles had. "Everybody in the industry hated submersibles," Simmons explained. "They were terribly old, but these were actually the newest form of offshore drilling rig because they had been built right around the end of the collapse of the jackup market."[12]

Simmons told Day that, at the very least, the submersibles would make terrific spares and that he could get Noble a great deal since Kerr-McGee just wanted to be rid of them. Noble saw diamonds in the rough and agreed to buy. As fate would have it, Noble's operations would excel in the late 1990s as a result of these very same triangular-shaped submersibles after Noble's engineers transformed them into EVA-4000™ design semisubmersibles for deepwater drilling. "Years later," Simmons said, "when Kerr-McGee signed a five-year contract for one of those semisubmersibles, I asked them, 'Did it pain you guys to think you could have owned that equipment?' They said, 'No, we just hope Noble makes a profit from them because they were not core assets to us.'"[13]

Expanding the Fleet

A public offering of Noble Drilling stock in August 1990 raised $44.5 million to fund capital improvements for international work. Another stock offering in November 1991 helped reduce debt from the Transworld acquisition and gave Noble more working capital. From 1991 to 1992, the company was able to reduce its long-term debt by 40 percent.[14]

"I think Jim [Day] was one of the first to realize that when things go down, the banks are the worst place to go," said Jay Courage, who, as a representative at Salomon Brothers, assisted Noble on the 1990 public offering. "Jim has always been incredibly prudent in financing his company in the public market. He's realized that sometimes in the equity market, you need to

spend money to make money, and it's more prudent to finance your company with equity. It's also not a bad thing if your investors make money with you."[15]

Another important acquisition was the assets of Western Oceanic from the Western Company of North America for $150 million in cash. Its fleet consisted of nine offshore jackups and related equipment. The purchase moved Noble to a new level and allowed it to expand into new markets: Zaire (now Congo) in West Africa and Lake Maracaibo in Venezuela. The acquisition, which was completed in October 1993, also expanded Noble's operations in the United States, the Mexican Gulf, and Nigeria.[16] A public stock offering and a warrant offering helped the company finance the deal.

That same month, Noble further enhanced its fleet after purchasing two offshore submersible rigs from Portal Rig Corporation for 626,410 shares of common stock. Located in the Gulf of Mexico, the rigs had been stacked for some time and had to be refurbished to bring them up to Noble's standards before going to work.[17]

By 1993, the oil-drilling market had strengthened enough, especially in the Gulf of Mexico, for Noble to take two offshore rigs, the *Jim Thompson*, a submersible, and the *Dick Favor*, a jackup, out of storage. After reactivation, the *Dick Favor* was sent for a long-term contract with Lagoven, a division of Petroleos de Venezuela S.A., to Lake Maracaibo, where the company already had a presence from the Western Company acquisition. Under the Lagoven contract, Noble moved one more rig to Venezuela, the *Carl Norberg*, making Noble the largest operator of jackup rigs in Lake Maracaibo.[18]

A Natural Succession

In April 1991, both Day and Sam Noble were reelected to the board of directors for three-year terms, but, sadly, Sam Noble would not live to see the entire term. He died on September 21, 1992, at his ranch near Ardmore, Oklahoma, after a long illness. He was 67.[19]

Upon Sam Noble's death, Day was elected chairman of the board in addition to his duties as president and CEO. "Sam's death was a tremendous loss for the industry," said Day. "Obviously words cannot describe the loss personally. I know he would be proud of what has evolved from the seeds he sowed."[20]

Restructuring

As Noble Drilling positioned itself to survive the depressed oil market, the company's executives restructured the divisions to better manage various contracts, rigs, and services. In 1992, with land drilling operations extremely slow, the company decided to close its Mid-Continent and Rocky Mountain operations to strengthen the focus on its international activities.[21] Day explained that closing them was a continuation of the company's strategy to emphasize offshore and international drilling.[22]

With the closing of the two land divisions, Noble's presence in Oklahoma, where it had set down its roots in the 1920s, came to an end. About 200 employees in Oklahoma, Texas, Michigan, North Dakota, and Wyoming were laid off, victims of the depressed market.[23] Twenty-nine land rigs were put in storage, 20 of which had been idle for some time. Around the same time, the company lost a valuable employee when Patty Elmore retired in 1993 after 16 years of service. She had served as Day's secretary and retired as manager of investor relations.

Before the Mid-Continent division closed, Charlie Yester, division manager, was able to demonstrate the company's dedication to improving drilling technology by installing a National-Oilwell power swivel for field-testing on the Mid-Continent division's rig *N-133* in the Arkoma basin in southeastern Oklahoma. Also in 1990, two of the division's rigs were involved in a research effort organized by Conoco to evaluate the downhole measuring devices of different companies under various operating conditions. The rigs were chosen for the project because they were small and offered a high degree of control and because they had accumulated stellar safety records.[24]

Gulf Coast Land

Unlike the Mid-Continent and Rocky Mountain regions of the United States, the land around the Gulf Coast was teeming with activity. Headquartered in Houston, the Gulf Coast Land division was led by Roger Lewis. In 1990, the division operated 15 rigs in Texas and Louisiana, one of which, rig *E-31*, was refurbished and leased to Venezuela.

Three of the division's rigs at that time were busily drilling in the booming Pearsall area of West Texas, where horizontal drilling in the Austin Chalk boosted oil production levels. Horizontal drilling rigs were a new technology that had the potential to transform the business because they could drill down thousands of feet and then turn to tap pockets of oil. For the next few years, the division continued to see a lot of activity in Texas. In 1992, six of its rigs were kept busy in south and east Texas,[25] and three more joined the scene in 1993.[26]

Gulf Coast Marine

As in the Gulf Coast Land area, the Gulf Coast Marine division, with offices in Lafayette and New Orleans and led by Division Manager Bill Rose, was a center of domestic activity in the early 1990s. In 1991, the division operated eight rigs in the Gulf of Mexico and added 12 more in January 1991 after the acquisition of Transworld Drilling. In 1990, a 200-foot mat-supported cantilevered jackup rig from Noble's GECC acquisition, the *Duke Hinds*, was modernized and refurbished for shallow-water drilling, making it more specialized and therefore more in demand. Shortly after the refurbishment, it went to work under contract with Arco Oil & Gas Company.

Noble Drilling experienced more good fortune when its Gulf of Mexico equipment escaped serious damage from Hurricane Andrew in August 1992. Located in the eye of the storm, the *Gus Androes* and the *Jim Bawcom* were hardest hit. Crews monitored the progress of the hurricane and secured the rigs before evacuating. Once the storm had passed, the crews quickly repaired the damage so they could begin producing for their customers again.[27]

By 1992, drilling activity in the Gulf of Mexico had begun to decline, and Noble responded by consolidating the administrative offices of its Gulf Coast Marine operations in Lafayette, Louisiana, where Transworld had been headquartered. "It was much easier for us at that time to move to Lafayette," said Bill Jennings, who retired as vice president of Western Hemisphere Operations in December 1999.

Rigs *OW-502* and *OW-503*, both of which could drill to 10,000 feet, drill simultaneous wells within 400 feet of each other. Both rigs were located at the Conoco Borehole Test Facility in Newkirk, Oklahoma, and were overseen by rig manager Therald Martin.

"The Transworld operation was actually bigger than the operation we had in New Orleans."[28]

This and other cost-cutting measures resulted in a division overhead decrease of 29 percent. During the year, drilling activity picked up again, and by August the division had improved its dayrates by 70 percent.[29] That strengthening continued throughout 1993.

Canada and Mexico

Throughout 1990, Noble's Canadian division, led by Division Manager Boris Ewanchuk, experienced steady activity in the Rocky Mountain foothills, and by the end of the year the division was able to purchase six rigs that it had been oper-

The *Frank Lamaison* was one of five mat-supported shallow-water jackups that Noble Drilling acquired from Transworld Drilling in 1991.

ating under a lease agreement, bringing its total number to 11.

Since 1986, the Canadian division had been providing drilling management and training for the Kenya Power Company to develop a geothermal field in southwest Kenya. The training program, taught to 120 students, was completed in 1992, when the Canadian drilling market was almost as depressed as the U.S. market.[30] The following year, however, strong natural gas prices translated into a sharp increase for Canada's drilling activity. By the end of 1993, all of the company's Canadian rigs were working, and the division had moved two rigs from the Rocky Mountains to North Dakota.[31]

Elsewhere in North America, the Mexican drilling market was showing promise by the end of 1992. Noble Drilling signed a bareboat charter contract in January 1993 for the *Red McCarty*, a 200-foot mat-supported jackup rig, with Compania Perforadora Mexico S.A. The *Red McCarty* was moved from the U.S. Gulf of Mexico to drill a four-well program in the Bay of Campeche.[32]

The United Kingdom

Vice President and Division General Manager Don Taylor headed up Noble Drilling (U.K.), which provided repairs and recertification for equipment in the North Sea through its subsidiary, called Noble Offshore Services Ltd.[33] The subsidiary also offered engineering support for offshore development and production facilities, which proved especially valuable in managing drilling operations in the North Sea.

The Continental Shelf Convention agreement, ratified in 1964, opened the way for drilling in the North Sea after it outlined what areas belonged to which countries. Shortly after, both natural gas and oil were discovered in large fields—including the Brent, the Auk, the Ninian, the Ekofisk, and the Forties—and these discoveries propelled the North Sea into the world oil spotlight.

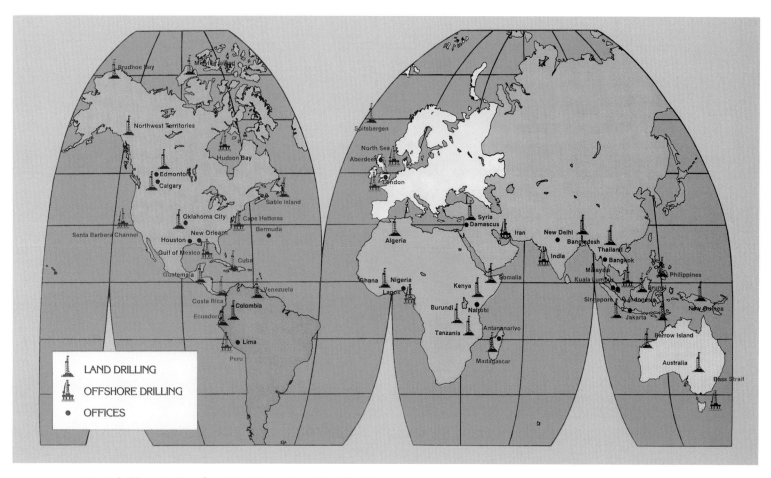

LAND DRILLING
OFFSHORE DRILLING
OFFICES

But drilling in the frontier domain of the North Sea presented its own set of challenges. Working in an area almost as far north as Alaska, drilling crews had to endure extremely cold, foggy weather with high seas and winds strong enough to knock workers from an offshore rig platform. "The North Sea is notorious for bad weather and rough storms," said Larry Perras, who, before he became area manager for Noble Drilling West Africa, worked extensively in the North Sea. "The sea conditions themselves can be quite horrendous. If you look from the top of the wave down to the bottom trough of the wave, sometimes there's a difference of 80 feet, so that's quite scary. And sometimes rain would come down horizontal, almost freezing."[34]

Still, the perilous waters proved to be a productive area for oil, and Noble was fortunate enough to have a big piece of the North Sea pie. In 1989, Noble held 25 percent of the platform drilling market in the U.K. sector of the North Sea, including a contract in the Hutton field for Conoco.[35] In 1991, the U.K. division won two of the area's five platform

Noble's worldwide presence, which was spread across the globe so that its assets were cushioned from market downturns, extended into more than 25 countries over the years.

drilling management contracts, one of which was a five-year agreement.[36] And by 1993, the division managed operations for 15 drilling rigs in the North Sea and continued its maintenance, rental, and certification of drilling equipment as well as its engineering design work.

More and more, Noble Drilling was realizing the benefits of alliances and partnerships as independent oil and gas companies sought to make their operations more efficient. In July 1993, the U.K. division formed a partnership with BP Exploration to help oversee operations in the Forties field, which Britain had discovered in 1970.[37] "With an alliance, everybody works more efficiently, and everybody works toward the same goals instead of their own individual company's goals," explained

Rig manager Larry King discusses safety performance with driller Gregory Peck on rig *OW-501*. Noble's supervisors and crew members were always taught with modern, effective training programs that helped ensure safe and reliable performance.

Perras, who managed the Forties field alliance in the mid-1990s.

As proof of the U.K. division's excellence, in July 1992 it won a prestigious award for its Quality Management System after earning the rigorous ISO 9001 certification. The International Standards Organization, or ISO, created industry standards regarding overall quality, management, and compliance with environmental laws. Noble Drilling was extremely proud of the certification—and for good reason. The entire process took about two years, during which Noble wrote its own operations manuals, presented the manuals to the ISO, and went through an audit that ensured it followed its own documented procedures. "If you have an ISO certification, any customer will know the standard of performance that you're capable of," explained Alan Hay, contracts manager. "It's a seal of approval."[38]

Applying for certification was voluntary, and by becoming certified, Noble Drilling (U.K.) had set the operating standard for its competition. The quality certification was the first for a U.K.-based drilling contractor.[39]

Noble Drilling International

The Noble Drilling International division, which covered the Far East, the Middle East, India, and Madagascar, was headquartered in Singapore and overseen by Vice President Don Wood. During 1989, the division had significantly expanded its frontier, drilling for the first time in Thailand, Bangladesh, and Syria and drilling a relief well in Brunei for Brunei Shell Petroleum.[40]

In 1989, the *Ed Holt*, a 300-foot independent-leg jackup rig, had begun a two-year bareboat charter agreement with Jindal Equipment Leasing in

Noble's intensive safety instruction included all aspects of drilling and covered topics such as conventional and specialized drilling methods, emergency procedures, and other custom programs to suit various clients' needs. Noble's hardhats even bore the logo for the International Association of Drilling Contractors (IADC) as a testament to the company's many safety awards.

Right: After winning four contracts with Shell Nigeria in 1990, the *NN-1* mat-supported slot jackup, which Noble jointly owned, was modified for shallow-water drilling. It worked for two years in Nigeria.

Opposite: The *Ed Holt,* a 300-foot independent-leg jackup with 450-foot legs, began work offshore India in 1989 and was the first originally owned Noble rig to work internationally. *(Photo courtesy Lewis Dugger.)*

offshore India for the Oil and Natural Gas Commission (ONGC). In the midst of such a depressed worldwide drilling market and as the first originally owned Noble asset to work internationally, the rig and its work in India were critical, helping to "carry the company for two years," according to Day.[41] Moreover, the *Ed Holt* provided a stepping-stone for future work in that area. "It was exciting because we were just getting our relationship started with ONGC," said Mark Burns, operations manager for the United Kingdom and Norway. "It was a very good way to increase our presence in India."[42] In 1992, the *Ed Holt's* bareboat charter agreement was renewed for a fifth year.[43]

Also in 1992, the International division won a turnkey contract with OMNIS, a department of the Madagascar government that was responsible for strategic industries. Under the turnkey arrangements, which paid a fixed amount upon completion, Noble mobilized a land rig from the Far East to drill the well; constructed roads, the drill site, and an airstrip; and mobilized the rig, crew camps, and all the drilling and project-related equipment.[44]

Nigerian Activities

Vice President and General Manager Doug Rourke headed the Noble Drilling West Africa division, which fared well in the early 1990s. Throughout 1992, the four rigs Noble had drilling in Nigeria were operating at 100 percent utilization. The contract for the *NN-1* expired and was not renewed due to the Nigerian National Petroleum Company's 1993 budget cuts, but the *Chuck Syring* and *Lewis Dugger* contracts would not run out until June 1994. The rigs performed so well—all four of them reported no lost-time accidents in 1992—that the division's western region, which included the Warri office, the *Gene Rosser*, and the *Chuck Syring*, was awarded Shell's first-place quarterly award for major contractors.[45]

Excellent Operations

Noble Drilling's focus on safety not only made for a safer work environment but also improved productivity and reduced its insurance costs. Throughout the downturn in the oil industry, Noble had been dedicated to training its staff in the safe handling of drilling equipment, resulting in one of the most impressive safety records in the industry. Noble's safety training was so impressive, in fact, that its domestic operations showed a 43 percent improvement year to year in lost-time injuries. International operations also showed a year-to-year improvement.[46]

In 1991, for the 11th consecutive year, the International Association of Drilling Contractors (IADC) awarded Noble top honors in its accident-prevention program. In 1993, 24 of Noble's rigs completed the year without a lost-time accident. That same year, the zero-discharge submersible *Paul Wolff* in the Gulf Coast Marine division was awarded the Safety Award for Excellence (SAFE) from the Minerals Management Service "for the exemplary manner in which [the rig's crews] conducted drilling operations."[47]

Since its earliest days, Noble had been committed to conducting business in such a manner that the environment was disrupted as little as possible. So when Congress passed the Oil Pollution Act in 1990 in response to the *Exxon Valdez* oil tanker accident in Alaska, Noble was scarcely affected. The act added regulations for domestic offshore rigs, specifically concerning leaks, spills, and blowouts.[48]

In addition to improving safety and minimizing effects on the environment, Noble began implementing programs developed in 1990 and 1991 to formalize its quality control. The company's Quality Assurance system ensured that Noble's personnel and equipment performed in the safest and most efficient manner possible and sought to prevent problems before they happened. Because the industry had no formal quality system requirements, Noble's formal system made it very attractive to potential customers and propelled it ahead of the competition.[49]

Also in 1991, the company implemented its Planned Preventive Maintenance System (PPMS), which formalized its standard maintenance program to safely preserve its assets. The PPMS used computerized inventory and maintenance systems, which not only made Noble's bidding process more efficient but also helped the company utilize its equipment in the best possible way and set a standard for the equipment's upkeep.[50]

Broadening Its Services

Throughout these difficult times, Noble succeeded, quite admirably, in diversifying its rig capabilities, thus making the company more attractive and allowing it to exact higher rates for its services. At the end of 1991, Noble's fleet included seven rigs with zero-discharge ratings, thirteen cantilever rigs, seven with top drives, nine with cascading solids control, and four with mast capabilities of at least 1.5 million pounds.[51]

Further broadening its range of services, Noble in 1992 gained a 50 percent interest in SeaHawk Services Ltd. A company called Offshore Logistics (OLOG) owned the other half.[52] SeaHawk provided platform and production management services, offshore medical support services, and temporary employees to the industry and operated mainly in the Gulf of Mexico.[53] The following year, Grasso Corporation and Noble Drilling combined their production management businesses so that Noble and OLOG jointly owned 55 percent of Grasso. SeaHawk and Grasso Production Management became wholly owned subsidiaries of Grasso Corporation.[54] At the same time, Noble combined its remaining marine services businesses and spun the new, publicly traded company off to its shareholders.[55]

A Will to Survive

By the end of 1993, the contract oil drilling market had begun to stabilize, and, thanks to the steps Noble's board and management team had taken, Noble Drilling was poised to reap great rewards. For the first time since 1982, the company was able to report positive earnings, with operating revenues reaching the highest in Noble's history: $195 million, a 39.6 percent increase over 1992's figures.[56] "While the return to profitability was a cause for celebration, the return to positive cash flow was even more exciting for a financial man," remembered Byron Welliver.[57]

By that time, Noble had become the largest offshore drilling contractor in the world in terms of drilling units, with 31 offshore rigs and 51 land rigs.[58]

Not only did Noble have a diversified offshore fleet with drilling operations all over the globe, but, unlike many other drilling contractors, its financial position had remained stable throughout the disastrous decade. Still, the company recognized the need to further consolidate the industry and to partner with other companies to seek more cost-efficient operations. Its wide array of service capabilities—which included remote logistics, engineering design and construction, training and safety programs, and production management—made it especially appealing to those companies that were seeking to contain costs through partnerships.

There was little doubt that Noble Drilling had taken on a different character from its earlier years. And if management had anything to say about it—and they had plenty—the company would continue boring through the dark down cycle, chipping away at obstacles, as determined as a drill in difficult terrain.

Noble crewmen connect components of a blowout-prevention stack on an offshore rig.

CHAPTER TEN

DEEPER ASPIRATIONS

1994–1997

I am proud of what our employees have accomplished and I know will accomplish in the years ahead. . . . We have the management talent that can continue to respond to new market opportunities, develop new ideas, and carry on the achievements we've experienced in the past.

—Jim Day, 1996

NOBLE DRILLING MUST HAVE entered the year 1994 with a sigh of relief, for the company had survived what Day termed the "toughest and longest downturn the oil service industry has ever experienced," and it had emerged stronger and more competitive than ever.[1] By the end of the year, Noble owned and operated the world's largest offshore mobile rig fleet, with 32 jackups, eight submersibles, and four posted inland drill barges, and its fleet operations spanned the globe, working in the Gulf of Mexico, Venezuela, Nigeria, Zaire, India, and the North Sea. In addition, Noble owned 46 land rigs strategically located in Alberta, British Columbia, Newfoundland, and along the Texas and Louisiana Coasts.

Noble's rig utilization rates had improved as well. Its domestic land fleet went from 39 percent utilization in 1993 to 51 percent in 1994, while its international land fleet's rate shot up from 43 percent to 77 percent. Noble's international offshore fleet topped the chart with 82 percent utilization in 1994, up from 73 percent the year before.[2]

There was no doubt that Noble Drilling's situation had improved dramatically since its spin-off from Noble Affiliates in 1985. Though the drilling market had recovered somewhat since those dismal days, it was Noble's strong management and its ability to grow and adapt to changing market conditions that allowed it to thrive where others had failed. Throughout the downturn, Noble Drilling had maintained its equipment and had broadened the services it offered while simultaneously keeping debt to a minimum. The result was a drilling company that maintained the largest fleet of jackup rigs in the U.S. Gulf of Mexico, had a dominant jackup presence in Venezuela's Lake Maracaibo, ran a quarter of all rigs in offshore West Africa, and operated two-thirds of the entire world's submersible fleet.[3]

But the industry outlook wasn't all rosy. Though Noble Drilling's operating revenues in 1994 had increased by 33 percent from the previous year—setting a record for the second consecutive year—energy prices had yet to recover, as natural gas prices dropped from $1.95 per million cubic feet at the beginning of 1994 to $1.47 by year's end.[4] Furthermore, the industry still suffered from overcapacity in drilling assets, despite the best efforts of Noble and other healthy drilling companies to consolidate.

The oil and gas industry may have needed a shot of adrenaline, but Noble Drilling refused to sit

---

Thanks to the strong leadership and forward-thinking vision of Jim Day, Noble Drilling had emerged from one of the industry's worst times as a formidable leader.

idly by and wait for recovery. The company had positioned itself to wade out of the industry turmoil by focusing its efforts on enhancing its operations, improving its finances, and expanding its fleet into promising areas. Jim Day and the rest of Noble's action-minded management team would continue these strategies, adapting and growing so that by 1997, Noble Drilling was far less susceptible than much of the competition to the fluctuating market conditions and, in fact, was a dominant player in the burgeoning realm of deepwater drilling.

Triton Engineering

Since 1988, when Noble had acquired Temple Marine and R. C. Chapman, the company had been seeking to expand its services through responsible growth—that is, acquiring assets and even entire companies that would make Noble a stronger player and doing so only when market conditions were favorable. In April 1994, Noble again augmented the organization with the purchase of Houston-based Triton Engineering Services, which provided engineering, consulting, and turnkey drilling services in 54 countries as well as manufacturing and renting oil-field equipment such as shale shakers. With Triton's assets, Noble was able to gain market share in the turnkey drilling market and in engineering services—an area that was growing as oil and gas companies sought to outsource with experts in order to reduce costs.

"Triton allowed us to approach our customers from a different perspective," explained Day. "Heretofore, drilling contractors typically were issued requests for bids on projects, and there was very little interface with the customer. Triton had more of an in-depth relationship with the operator because it had to get familiar with the project. Through this acquisition, we were able to get closer and have more interface with some of our clients."[5]

Furthermore, the Triton acquisition gave Noble more engineering expertise. "While we had a staff of engineers in Houston and in the North Sea, most of our experience was from the mudline up," explained Larry Richardson, Noble's manager of turnkey contracts. "In other words, all of our expertise was in the drilling rigs, the platform, the production facilities, things of that nature, but not in drilling wells

below the mudline. We wanted to acquire that technology and also to have that in our toolboxes so we could offer customers more services."[6]

Since its founding in 1976 by a proactive visionary named Joseph E. Beall, Triton Engineering had

After buying Triton Engineering in 1994, Noble again expanded its offshore presence when it acquired 13 drilling rigs from Chiles Offshore.

been outsourcing its valuable engineering and project management services to oil and gas companies that would not otherwise have those capabilities. It was one of the first companies to offer turnkey drilling services and had experience drilling offshore with drill barges, semisubmersibles, jackups, and platform rigs. Its remarkably capable management and personnel had experience in a vast array of projects and services, including drilling, field development design and installation, project management and consulting, and engineering. Given the emphasis Noble placed on upgrading its equipment and training its personnel, Triton's ability to design equipment and its experience in training and preparing training manuals made Triton even more appealing to Noble.

Triton became a wholly owned subsidiary of Noble Drilling, and Joe Beall and his team became part of the Noble team. "Noble allowed Triton to operate very autonomously," said Kurt Hoffman, who at that time was Triton's vice president of international operations. "However, when opportunities arose, Triton would use Noble rigs."[7]

When Noble acquired the company, Triton already had 200 turnkey wells in the Gulf of Mexico and 17 international turnkey wells under its belt. During its first year with Noble, it added nine new oil and gas companies to its already impressive client list and signed an additional 35 turnkey contracts. Furthermore, Triton was able to maintain a focused turnkey drilling effort to optimize returns, unlike other turnkey services companies that sought only specific market share. By 1996, Triton was offering turnkey services in the lucrative markets of Mexico, Nigeria, Gabon, and the North Sea.

Larry Richardson pointed out that the Triton acquisition would also help maintain Noble's operations during down cycles. "In a downward market when Noble's rigs were idle, Noble could look to Triton to help put some of those rigs to work by getting a contract to drill a turnkey well and then using one of Noble's rigs to drill that well," he said.[8]

Chiles Offshore

Triton Engineering wasn't the only acquisition on the horizon. Continuing with its strategy of expanding its offshore fleet, in September 1994 Noble finalized a deal with Chiles Offshore Corporation in which Chiles was merged with Noble's Noble Offshore Corporation subsidiary to form the largest drilling contractor in the Gulf of Mexico. The merger gave Noble 13 strategically located drilling units, 11 of which were in the Gulf of Mexico and two in Nigeria. Moreover, the purchase helped consolidate the scattered offshore drilling industry, which still suffered from too little demand for rigs. "Although our industry will continue to experience volatility, this acquisition will enhance an already strong Noble Drilling balance sheet and provide fur-

Left: Joseph E. Beall founded Triton Engineering in 1976 and joined Noble after it acquired Triton in 1994.

Right: Danny Adkins was Chiles Offshore's vice president of operations when Noble acquired it. He advanced through various positions and in 2000 was named senior vice president of operations.

ther financial flexibility to expand our significant international operations," Day said.[9]

Analysts agreed. "The merger is certainly going to help Noble because they will have the largest jackup fleet in the Gulf of Mexico, so they will be very highly leveraged, particularly to natural gas drilling," said NatWest Securities analyst Michael K. LaMotte.[10]

The merger with Chiles Offshore brought some excellent operating people to Noble Drilling. Danny W. Adkins, who previously served as Chiles Offshore's vice president of operations, initially held the same title with Noble Drilling before becoming senior vice president of engineering and later senior vice president of worldwide operations. John T. Rynd, formerly vice president for domestic marketing and contracts for Chiles Offshore, was promoted to vice president for marketing and contracts prior to moving into investor relations in 2000.

From within Noble, Julie J. Robertson was appointed vice president for administration while still retaining her position as corporate secretary. The promotion made her the highest ranking woman in the drilling sector. Alan Krenek, previously controller, was named controller of reporting; and Doug L. White, formerly with Amoco Production, became director of operations and was promoted to

Left: John Rynd was Chiles Offshore's vice president for domestic marketing and contracts and later became Noble's vice president of investor relations.

Right: Julie Robertson worked at Peter Bawden Drilling when Noble acquired it in 1988. She moved up the Noble ranks, being named senior vice president—administration and corporate secretary.

vice president of international operations the following September. Other officers of Noble Drilling included Byron Welliver, treasurer and senior vice president for finance; and Warren L. Twa, senior vice president for international operations.[11]

Over the years, Noble had learned the right and wrong ways of integrating a new company into the organization, and those who came from Chiles Offshore maintained that Noble had a very people-oriented approach. "Noble was very tolerant, very patient, very forgiving, and very understanding when it came to Chiles people learning to do things the Noble way," said Danny Adkins. "When acquiring, it's very easy for people, for companies, to lose focus on their operations, on safety, and on maintenance. Noble has tried to manage these types of problems that are involved with acquisitions and has become very experienced at it."[12]

"When we did acquisitions, we went out and welcomed the new group and the new crews to Noble Drilling," said Bill Jennings. "We told them what our

Noble had a strong presence in Lake Maracaibo, Venezuela, where the *Dick Favor* was at work for the state oil company in the late 1990s.

policies and rules were, and we also left one of our Noble rig managers out there. We looked at the way they did things—safety, maintenance—and if we saw something that would improve Noble's processes, we adopted it. We also taught them over a period of time how we did our paperwork, how we did our budgets, etc. And it took time. But it was the Noble way, and it was the right way."[13]

Geographic Expansion

In addition to its offshore operations, Noble continued to maintain its labor contracts in the North Sea. Under a labor contract, Noble does not own or lease the drilling units but provides personnel to manage and perform drilling operations for other companies. In 1994, Noble was awarded an offshore labor contract in the Middle East by Qatar General Petroleum Corporation (QGPC) to operate its drilling unit the *Dana* (which later became the *Noble Chuck Syring* after Noble purchased it in 1996), marking the first time Noble operated in that part of the world. The following year, Noble broadened its presence in the Middle East with its own rig, the *Noble George McLeod*, a 300-foot independent-leg cantilever under a footage contract with QGPC in Qatar.

Drilling activity in Nigeria was on the rise, especially for jackups that could operate in up to 300 feet of water—a market sector that Noble had a large share of. In 1994, the *Ed Noble*, which had been drilling offshore Nigeria, received an extended contract for one year, while Mobil Nigeria secured the *Tommy Craighead* for two years. Shell Nigeria also extended the *Chuck Syring*'s contract for two more years in 1994. In 1995, Noble's 300-foot independent-leg cantilever unit the *Percy Johns* was mobilized from the Gulf of Mexico to work under a three-year contract with Mobil Nigeria, while the *Lloyd Noble*, a 250-foot independent-leg cantilever, journeyed from the Gulf of Mexico to Africa's west coast to begin drilling for Chevron. The addition of those two units in Nigeria made Noble the second-largest drilling contractor along the west coast of Africa.[14] Also in 1995, the *Don Walker* jackup began a three-year contract with Mobil Nigeria.[15]

At Venezuela's Lake Maracaibo, the *Dick Favor* and *Carl Norberg* rigs began new five-year contracts in 1995 with Lagoven, an affiliate of Petroleos de Venezuela (both rigs had been working in Venezuela under separate contracts since 1994), while Shell Venezuela S.A. contracted for the *Charles Copeland*.[16]

Upgrades and Enhancements

As Noble Drilling continued to acquire rigs from other companies, it refurbished the new units to bring them up to its operating standards and to make them more competitive. In 1994, Noble completed its refurbishment of the *Linn Richardson* and began transforming the 300-foot slot-type independent-leg *John Sandifer* into a cantilevered unit with a new top-drive system and cascade mud system, which would make it more versatile. The *Eddie Paul* went through a similar refurbishment and was also equipped with a 70-foot extended-reach cantilever (ERC™) that would allow it to drill over larger platforms and in water depths of 390 feet. The ERC™ was an innovative design created by Noble's skilled engineering staff. It allowed Noble to save money by enhancing existing drill units rather than investing in newbuilds. "We did the very first one," said Dave Beard, vice president for engineering. "When we first did the ERC™ projects, some of our competitors didn't think they'd succeed, and now the design is being copied. We license the name."[17]

Both the *John Sandifer* and the *Eddie Paul* were tailored according to Noble's new I.D.E.A.S.™ (Improved Drilling Efficiency and Accountability System), which was developed to improve drilling performance. I.D.E.A.S.™ was designed to use operators' input to find better ways to determine a well's critical path, reduce drilling time, improve operating efficiency, provide safer working conditions, and meet return on investment.

The idea took root when Bill Jennings, who at the time was division manager for Gulf Coast Marine operations, and Charles H. "Buddy" King, vice president of Noble Engineering & Development, started discussing ways to become more efficient. "Buddy had some great ideas," said Jennings. "We sat down with our whole operating group in Lafayette and started discussing what we could do to become more efficient on a drilling rig. All our superintendents came up with certain ideas, and that's when we came up with the phrase 'I.D.E.A.S. program.'"[18]

The I.D.E.A.S. team took photographs of each rig operation and made them into slides for study and evaluation. "It was amazing what we could see

The *Eddie Paul* jackup was refurbished in 1994
with a 70-foot extended-reach cantilever, or ERC™,
which was a unique Noble Drilling design copied
by several competitors.

from the slides," said Jennings. "It was like a time-in-motion study, and we started step by step, breaking down the operation and making it into a continuous operation so that we didn't have redundant time. It's an ongoing process that provides our clients with the most efficient rigs around the world."[19]

According to the company newsletter, the I.D.E.A.S.™ program gave Noble's customers "the most efficient rig crews in the Gulf of Mexico by focusing on planning the mutual task of drilling a well and providing measurable cost savings."[20] When the rig conversions were completed in the spring of 1995, both units went to work in the Gulf of Mexico.

While the I.D.E.A.S.™ program improved Noble's fleet, the Noble Enabler Financial System improved its information systems by providing better real-time financial and operating information at the rig level. This feature was especially attractive to Noble's larger customers, the major oil and gas companies, because it closely matched the systems they used, thus providing specific, accurate information.

Standing Out

Noble Drilling's efforts to stand out among its competitors paid off quite well. In 1994, Noble Offshore beat out four other bidders to win a five-year contract with Hibernia Management and Development Company for the Hibernia Project, located in the eastern waters offshore Newfoundland. The Hibernia Project included building the first offshore oil facility in North America to use a gravity-based design—an engineering feat in and of itself—and was the only platform in the world with an iceberg-resistant ice wall.[21] For the first part of the project, which began in September, Noble provided specialized consulting services related to the assembly and hookup of two platform drilling rigs that would be installed on the concrete gravity-based

structure. Beginning in 1997, Noble began operating and maintaining the two rigs,[22] and by the end of 2000, the Hibernia project was producing anywhere from 110,000 to 150,000 barrels of oil a day![23]

"The Hibernia project is very challenging, not only from the drilling engineering perspective but also from an equipment perspective," said Kurt Hoffman, who became vice president of Noble's Western Hemisphere operations in 1999. "The formation is quite deep, anywhere from 22,000 feet to 26,000 feet, and with 60 to 70 wells in this one location, they're not all straight holes; they're directional wells. So we're drilling as much as 26,000 feet at as much as 70 degrees to 80 degrees deviation."[24]

Also in 1994, Noble's *OW-842* rig began drilling the deepest well ever drilled in western Newfoundland under a contract with Hunt Oil Company and its partner, PanCanadian Petroleum. The well was targeted to be 15,000 feet deep.[25] That same year, Chevron chose Noble to drill a natural gas well in the Destin Dome area offshore Florida's Panhandle. This was an environmentally sensitive area, but Noble's environmental policies helped it win the contract, and indeed Noble went beyond Chevron's expectations.

Furthermore, Noble was one of nine drilling service companies chosen to become part of Amoco Production Company's exclusive Amoco Supplier Alliance Program (ASAP 2000). Amoco's goal was to reduce its supplier/vendor base from more than 12,000 to a small, select group of allied suppliers. ASAP 2000 members sought to reduce Amoco's exploration and development costs so that Amoco could continue its activities in existing fields.

Amoco chose Noble Drilling for, among other reasons, its commitment to providing quality service and its willingness to share information regarding costs. Shortly after it was granted approved-vendor status in the summer of 1994, Noble was awarded

Amoco's Cotton Valley program, which was a 10-well pilot alliance in the East Texas field.[26]

Noble's emphasis on creating a safe working environment was once again recognized in 1996 when the Department of Interior's Minerals Management Service (MMS) awarded Noble its National Offshore Safety Award for Excellence for the *Tom Jobe*, which was working in the Gulf of Mexico. That same year, Dr. Roy Rhodes joined the company full-time as vice president of organization development. In his new position he was charged with developing programs to bring in a new generation of Nobleites who could uphold the company's future.[27]

Fancy Fleetwork: EVA-4000™

In the wild ups and downs of a cyclical industry, the company had succeeded where many others had failed. But Jim Day was not content to bask in the glory of Noble's recent accomplishments. Rather, he and the rest of the Noble team were continuously planning for the future.

Noble's future was to be in deepwater drilling, for deepwater was where many of its key customers had directed their resources. "Jim's vision for the company was to take rigs offshore, take them into deeper water, which is more the niche markets where we could expect a better return on capital," said Danny Adkins. "Jim had the long-range vision that deepwater was where we really needed to go."[28]

Throughout the 1990s, Noble Drilling achieved many milestones and was widely recognized for standing above much of the competition. In 1994, for example, rig *OW-842* completed the deepest well ever drilled in western Newfoundland.

"Our management team felt like the deepwater market provided us with a niche opportunity," said Day. "There were competitors that were in shallower water, but in deepwater, there was really not one dominant player. When we looked at the market, we saw an opportunity for Noble to step up, particularly with our engineering expertise, and move into that important sector."[29]

Noble's 1996 annual report explained why the oil and gas industry was moving more toward deepwater drilling:

Deepwater is one of the last unexplored frontiers where large hydrocarbon deposits await discovery. Activity has grown dramatically over the last several years due to a stable commodity price outlook, improvement in technology, such as 3-D seismic, and development of a more cost effective means of exploiting these deposits enabling operators to reduce dryhole costs. Major successes in deepwater exploration and development coupled with improving lease term on concessions in most deepwater markets will further tighten the deepwater semi and drillship market.[30]

Above right: Dr. Roy Rhodes became Noble's vice president of organizational development in 1996. His duties include leading Noble's safety workshops.

Below: While the company built its strength, it continued to serve the community. In 1997, for example, Nobleites and their families participated in the Juvenile Diabetes Foundation Walk.

As chairman of the National Ocean Industries Association, Day explained how important the Gulf of Mexico deepwater area was to the future of the oil

industry. "The deepwater Gulf of Mexico contains huge reserves—as high as 15 billion barrels of oil equivalent—and has the potential to dramatically increase exploration and production activities in the U.S. offshore," he said. "However, the costs to explore in and develop from the deepwater are extremely high. . . ."[31] Day was talking about extreme and costly government restrictions on exploration and drilling, in addition to the millions of dollars it would take to construct a rig capable of deepwater drilling.[32]

Noble, however, found a way to capitalize on the deepwater boom while keeping costs to a minimum. "Jim asked me if any of our assets, particularly our triangular submersibles, could be converted for use in deepwater," said Adkins, who had a lot of experience working with triangular semisubmersibles. "I said yes, that I had actually worked on triangular semisubmersibles some time ago." Subsequently, the decision was made to perform feasibility studies. "So we got into it, and sure enough it was very feasible. It was very innovative as well.

In 1996, Bill Jennings presents Slim Peters with a watch to commemorate Peters's 30 years of service with Noble Drilling. Noble Gulf Coast Marine employees, from left, are Robert Spence, operations manager; Ken Nettles, drilling superintendent; Slim Peters; Bill Jennings, vice president and general manager; and Ken Delaney, assistant division manager.

Three of Noble's triangular-shaped semisubmersibles undergo the EVA-4000™ conversion, which Noble pioneered, to turn them into submersibles capable of drilling in ultradeepwater.

We called it 'imagineering,' and we very quickly came up with a design of converting the submersibles, which we had a low-cost-basis in, to ultradeepwater assets. The conversions fit with Noble's strategy of converting low-cost-basis assets to compete in niche-market sectors."[33]

The conversion design was called EVA-4000™. EVA stood for economic value advantage, while 4000 indicated the original water depth and tonnage load that the drilling units would be designed for. (As the design progressed, however, Noble's engineers discovered that the rigs could be converted to drill much deeper than 4,000 feet.) Using the EVA-4000™ design, Noble planned to convert all of its existing triangular three-column-design submersibles, which it had acquired as part of the Transworld Drilling deal in 1991, into semisubmersible deepwater jackups.

"The industry thought Noble was crazy," said Jitendra Prasad, Noble's vice president of technical engineering, who was a member of the team of engineers that came up with the successful design. "The industry was laughing, but I had come from a company [the engineering arm of Sedco] that owned triangular semisubmersibles, and I was very familiar with how this would work—how to make it work."[34]

The industry's skepticism didn't last long. Noble's engineering team did, indeed, pioneer a way to rework a drilling unit that formerly was sunk to the bottom of the water to drill in less than 100 feet, making it capable of drilling in depths of 6,000 to 8,900 feet.

EVA-4000™ had several advantages over newbuilds. The EVA-4000™ system not only extended the life of existing rigs, which Noble had purchased when prices were low, but also ensured that Noble would not repeat the overcapacity cycle of a few years earlier. The engineers at Noble had spent over 18 months refining the design so that initial project costs for deepwater exploration and development could be kept to a minimum. Moreover, each deepwater semisubmersible could be designed to specific customer requirements.[35]

"The economics of the upgrade and conversion of the EVA-4000™ are clearly superior to the newbuild alternatives that have been proposed to the market," said Day.[36] Byron Welliver, who at that time was Noble's senior vice president of finance and CFO, told the *Oil Daily* that "most of the

numbers we've seen for newbuilds are $200 million or more and took over two years to complete. We can convert our rig for less than half of that and in half the time."[37] And Dave Beard said that though technically EVA stood for economic value advantage, "what it really stands for is getting the most bang for your buck."[38]

Still, Welliver recalled that there was not a lot of confidence or support outside of Noble for building the rigs. "Triangular rigs were not in widespread use in the industry," he said, "and the principal reaction was skepticism as to whether or not the concept would work."[39]

Noble wanted to find a buyer before it began the actual conversions. John Rynd, vice president of marketing, Bill Jennings, vice president and manager of Western Hemisphere operations, and Danny Adkins, who by that time had become senior vice president for engineering, formed a team to introduce the concept. "We had no deepwater operations when we started," said Rynd. "So we not only had to overcome a unique design; we also had to overcome a nondeepwater background."[40]

It was a testament to Noble's reputation and the strength of the EVA-4000™ design that the three men were able to find a willing buyer so soon. Shell Oil, which had been drilling in deepwater since the mid-1980s, signed a letter of intent to contract for the first EVA-4000™ conversion, the *Noble Paul Romano.*

"We were at a point in the designs at which we could give the customer some of the things they didn't have on other rigs," said Jennings. "They came up with ideas themselves. They'd say, 'Here's what's happened to us. Here's the problem we're having out there with the rigs we have presently.' And we would come back and say, 'Okay, we understand the problem you're having. Here's what we have for a solution.' And they'd say, 'Hey, great idea. Let's incorporate that.' So we went back to the drawing table and were able to incorporate the majority of their ideas."[41]

"We were very fortunate that Shell, being the major deepwater player in the Gulf of Mexico, showed an interest very early in the process," said Adkins. "Our focus was on economic value advantage, and we were very honest about that. We knew we had to bring value not only to our shareholders, but to Shell and Shell's shareholders. We wanted to avoid building cost into these projects that was not value

The *Noble Paul Romano,* shown here before its conversion, was the first submersible to be converted using the EVA-4000™ design.

Noble employees visit the Hibernia platform during its christening in May 1997. From left are Bill Mooney, board director for Noble Drilling Canada; Bill Jennings, vice president and managing director, Western Hemisphere; Tommy Craighead, Noble board director; George McLeod, chairman of Noble Drilling Canada; and Boris Ewanchuk, general manager of Noble Drilling Canada.

added, and Shell shared that philosophy. They had a lot of experience in deepwater, a lot of confidence, and they realized that you didn't have to have a $300 million investment to go do this deepwater work—and we did too."[42]

By the fall of 1998, the *Noble Paul Romano* would be ready to begin its contract in the Gulf of Mexico with Shell Deepwater Development as a semisubmersible unit capable of drilling in 6,000 feet. The opportunity with Shell led to Petrobras of Brazil being interested, and from there the interest snowballed. "Both Shell and Petrobras were probably the leaders in deepwater drilling," said Jennings. "We knew that if they accepted the design, it was like having a blessing."[43] Or, as Day pointed out, it "was like getting a Good Housekeeping seal of approval."[44]

By the end of 1997 Noble Drilling had commitments for six long-term contracts for its EVA-4000™ conversions.[45]

In Deepwater

Noble sought to further expand its presence in the deepwater drilling sector through acquisitions and refurbishments. In 1995, the company had acquired the *Azteca*, renamed the *Noble Gene Rosser*, and the *Maya*, renamed the *Noble Lewis Dugger*. Both were independent-leg 300-foot slot-type jackups that would be converted to cantilever rigs before beginning work in 1996.

In 1996, Noble added four more deepwater jackups to its offshore fleet, starting with the 300-foot cantilever jackup *Odin Explorer*, renamed the *Noble Gus Androes*. Located in the Arabian Gulf, the *Noble Gus Androes* increased Noble's presence in the Middle East and even set a world record in December for cumulative footage on one bit, drilling 15,774 feet in 67.1 hours.[46] Noble also added the *Noble Kenneth Delaney* and the *Noble Jimmy Puckett*, both 300-foot independent-leg cantilever units, and the *Noble Chuck Syring*, a 250-foot independent-leg cantilever, formerly the *Dana,* which had been drilling in Qatar. (Since 1981, the rig later known as the *Noble Chuck Syring* had been displayed on Qatar's largest denomination of currency, the Qatari riyal 500 banknote, as a symbol of the country's oil and gas industry.)

Going Dutch

At the same time as the initial EVA-4000™ designs, Noble took another big step into deepwater when, after nearly two years of on-and-off talks, it acquired the highly respected Dutch drilling contractor Neddrill. Headed at the time by F. W. "Frits" van Riet, Neddrill was the drilling subsidiary of Royal Nedlloyd N.V., a shipping giant headquartered in Rotterdam, the Netherlands. Neddrill had a notable presence in the North Sea and in the deepwater offshore Brazil and owned two drillships, six harsh-environment jackup drilling units, and one semisubmersible. Because drillships are self-propelled and have a ship-shaped hull, they are very mobile and can carry a lot of equipment, making them ideal for drilling in remote locations. All of Neddrill's drillships were dynamically positioned, which meant they used computer-controlled thrusters and special sensors rather than anchors to keep them in position. With thrusters and sensors on the ship's hull below the waterline, a technician could tell the computer where to keep the rig positioned. The sensors detected wind, wave, and current, and the thrusters, controlled by the computer, would offset those forces to keep the rig in place. In addition, Neddrill operated and jointly owned a third drillship and ran a jackup hotel accommodation unit under a bareboat charter agreement.[47]

Neddrill greatly influenced Noble's activity in the North Sea. "The deepwater assets were very important to us," said Bill Jennings. "Deepwater jackups are at the upper end of the food chain when you're starting in that business."[48]

"These were the first mobile rigs we had," said Bill Rose. "Up until that time, our North Sea operation that came from the Bawden acquisition was all contracted platform rigs. Basically, we had been a labor contractor there. But the Neddrill acquisition gave us owned assets in the North Sea."[49]

Additionally, the acquisition increased Noble's size by about 25 percent, making it one of the largest offshore drilling contractors in the world, and added about 500 employees in countries including Brazil, Argentina, Denmark, and the Netherlands. Noble paid $300 million in cash plus 5 million shares of stock.[50] Four years after the acquisition, John Rynd reflected that the Neddrill acquisition also gave Noble "credibility in deepwater and floating operations that we previously didn't have, not just from the day-to-day operations but from an engineering side as well."[51]

Day told stockholders in the company's 1996 annual report that "the company has an excellent reputation, outstanding personnel, and well-maintained equipment. We are very excited about the addition to our operation and what it will mean to the future of the company."[52]

It seemed Wall Street was excited as well. On March 29, 1996, three months before the Neddrill acquisition was finalized, Noble Drilling began trading on the New York Stock Exchange, and analysts cheered the wisdom of adding Neddrill's significant deepwater presence to Noble's assets. Both Moody's Investors Service and Standard & Poor's (S&P) upped their ratings of Noble's senior notes. Moody's predicted that the Neddrill acquisition would make Noble more competitive, while S&P praised the company for its fleet upgrades and enhancements and put Noble on its watch list.[53] "S&P takes a positive view toward the acquisition because it not only strengthens Noble Drilling's position as the largest public offshore drilling contractor in terms of the number of rigs, but also materially reduces its dependence on the more volatile Gulf of Mexico markets while adding harsh environment and deepwater capabilities to the Houston company's fleet," wrote *Petroleum Finance Week.*[54]

In December 1996, Noble bought the *Essar Explorer,* a 300-foot independent-leg cantilever unit operating offshore India. The unit was later renamed the *Noble Jimmy Puckett.*[55] By the following summer, the Neddrill division had been renamed Noble Drilling (Nederland).[56]

Good Rationale

At the same time as it was building up its deepwater jackup fleet, Noble began an ongoing rationalization program of disposing of its

After its deepwater conversion, the *Noble Paul Wolff* would be capable of drilling in water depths of 8,900 feet and would be Noble's first dynamically positioned deepwater semisubmersible.

less-competitive noncore assets such as barges and land units so that it could focus on its higher-end assets in offshore drilling.

In January 1996, Noble sold two of its posted barges, the *Gus Androes* and the *Gene Rosser* (not to be confused with the cantilever jackups, the *Noble Gus Androes* and the *Noble Gene Rosser*). In September it sold two more posted barges, the *Lewis Dugger* and the *Chuck Syring.*

But the big move came in December, when Noble sold its remaining 47 land rigs, 28 of which had been stacked, to Nabors Industries for $60 million in cash. An internal report that assessed the value and condition of the company's land rigs had clinched Day's decision to focus solely on marine offshore operations. When the final sale was announced, Gene Isenberg, chairman and CEO of Nabors, reconfirmed to the industry Noble's propensity for keeping its rigs in top condition, even when stacked. "The condition of the assets [has] exceeded our expectations as we have completed our due diligence," he said.[57]

"We knew we weren't going to get the economic returns from the land business," explained Roger Lewis. "Even though the land business may have been doing well at the time, we had gone through 15 years of very difficult times to get to that one or two years that it blossomed. So we didn't see a long-term growth perspective."[58]

"The land business is a very low-margin, very low-return business," explained Danny Adkins. "Noble was one of the best land drillers and managed to make money and run a premium operation in the worst of times, but it wasn't a long-term business to put money into. Our most valuable resource is our people, and we felt like if we could take those skill sets, that talent, and put it on assets that would bring a higher return, we'd add more value long term for shareholders and employees. It was a tough decision, but it was the right decision. That's why Noble is where it is today. Management had the vision and knew that we had to transition the company away from that kind of business."[59]

Noble recognized the irony of selling its land rigs in the same year that it was celebrating its 75th anniversary and thus remembering its roots in land drilling. But land drilling had grown much less significant for Noble as its international foot-print grew larger and larger and as it continued its offshore expansion.

Noble had intended to sell its low-margin assets for some time but was waiting until the market improved so it could get an optimal return. "The company did a fabulous job of timing the divestments where we were able to reap the greatest dollars from selling the land units," observed Roger Lewis. "We picked the peak time to sell the land rigs—when we finally had an up cycle."[60]

Forward Momentum

By the end of 1996, Noble was on top of the world—or at least 13 countries worldwide—and with 57 mobile drilling units, it had the largest fleet in the industry.[61] Moreover, Noble had become a leader in the deepwater jackup market with 19 independent-leg cantilevered jackup units rated at 300 feet and over, and it held a third of the world's jackups that could drill in water depths of more than 350 feet. Operating revenues for 1996 reached $514 million, an amazing 57 percent increase over the previous year.[62]

Noble's forward momentum continued throughout 1997 as demand for drilling and related services at last caught up with—and in some areas even surpassed—supply. In June of that year, it realized its stock was undervalued, despite a 52-week high of $24 in January, so the board authorized the company to buy back up to 10 million of its common shares, or about 8 percent of its outstanding stock. "Analysts have been saying for months that the entire offshore oil service sector is currently a huge bargain," reported *Offshore* magazine. "With little debt and no inclination to build or upgrade on speculation, these contractors, manufacturers, and service companies are putting their money where they know it will grow."[63]

The company's enviable financial situation was even more impressive in light of the market conditions it had survived. The period in the 1980s and 1990s when Noble had acquired so many of its assets was, as Byron Welliver pointed out, "characterized by low to negative cash flow, which would not support the addition of debt." Except for working-capital lines, it had been Noble's basic philosophy to avoid debt. "Fortunately, we were a public company, which provided us another currency to

Jim Day (far right) presents Roger Eason (second from right) with a watercolor painting of his namesake rig at the rig's dedication dinner in October 1997. With Eason are his son and daughter-in-law, Lynn and Nancy Eason.

use in our objective to expand during the period that assets were inexpensive," Welliver said. "The majority of the early acquisitions were made by issuing Noble stock. Care was taken in establishing the number of shares to be issued to ensure that the acquisitions would be accreditive."[64]

The year 1997 was critical and busy for Noble Drilling as the company continued stressing deepwater drilling through reactivation of rigs and its exclusive EVA-4000™ conversions. The success of the conversion program was a tribute to many Noble people, represented by such key team leaders as Neil Mendoza, Scott Marks, Aldert Schenkel, Tom Foyt, Norton Haviland, Francis Tubbs, Harvey Duhaney, Greg Castleman, Jim Gormanson, and many others who worked in close cooperation with the Friede & Goldman/Halter yard in Pascagoula, Mississippi, and the yard in Sabine Pass, Texas. The EVA program's development, including design and construction, was led by Dave Beard, Jitendra Prasad, Hans Deul, and Danny Adkins.

The *Noble Bill Jennings* was reactivated in 1997 after being converted into a 390-foot independent-leg cantilever with extended reach and was mobilized to the Gulf of Mexico to begin a one-year

contract with Mesa Operating Company. In addition, the *Noble Joe Alford* and the *Noble Lester Pettus*, both 85-foot cantilever submersibles, began working in the Gulf of Mexico after being reactivated and upgraded.[65]

Noble was able to keep its fixed costs down by purchasing these units when rig prices were at a minimum, and the company drove up its competitive edge by passing those savings on to its customers. Noble's customers also saved money by contracting with the EVA-4000™ semisubmersible units since Noble's deepwater conversion cost much less than a newbuild. In June 1997, Noble's second EVA-4000™ semisubmersible conversion, the *Noble Paul Wolff*, signed a six-year contract with Petrobras in Brazil. The *Noble Paul Wolff* would be the company's first dynamically positioned conversion project, and when completed in June 1998, the unit would be capable of operating in water depths up to 8,900 feet.[66] Also in the summer of 1997, the *Noble Amos Runner* received a five-year contract in the Gulf of Mexico. When its EVA-4000™ conversion was completed in January 1999, it would be capable of drilling in up to 6,600 feet of water. In addition, the *Noble Max Smith*, which would be rated at 6,000 feet once its EVA-4000™ conversion was completed in July 1999, would begin its five-year contract in the Gulf of Mexico with Amerada Hess Corporation. And the *Noble Jim Thompson*, another EVA-4000™ unit, would begin a three-year contract in 1999 with Shell Deepwater Development, drilling in water depths of up to 6,000 feet in the Gulf of Mexico.[67]

Elsewhere, the *Noble Al White* jackup was upgraded and began an 18-month production drilling contract for SAGA Petroleum in the Norwegian sector of the North Sea, while the *Noble Kolskaya* harsh-environment jackup began drilling under contract in Denmark.[68] In offshore Brazil, three Noble units began long-term contracts with Petrobras after major upgrades and modifications: the *Noble Roger Eason*, the *Noble Leo Segerius*, and the *Noble Muravlenko*.[69] The *Noble Leo Segerius* and the *Noble Roger Eason*, in fact, were both involved in breaking the world record for deepwater completion and production in early 1997.[70]

Noble's rationalization program continued as the company reduced its exposure in the recently volatile Gulf of Mexico market. In the spring of 1997,

Noble divested itself of many of its older-technology rigs when it sold its 12 mat-supported jackups, most of which had been operating in the Gulf of Mexico, to Pride Petroleum for $265 million in cash. Day said that the proceeds would be invested in assets that would provide long-term profits, such as the EVA-4000™ conversions.[71]

The sale, which completed Noble Drilling's transformation into a premium jackup and deepwater-focused company, was viewed as a wise decision. "Usually CEOs want to hold on to all their assets," explained Jay Courage, senior managing director at Jeffries & Company investment firm and a key banker involved in the sale. "They're reluctant to do any pruning, but Jim has always been willing to prune if he can get good prices and then put that money into higher-value-added assets."[72]

Positioned for Success

Noble Drilling's operating revenue for 1997 reached $713.2 million, beating 1996's results by 39 percent.[73] Though part of Noble's vastly improved 1997 results could be attributed to a more favorable market, the company's continued strategies of conservative financing and an emphasis on deepwater and international drilling most definitely had positive effects as well.

Noble wasn't letting itself be fooled into resting on its laurels, for the company knew that a tighter rig market would bring potential shortages in qualified personnel, delays in equipment delivery, and the threat of speculative construction that could spark a new overcapacity cycle.

To help remedy the employment challenges, Dr. Roy Rhodes began an aggressive training program in which engineers and other personnel would be enlisted from around the world and placed in a three-year training program that focused on technical, business, and leadership skills—all to prepare them for the challenging conditions of the drilling industry. Other employees would have opportunities to refine their skills for future promotions through three-year training programs and through the computer-based training modules installed on each of Noble's rigs.[74]

"We recognized that our workforce was getting older," explained Day. "In order for this company to exist for another 80 years, we knew we needed to train and mentor that next generation. That's what it's all about, and that's truly a unique effort."[75]

Noble, in fact, had positioned itself to survive almost anything the industry could throw at it by converting many of its rigs to deepwater semisubmersibles, disposing of its low-return, noncore assets, and keeping a healthy balance sheet. By the end of 1997, Noble owned seven semisubmersibles for the growing deepwater segment; three dynamically positioned drillships; 32 jackups operating in the lucrative offshore sector; and three submersibles, which could be converted to deepwater using the innovative EVA-4000™ design. Noble's rig fleet was capable of drilling in water depths ranging from 70 feet to 8,900 feet, and the company maintained operations in 13 countries and with a wide range of operating companies. In addition to its offshore and turnkey drilling services, Noble offered engineering and production management services and, in fact, managed the Hibernia offshore platform in Canada and 14 others in the North Sea.

Once again, the industry's prospects looked bright, but management was wise enough to realize that the market could swing in the other direction quicker than a drill bit could rotate. "If you're investing in this sector, grab a seat belt because we're going to have a ride," Day said at an oil conference in the fall of 1997. "This doesn't mean we won't make money. But there will be pauses."[76]

Pauses indeed—and not far off. Yet Noble Drilling's efforts to maximize its potential in the cyclical industry were about to pay off even more as the next year brought another dramatic drop in the price of oil and natural gas.

THE PEOPLE BEHIND THE RIGS

*N*OBLE DRILLING NAMES ITS RIGS AFTER *individuals who have been especially valuable to the company. Following is a short biography of those individuals, along with information about their namesake rig. The names are arranged in the order that the rigs were christened.*

Ed Holt

Ed Holt's career with Noble Drilling started in 1930, when he joined the company as an engineer. He rose through the ranks to senior management positions and was instrumental in the Sherwood Forest drilling project during World War II. In 1950 Holt returned from retirement to assist with the management transition after Lloyd Noble's death; he continued as an officer and trusted advisor for many years. Holt served on the board of directors until his death in 2001 and ultimately enjoyed over 70 years of association with the company.

The *Noble Ed Holt* is a Levingston III-C independent-leg jackup. The rig is rated to work in up to 300 feet of water and drill to 25,000 feet. In 2001 the unit was drilling offshore India.

Sam Noble

Due to the untimely death of Lloyd Noble in 1950, Sam Noble was thrust into a senior management role that few 25-year-olds experience. Having just completed his masters degree at Dartmouth in Massachusetts, he was appointed to head up Samedan in addition to serving on its board of directors. In 1954 he was appointed to Noble Drilling's board and also served on the board of trustees of the Samuel Roberts Noble Foundation. He served as Samedan's president from 1952 to 1965 and continued to serve as chairman of the boards of Noble Drilling Corporation and Noble Affiliates and as a trustee of the Noble Foundation until his death in 1992. In addition to his responsibilities with the Noble companies, Sam Noble was involved in successful ranching and oil and gas ventures. He served on the boards of approximately 25 philanthropic organizations.

The *Noble Sam Noble* is a Levingston III-C independent-leg jackup rated to work in up to 300 feet of water and drill to 25,000 feet. In 2001 the rig was at work in the Gulf of Mexico.

Johnnie Hoffman

Johnnie Hoffman's career with Noble started in 1947, when he joined as a roughneck in the Gulf Coast division. He worked his way up to toolpusher and superintendent before serving for many years as Gulf Coast division manager. He retired in 1986, after 39 years of service, and served on the board of directors of Noble Drilling from 1983 until his death in 1996.

The *Noble Johnnie Hoffman* is a Baker Marine independent-leg cantilever jackup capable of working in up to 300 feet of water and drilling to 25,000 feet. In 2001 the rig was operating in the Gulf of Mexico.

Fri Rodli

Fri Rodli began his oil-field career in 1955 in Canada and in 1959 went to work for Peter Bawden Drilling, which was acquired by Noble in 1988. Over the years he served the company in various financial and administrative functions.

The *Noble Fri Rodli* is a Transworld column-stabilized, offshore submersible rig capable of drilling to 25,000 feet in water depths up to 70 feet. Formerly known as *Rig 65*, it was built in 1979 and in 2001 was serving in the Gulf of Mexico.

Amos Runner

Amos Runner began working for Noble Drilling in 1960 as a welder's helper in the Gulf Coast Marine division. He was promoted over the years through various rig positions, including toolpusher and drilling superintendent, and served as manager of the Gulf Coast Marine division. When he retired in 1993 after 31 years of dedicated service, he was vice president of domestic operations.

The *Noble Amos Runner* is a Noble EVA-4000™ semisubmersible capable of drilling in water depths up to 6,600 feet. In 2001 the rig was working in the Gulf of Mexico.

Paul Romano

After graduating from the University of Texas in 1949, Paul Romano began working as an engineer for Delta Drilling. In 1952 he joined Kerr-McGee as a drilling engineer and in 1965 was named general manager of Kerr-McGee's drilling operations. He was named vice president of Transworld in 1969 and president in 1973. When he retired in 1990, Romano was senior vice president of Kerr-McGee Corporation and president of the Transworld subsidiary.

The *Noble Paul Romano* is a Noble EVA-4000™ semisubmersible capable of drilling in water depths up to 6,000 feet. In 2001 the rig was drilling in the Gulf of Mexico.

Max Smith

Max Smith commenced his career with Noble in 1959 as a roughneck in the Gulf Coast Marine division. Over the years, he served Noble as driller, toolpusher, drilling superintendent, assistant division manager, and division manager. He retired from the company in 1991 after 32 years of service.

The *Noble Max Smith* is a Noble EVA-4000™ semisubmersible capable of drilling in water depths up to 6,000 feet. In 2001 the rig was working in the Gulf of Mexico.

Jim Thompson

Jim Thompson's participation in Noble activities began in 1943, when he became general attorney of Noble Drilling. In that position he oversaw the legal matters and war regulations concerning manpower and materials related to the company's participation in the Sherwood Forest project in England and the Canol project in the Arctic Circle. Thompson transferred to Ardmore in 1945 as general counsel for all of the Noble enterprises, serving as executive vice president and director. He was instrumental in the formation of Noble Affiliates and served as a director until 1986. He was president of the Noble Foundation from 1952 until 1965 and one of its trustees until 1972.

The *Noble Jim Thompson* is a Noble EVA-4000™ semisubmersible capable of drilling in water depths up to 6,000 feet. In 2001 the rig was drilling in the Gulf of Mexico.

Paul Wolff

Paul Wolff's career as a mechanical engineer has yielded many innovations in drilling technology for the energy industry. Wolff designed the first mobile offshore drilling rig and is considered the father of the column-stabilized mobile unit, which was the catalyst for the modern semisubmersible. Over a span of 40 years, Wolff served as both a direct employee and a consulting engineer to Kerr-McGee companies. He holds 10 patents for a wide range of devices, including rig designs and operating methods, a liquid-level monitoring instrument, and a weighing device used in running oil well logs.

The *Noble Paul Wolff* is a Noble EVA-4000™ dynamically positioned semisubmersible capable of drilling in water depths up to 8,900 feet. In 2001 the rig was working offshore Brazil.

Dick Favor

Dick Favor first worked for Noble Drilling as a roustabout while playing football for the University of Oklahoma in a summer work program. He worked his way up in the Gulf Coast division, eventually becoming division manager. When he retired in 1960, he had been associated with the company for more than 25 years.

The *Noble Dick Favor* is a Baker Marine independent-leg cantilever jackup capable of working in up to 150 feet of water and drilling to 20,000 feet. In 2001 the rig operated offshore Nigeria.

Roy Butler

Roy Butler began his career with the Continental Oil Company and joined Samedan's production department in 1955. Ten years later he was promoted to president of Samedan. In 1975 he was named president of Noble Affiliates and in 1984, after 29 years with Noble, retired as president and chief executive officer of Noble Affiliates.

The *Noble Roy Butler* is a Friede & Goldman L-780 Mod. II independent-leg cantilever jackup rated to work in up to 300 feet of water and drill to 25,000 feet. The rig was built in 1982 and in 2001 was located offshore Nigeria.

Charles Copeland

Charles Copeland began his career with Noble as an accountant in 1957 and after several assignments became head of the contracts billing department. In 1980 he was named director of administration and was later promoted to vice president and corporate secretary. He retired in 1989 after 32 years of service.

The *Noble Charles Copeland* is a Marathon LeTourneau Class 82-SD-C independent-leg cantilever jackup capable of drilling to 20,000 feet in water depths of up to 250 feet. Built in 1979, the rig was located in the Middle East in 2001.

Earl Frederickson

Earl Frederickson joined Noble Drilling as a roughneck in 1946 and worked through the ranks, filling virtually every position on a rig, including rig manager and drilling superintendent. After 33 years with Noble, he retired in 1979 as manager of the West Texas division.

The *Noble Earl Frederickson* is a Marathon LeTourneau Class 82-SD-C independent-leg cantilever jackup capable of working in up to 250 feet of water and drilling to 20,000 feet. The rig was built in 1979 and in 2001 was located in the Gulf of Mexico.

Percy Johns

Percy Johns joined Noble Drilling in 1933 in office administration. He rose through the ranks, becoming assistant treasurer in 1939, vice president in 1948, and president in 1953. Johns became vice chairman in 1963 and retired in 1969 after 36 years with Noble.

The *Noble Percy Johns* is a Friede & Goldman L-780 Mod. II independent-leg cantilever jackup rated to work in up to 300 feet of water and to drill to 25,000 feet. Built in 1981, the rig was located offshore Nigeria in 2001.

George McLeod

George McLeod joined Samedan in the Canadian office in 1960 and was promoted to division manager and later vice president. In 1974, he became president of Samedan and in 1984 was named president and chief executive officer of Noble Affiliates, a position he held until his retirement in 1986.

The *Noble George McLeod* is a Friede & Goldman L-780 Mod. II independent-leg cantilever jackup rated to work in up to 300 feet of water and drill to 25,000 feet. The rig was built in 1981 and in 2001 was located offshore Abu Dhabi.

Carl Norberg

Carl Norberg joined Noble Drilling in 1936 as a roughneck and retired 44 years later as toolpusher. He was one of the Noble employees who went to England during World War II to work in Sherwood Forest.

The *Noble Carl Norberg* is a Marathon LeTourneau Class 82-C independent-leg cantilever jackup capable of working in up to 250 feet of water and drilling to 20,000 feet. The rig was built in 1976 and in 2001 was working in the Gulf of Mexico.

Don Walker

Don Walker joined Noble Drilling in 1942 as administrative manager of the Sherwood Forest project. He later implemented and directed the company's safety program for many years. Walker retired from Noble Drilling in 1969 after 27 years of service.

The *Noble Don Walker* is a Baker Marine independent-leg cantilever jackup capable of working in up to 150 feet of water and drilling to 20,000 feet. The rig, built in 1982, was located offshore Nigeria in 2001.

Tommy Craighead

Tommy Craighead began working for Samedan Oil in 1949 as mail clerk, coffee room manager, and photocopy clerk. In 1951 he was transferred to a district office as a roustabout and became chief clerk of all Samedan operations in 1954. In 1957, Craighead was transferred to the land department as a scout and was later promoted to assistant landman and then district landman. He resigned in 1962 to become an independent oil and gas broker, forming his own company. Craighead was appointed to the board of directors of Noble Drilling in 1988.

The *Noble Tommy Craighead* is a Friede & Goldman L-780 Mod. II independent-leg cantilever jackup. The rig, built in 1982, can work in water depths ranging from 14 feet to 300 feet and can drill to 25,000 feet. In 2001 it was working offshore Nigeria.

Tom Jobe

Tom Jobe's association with the Noble family began in 1944, when he and Sam Noble were roommates at officer training at the University of Oklahoma. Jobe received his commission in the navy in 1946 but resigned in 1947 to complete a degree in geological engineering and geology. In 1955 Sam Noble offered him the opportunity to open Samedan's Gulf Coast division in Lafayette, Louisiana. Jobe moved to Ardmore, Oklahoma, in 1961 as exploration manager and retired in 1986 after 31 years with Samedan.

The *Noble Tom Jobe* is a Marathon LeTourneau 82-SD-C independent-leg cantilever jackup rated to work in water depths ranging from 11 feet to 250 feet and to drill to 25,000 feet. The rig, built in 1982, was operating in the Gulf of Mexico in 2001.

Ed Noble

Edward E. Noble, chief executive officer of Noble Properties, had an extensive entrepreneurial career. He moved to Atlanta at the age of 28 to develop Lenox Square, the first major regional shopping center in the southeastern United States, and managed the center until its sale in 1976. During that same period, he owned and managed an award-winning chain of independent hotels and motels. Ed Noble developed properties in eight states and has been owner/director of a wide range of entities in addition to his active civic involvement. He also served under President Ronald Reagan as chairman of the Synthetic Fuels Corporation.

The *Noble Ed Noble* is a Marathon LeTourneau 82-SD-C independent-leg cantilever jackup capable of working in water depths as shallow as 11 feet and as deep as 250 feet. The rig was built in 1984 and in 2001 was working offshore Nigeria.

Lloyd Noble

As a college student, Lloyd Noble teamed up with Art Olson. They drilled their first well using a secondhand rig in 1921 in Carter County, Oklahoma. Though the business faced tough times during its first few years, it prospered during the oil boom in southern Oklahoma. Lloyd Noble also drilled in Alberta, Canada (where the company was still active in 2001). In 1930, after acquiring 38 rigs, he and Olson amicably parted ways, dividing the assets. Lloyd Noble then formed several drilling companies and bought, merged, and combined several more to form Noble Drilling Corporation and several producing companies, including Samedan Oil.

The *Noble Lloyd Noble* is a Marathon LeTourneau 82-SD-C independent-leg cantilever jackup rated to work in water depths ranging from 11 feet to 250 feet. Built in 1983, the rig is capable of drilling to 20,000 feet. In 2001 the unit was working offshore Nigeria.

Eddie Paul

Eddie Paul began his 34-year career with Noble Drilling in the winter of 1952 as a boiler fireman on a rig in North Dakota. He worked at all positions on the rig and was promoted to toolpusher in 1959 and to assistant drilling superintendent in 1967. In 1973 he was promoted to Rocky Mountain division drilling superintendent and assistant division manager. He was named Rocky Mountain division manager in 1982, a position he held until his retirement in 1986.

The *Noble Eddie Paul* is a Marathon LeTourneau Class 84 independent-leg cantilever jackup. In 2001 the rig was being extensively modified with the installation of a unique 70-foot extended-reach cantilever (ERC™) to drill over large platforms. The *Noble Eddie Paul* also was modified with additional leg to work in up to 390 feet of water. The rig, capable of drilling to 25,000 feet, was located in the Gulf of Mexico in 2001.

John Sandifer

John Sandifer joined Noble Drilling in 1960 as a roughneck. In 1964 he was promoted to toolpusher, and he worked on land rigs until 1980, when he was transferred to the *Sam Noble* offshore jackup rig. Sandifer retired in 1984 after 24 years with Noble Drilling.

The *Noble John Sandifer* is a Levingston III-C independent-leg jackup that was upgraded and converted to a cantilever unit. Originally built in 1975, the rig is rated to work in up to 300 feet of water and drill to 20,000 feet. In 2001 the unit was working in the Gulf of Mexico.

Joe Alford

Joe Alford joined Noble Drilling in 1953 as a roustabout and was promoted through the ranks to rig manager. He spent his entire career with Noble in the Gulf Coast division. Alford retired in 1986 after 33 years of service.

The *Noble Joe Alford* is a column-stabilized submersible capable of drilling in up to 85 feet of water to a depth of 25,000 feet. The rig was built in 1982 and in 2001 was located in the Gulf of Mexico.

Lester Pettus

Lester Pettus worked his entire career with Noble Drilling in the Gulf Coast division. He began as a roughneck in 1935 and rose through the ranks to toolpusher. He retired in 1981 after 46 years of service with Noble.

The *Noble Lester Pettus* is a column-stabilized submersible rated to work in up to 85 feet of water and drill to 20,000 feet. The rig, built in 1982, was working in the Gulf of Mexico in 2001.

Gene Rosser

Gene Rosser's career with Noble started in the Gulf Coast. In 1942, just after his transfer to the Rocky Mountain division, he was recruited for the famed Sherwood Forest drilling project, which he led. Rosser later retired from Noble to continue as a consultant in the industry.

The *Noble Gene Rosser* is a Levingston III-C independent-leg jackup. The rig is rated to work in up to 300 feet of water and drill to 20,000 feet. In 2001 it worked in the Gulf of Mexico.

Lewis Dugger

The 43-year career of Lewis Dugger commenced in 1940, when he hired on as a roust-

about. He was recruited by Ed Holt to be part of the Sherwood Forest drilling project during World War II and after his return was promoted to toolpusher in 1945. Dugger spent 22 years as a superintendent in the Gulf Coast division and spent the final nine years of his career as Gulf Coast safety supervisor. He retired in 1983.

The *Noble Lewis Dugger* is a Levingston III-C independent-leg jackup. The rig is rated to work in up to 300 feet of water and drill to 20,000 feet. In 2001 the rig was working in the Bay of Campeche, Mexico.

Gus Androes

Gus Androes began at Noble as a roustabout in the Gulf Coast division in 1948. He worked his way through several rig positions, serving as toolpusher and superintendent. Androes served as superintendent of operations for the Gulf Coast area and retired in 1986 after 38 years of service.

The *Noble Gus Androes* is a Levingston III-C independent-leg jackup. The rig is rated to work in up to 300 feet of water and drill to 25,000 feet. In 2001 it was operating offshore Qatar.

Chuck Syring

Chuck Syring's Noble career started in 1948. He worked through various rig positions and served as toolpusher and superintendent before being promoted to manager of the Rocky Mountain division. In 1982 he was appointed a vice president. He retired that same year after 34 years of service.

The *Noble Chuck Syring* is a Marathon LeTourneau Class 82-C independent-leg cantilever jackup capable of working in up to 250 feet of water and drilling to 20,000 feet. The rig was built in 1976 and refurbished in 1996. In 2001 it was working offshore Qatar.

Leonard Jones

Leonard Jones joined Noble Drilling in 1961 as a roughneck. He was promoted to toolpusher in 1974 and district superintendent in 1978. In 1984 he was promoted to division superintendent. After 38 years of service, Jones retired in 1999 as drilling superintendent.

The *Noble Leonard Jones* is a Marathon LeTourneau Class 53 jackup that was converted with an ERC™. It is capable of working in depths up to 390 feet and drilling to 25,000 feet. In 2001 it was working in the Gulf of Mexico.

Bill Jennings

William F. "Bill" Jennings began his oil-field career with National Supply in Houston and later joined R. C. Chapman Drilling. When Noble acquired R. C. Chapman in 1988, Jennings became Noble's general manager of the Gulf Coast Land division and later moved to the corporate office as vice president of worldwide marketing. In 1992 he was named vice president and general manager of the Gulf Coast Marine division and in 1996 was promoted to vice president of Western Hemisphere operations. He retired in 1999 after 11 years of service with Noble.

The *Noble Bill Jennings* is a Marathon LeTourneau Class 84 jackup. Built in 1975, it was converted to an ERC™ in 1997 and can drill to 25,000 feet in water depths up to 390 feet. In 2001 it was working in the Gulf of Mexico.

Kenneth Delaney

Kenneth Delaney began his drilling career with Noble in 1961, working as a roughneck on a completion rig until he moved to a drilling unit. Two years later he was drafted into the U.S. Army, and after completing duty in 1966, he returned to Noble Drilling. He became a driller in 1971 and was promoted to toolpusher in 1976 and superintendent five years later. In 1988 Delaney was appointed assistant division manager along with his superintendent duties. He moved to Lafayette in 1991 as assistant division manager and operations manager and served in this position until becoming division manager of Gulf Coast Marine in 1997. He retired in 1999 after 34 years with the company.

The *Noble Kenneth Delaney* is a Friede & Goldman L-780 Mod. II jackup. Built in 1983, it performs in water depths up to 300 feet and drilling depths up to 25,000 feet. In 2001 the unit was drilling offshore Abu Dhabi.

Jimmy Puckett

Jimmy Puckett began his career with Noble Drilling in 1973 as a floorman. When the *Ed Holt* embarked on Noble's first international marine work, Puckett joined the operation, working four years in India, where he was promoted to superintendent. He transferred back to the Gulf Coast division in 1992 and took charge of moving the *Red McCarty*, Noble's first rig in Mexico in the Bay of Campeche. Puckett served as project manager of several refurbishment projects before being promoted to operations manager of the Gulf Coast Marine division. In 1999 he was promoted to division manager of that same division.

The *Noble Jimmy Puckett* is a Friede & Goldman L-780 Mod. II independent-leg cantilever jackup rated to work in up to 300 feet of water and drill to 25,000 feet. In 2001 the rig was located offshore India.

Lynda Bossler

Lynda Bossler began working for Noble Drilling in 1972 in the contracts and billing department. After four years she moved into the purchasing department and later into payroll. Beginning in 1987, Bossler served as secretary in the operations, marketing, and training departments, and in 1989 she accepted the position of manager of payroll, concurrent with her transfer to Houston. She retired in 1999 after 27 years with the company.

The *Noble Lynda Bossler* is a Marine Structure Consultants CJ46 jackup. It was built in 1982 to work in water depths up to 205 feet and drill to 25,000 feet. In 2001 the unit was working in the North Sea.

Roger Eason

A native of Pauls Valley, Oklahoma, Roger Eason began his working life as a roughneck for Noble Drilling prior to attending the University of Oklahoma from 1938 to 1942. At OU, he played football with other Noble notables, including Dick Favor, Red McCarty, and Bob Seymour. Eason served three years in the army during World War II and played professional football from 1945 to 1950 for the Cleveland Rams, which later became the Los Angeles Rams. He worked briefly for Hughes Tool in the late 1940s before beginning a 32-year career with Associated Oilfield Rentals, where he held numerous worldwide executive positions including president of A-1 Bit & Tool Company. He was a trusted advisor to Noble Drilling for many years and worked with the marketing group until his death in 1998.

Built in 1977, the *Noble Roger Eason* is a Neddrill drillship that can work in water depths from 300 feet to 6,000 feet in DP mode and drills in depths up to 25,000 feet. In 2001 the unit was working offshore Brazil.

Ronald Hoope

Ronald Hoope began his career with Nedlloyd in 1963 and joined Neddrill (acquired by Noble in 1996) when it was founded in 1974. He worked in seven different ranks on Neddrill rigs and worked in Houston from 1985 to 1990 as Neddrill's representative in the United States. He also served as commercial affairs manager for Europe, beginning in 1990.

The *Noble Ronald Hoope* is a Marine Structure Consultants CJ46 jackup. Built in 1982, the unit works in water depths up to 210 feet and drilling depths to 25,000 feet. In 2001 it was working in the North Sea.

George Sauvageau

George Sauvageau began his career with Noble Drilling in 1964 as a floorman in North Dakota. He worked through all rig positions and was promoted to drilling superintendent in 1990. Sauvageau served for several years in Nigeria as drilling superintendent before returning to Houston in the operations and engineering groups to serve as project manager on several reactivation projects.

The *Noble George Sauvageau* is a Neddrill four-leg jackup and is rated for water depths up to 225 feet and drilling depths up to 25,000 feet. The unit was built in 1981 and in 2001 worked in the North Sea.

Leo Segerius

Leo Segerius began working for Neddrill in 1976. He spent the majority of his career working overseas, primarily in remote areas. After Noble

acquired Neddrill in 1996, he became vice president of business development for South America, with headquarters in Macae, Brazil.

The *Noble Leo Segerius* is a Gusto Engineering Pelican Class drillship. Built in 1981 and rated to 25,000 feet, it can drill in water depths of 100–1,700 feet when anchored or, when in DP mode, in water of 4,250–4,950 feet. In 2001 the unit was working offshore Brazil.

Piet van Ede

Beginning in 1962, Piet van Ede was employed in various Nedlloyd subsidiaries, including Neddrill Rotterdam, where he became director of administration in 1982. He continued that role from the Beverwijk office after Noble bought Neddrill in 1996.

The *Noble Piet van Ede* is a Marine Structure Consultants CJ46 jackup. Built in 1982, it is rated for water depths up to 205 feet and drilling depths up to 25,000 feet. In 2001 the unit was at work in the North Sea.

Ton van Langeveld

Ton van Langeveld joined Royal Rotterdam Lloyd as a mate and worked his way into Nedlloyd's management. Van Langeveld served as managing director of Neddrill from 1985 to 1989 and retired in 1994 as managing director of Nedlloyd Lines, having worked his entire career for Nedlloyd. He was an active member of the supervisory board of directors of Neddrill Nederland B.V. until his retirement in 1996.

The *Noble Ton van Langeveld* is an Offshore Company SCP III Mark 2 semisubmersible. Built in 1979, it was modified for harsh-environment North Sea service in 1986. It works in 1,500-foot water depths and drills up to 25,000 feet. In 2001 the unit was active in the North Sea.

Byron L. Welliver

Byron Welliver began his career with Noble Drilling in 1985 as controller after working at Noble Affiliates as tax manager, controller, and treasurer. He was appointed vice president—finance and treasurer in 1986. Upon his transfer to Houston in 1989, he was promoted to senior vice president—finance and treasurer. Welliver retired in 1999 after 18 years with the company.

The *Noble Byron Welliver* is a CFEM T-2005-C jackup. Built in 1982, it works in water depths up to 300 feet and drills to depths up to 25,000 feet. In 2001 the unit was working in the North Sea.

Al White

Al White began his career with Neddrill in 1983. He worked as a rig superintendent from 1983 to 1995. After that he gained floater experience with drillships and in 2001 served as senior rig manager on the *Noble Ton van Langeveld.*

Built in 1982, the *Noble Al White* is a CFEM T-2005-C jackup. It works in water depths up to 360 feet and drills to depths up to 25,000 feet. In 2001 it was at work in the North Sea.

Homer Ferrington

Homer Ferrington began his 30-year career with Noble in 1969 as a roughneck on Noble platform AW25. He worked his way through the ranks on the rig and was promoted to rig manager in 1978. In 1989 Ferrington became drilling superintendent and served in that position until he retired in 1999.

The *Noble Homer Ferrington* is a Friede & Goldman 9500 Enhanced Pacesetter rig, capable of drilling in water depths up to 6,000 feet. In 2001 the rig was drilling in the Gulf of Mexico.

Dave Beard

After receiving a petroleum engineering degree from Montana Tech, Dave Beard started his oilfield career as a drilling engineer in 1970 with Gulf Oil. He joined Kerr-McGee as senior drilling engineer in 1976 and transferred to Transworld Drilling in 1979 as manager of engineering. After Noble bought the Transworld drilling assets in 1991, Beard served as Noble's manager of engineering and was involved in all rig refurbishment and upgrade projects begin-

ning in 1992. He was instrumental in the conversion of the EVA-4000™ units and was promoted to vice president of engineering in 1998.

The *Noble Dave Beard* is a Friede & Goldman 9500 Enhanced Pacesetter that will be capable of drilling in water depths up to 8,000 feet when its conversion for ultradeepwater is complete.

Julie Robertson

After graduating from the University of Texas, Julie Robertson started her career in the drilling industry in 1979 with Peter Bawden Drilling. She worked in the engineering department, writing maintenance and drill pipe manuals, and later moved into the areas of risk management and human resources. After Noble acquired Bawden in 1988, she served as benefits manager and director of administration. Robertson was named corporate secretary in 1993 and was elected vice president of administration in 1994. In 2001 she was promoted to senior vice president—administration and corporate secretary.

The *Noble Julie Robertson* is a Baker Marine Europe Class harsh-environment rig. Refurbished in 2000, the unit works in water depths up to 390 feet and drilling depths up to 25,000 feet. In 2001 it was drilling in the North Sea.

Clyde Boudreaux

Clyde Boudreaux started his oilfield career in 1963 as a roustabout with Kerr-McGee. He worked in numerous positions in the field until 1975, when he was placed in charge of maintenance for Transworld Drilling. Boudreaux continued to work in various maintenance and operational roles, and after Noble acquired Transworld assets in 1991, he was put in charge of maintenance for the Gulf Coast Marine division. In 1998 he was promoted to worldwide maintenance manager.

The *Noble Clyde Boudreaux* is a Friede & Goldman 9500 Enhanced Pacesetter rig that, after refurbishment, will be capable of drilling in water depths up to 8,000 feet.

In 1999, after being converted for ultradeepwater drilling with Noble's proprietary EVA-4000™ design, the *Noble Amos Runner* semisubmersible began drilling in the Gulf of Mexico.

CHAPTER ELEVEN

LEAN AND MEAN

1998–2001

Wall Street, to a large extent, is a show-me group, and you can tell them what you're going to do over time, but you've got to demonstrate that you can do what you're saying. We have been able, over many years, to share our vision and then deliver, and I think that Wall Street has recognized that.

—Jim Day, December 2000

ALL WAS GOING WELL FOR THE oil-service industry until the second quarter of 1998, when demand for offshore drilling rigs in the U.S. Gulf of Mexico declined, sending dayrates and rig utilization rates tumbling. A few months later, international demand dropped off as well. Noble's average rig utilization rate for international offshore activity dropped from 95 percent in 1997 to 90 percent in 1998, while its domestic rig utilization rate went from 98 percent to 78 percent.[1] Much of the decline in activity could be blamed on a 33 percent drop in the price of oil and a 22 percent drop in natural gas prices. As always, the market conditions were out of Noble's control, and the company sought to prepare itself for both the worst of times and the best of times so that when the market did recover, Noble Drilling would be positioned to pull ahead of the competition.

Noble's conservative philosophy proved fruitful when it came time to report 1998's operating results. Thanks to the company's emphasis on deepwater and international operations, along with its balanced rig portfolio and conservative financial practices, Noble finished the year with operating revenues of $788.2 million, an 11 percent increase over the previous year.[2]

Underscoring Noble's healthy performance, in April 1998 Standard & Poor's raised its corporate credit rating on Noble Drilling and its rating on Noble's $125 unsecured notes due in 2006 from BBB to A-. The rating upgrades were a result of Noble's growing contractual revenue base and its trend of firm pricing, despite depressed oil pricing conditions.[3] That year Noble also received Mitchells & Company investment group's Top 100 award for its stock price leadership.

Moreover, in September 1998 *Fortune* magazine put Noble Drilling at the top of its annual list of the 100 fastest-growing companies in America. The list was based on three-year earnings growth. Over the past three years, Noble's earnings-per-share growth had averaged 394 percent annually.[4]

Cost Cutting

The entire oil drilling and services industry was being affected by the low oil prices, and a slew of industry-wide layoffs and cost-cutting measures ensued. Though Noble Drilling had fared better than many in the most recent down cycle, the company did consolidate some of its European operations in late 1998,[5] and Day asked employees to "watch expenses of all types so that we can continue to improve our financial results."[6] Further consolidating costs, in 1999 Noble began relocating its Gulf Coast Marine division office from Lafayette,

As its logo indicated, Noble Drilling had become a truly international company by the late 1990s.

Louisiana, to Houston. Triton Engineering Services Company began relocating to the Houston head-quarters as well.[7]

The Fleet Expands

As oil prices dithered around $12 a barrel, their lowest since 1986, drilling companies' earnings dropped as well, making them more affordable as potential acquisitions. In the resulting shootout, only the strongest survived, but even those left standing were finding that competition had become astonishingly fierce. The situation didn't improve when, in December 1998, Exxon and Mobil announced they were merging, further reducing the number of companies that contracted Noble's rigs. It made sense that those companies that could provide a wider range of rigs and services would get more of the drilling contracts. "The more rigs you have, the better able you'll be to respond to . . . drilling requirements," Day said.[8]

Thus Noble's strategy of smart shopping for rigs began paying off further. In June 1998, Noble had purchased the *Ilion* (renamed the *Noble Clyde Boudreaux*), a rectangular Friede & Goldman 9500 Enhanced

These longtime employees accepted Noble's early-retirement package. The group was honored at a dinner in Lafayette, Louisiana, in November 1999. Representing 322 years of service with Noble, the retirees included (standing, from left) John Douglas, W. R. Ford, Gwyn Howard, Vernon Pippen, Leonard Jones, Kenneth Delaney, Bill Jennings, Jerry King, Billy Johnson, and (seated from left) Freddie Harveston, James Fish, Allen Taylor, and Homer Ferrington. Jim Day (seated far right) hosted the dinner and presented awards.

Pacesetter semisubmersible located in Pascagoula, Mississippi. Noble made the purchase by setting up a limited liability company with an initial 50 percent equity interest and an option to increase its equity interest to 70 percent. The following month, Noble bought the *Shelf 6*, subsequently renamed the *Noble Dave Beard*, also a rectangular Friede & Goldman 9500, located in Wakkanai Harbor, Japan. Noble planned to convert both rigs for ultradeepwater drilling (for water depths up to 10,000 feet) after securing long-term contracts and, in anticipation of a strong market, began engineering studies in 1999 on several rigs that had deepwater potential.[9]

Meanwhile, Noble continued upgrading its current fleet. In late 1998, the *Noble Leonard Jones* was reactivated and upgraded with a 390-foot extended-reach cantilever to begin work in the Gulf of Mexico,[10] while the *Noble Kenneth Delaney* jackup was upgraded for work in the Persian Gulf for the country of Qatar.[11] In the North Sea, the *Noble George Sauvageau,* a harsh-environment jackup, finished having its water depth upgraded and began working offshore Denmark.[12] And the *Noble Jimmy Puckett* jackup was upgraded and refurbished in Sharjah to begin a contract with ONGC offshore India in April 1999.[13]

Conversions Complete

Noble's EVA-4000™ conversions of three-column submersibles into ultradeepwater semisubmersibles had carved a niche for Noble Drilling in the ultradeep-drilling market, and Noble proved that the innovative design did indeed save time and money over newly constructed rigs.

"It's become clear that Noble's [newly converted] rigs are operating at the very high level [that management] said they would operate at," said Matt Packard, an oil-service analyst at MFS Investment Management in Boston.

Other analysts agreed. "Noble has clearly demonstrated that their engineering and shipyard management has been superior," said Matthew Conlan, an analyst at Prudential Securities in Houston, adding, "[Noble] is one of the very few companies which did not destroy capital during their [rig] upgrade program."[14]

Despite delays and damage caused in the fall of 1998 by Hurricane Georges, which struck the central Gulf Coast where two of Noble's EVA-4000™ conversions were taking place, the *Noble Paul Romano*'s conversion was completed in November 1998, and the unit was delivered to Shell Deepwater Development for a five-year contract in Mississippi Canyon 985 in the Gulf of Mexico.[15] The newly converted semisubmersible was capable of working in water depths up to 6,000 feet. "The success of the *Noble Paul Romano* has been sort of the 'proof in the pudding' for all involved," said Danny Adkins, who became senior vice president of operations in August 2000. "Members of the project, operations and design teams, have been able to see their efforts pay off."[16]

Likewise, the *Noble Paul Wolff* finished its EVA-4000™ conversion and was mobilized to offshore Brazil in May 1999 to begin a six-year contract

---

The *Noble Leonard Jones* (left) was capable of drilling down 25,000 feet in water depths up to 390 feet after its ERC™ upgrade in 1998. The *Noble George Sauvageau* four-leg jackup (right) was upgraded in 1998 so that it could drill in water depths of 225 feet.

guess it's great to set world records, but I sure hate to do it on the first well.' Well, we went down there and actually did a great job." Noble's record was since broken by a drillship, but by the end of 2000 the *Noble Paul Wolff* still held the depth record for a semisubmersible.

Even after breaking three world records with the *Noble Paul Wolff*, Noble continued trying to reach depths of 10,000 feet or more. "We're going after that deeper water all the time," said Hans Deul, who joined Noble from Neddrill and became director for deepwater drilling systems. "There doesn't seem to be a limit anymore. We've set a target for 10,000 feet, and I'm sure that as soon as they reach that, they're going to be talking about 12,000, maybe deeper."[19]

To enable the *Noble Paul Wolff* to reach such astounding depths, Noble's engineering team began developing an alloy riser that could be as much as 40 percent lighter than regular steel risers. The lighter riser would help offset the extra weight of the mud that came from drilling deeper wells.[20]

"The *Noble Paul Wolff* has been very successful," said Adkins. "It has some really extraordinary characteristics. It is the first and still the only dynamically positioned triangular semisubmersible ever built, and it has very good station-keeping characteristics. Because it's triangular, it really doesn't matter which way the weather comes from. It doesn't have to orient itself to the force that wind

with Petrobras. Rated at 8,900 feet, the *Noble Paul Wolff* could drill deeper than any of Noble's other rigs. Additionally, the rig was given a new compact power system and dynamic-positioning capabilities to keep it postured over the wellhead.[17]

It didn't take long for the *Noble Paul Wolff* to prove itself. By the end of 1999, it had set three successive world water-depth records while drilling offshore Brazil. Ultimately, the *Noble Paul Wolff* went down 8,816 feet, which beat Global Marine's record of 7,718 feet by over 1,000 feet.[18] "When Leo Segerius called me and told me that the first location for the *Paul Wolff* was going to be in over 8,000 feet of water, which would set a new world record, I was stunned," said Bill Jennings. "I told Leo, 'I

Left: Throughout the late 1990s, Noble Drilling continued to improve its position by upgrading its fleet. Here a semisubmersible sits in dry dock during its EVA-4000™ conversion.

Right: In 1999, the *Noble Paul Wolff* set a new world water-depth record by drilling in 8,816 feet of water while working offshore Brazil for Petrobras.

and wave and current impose on it, like a ship does. And it also has very good motion characteristics."[21] *Offshore* magazine, in fact, reported that the *Noble Paul Wolff*'s "motion characteristics are among the most efficient of any rig."[22]

"The positive results we've experienced from [the EVA-4000™ conversions] have helped the Noble teams establish credibility for meeting and surpassing the design and operations standards we set," said Adkins. "We are also very relieved to know that the program is achieving its objectives. . . . Everyone at Noble Drilling should be excited and proud of the current success rate and the developments to come. The EVA-4000™ program continues to set Noble Drilling apart from its peer group, thanks to the ingenuity and dedication of Noble people."[23]

New Officers

In November 1998, Jim Day announced that Robert D. Campbell would succeed him as president of Noble Drilling effective January 1, 1999, as part of the company's succession planning. Campbell, who held a bachelor of science degree in chemical engineering and a doctor of jurisprudence degree from the University of Texas at Austin, had been associated with Noble since 1977 while he practiced corporate/securities law at Thompson & Knight, PC in Texas. At that time, Noble Affiliates did not have an in-house legal staff, and Thompson & Knight served as the principal firm representing the parent company's corporate and business matters. After Noble Drilling was spun off from Noble Affiliates in 1985, Campbell continued to serve Noble Drilling as outside general counsel.

"I was always very impressed with the people at Noble," said Campbell nearly

Robert Campbell, who served for many years as Noble Drilling's outside general counsel, became president of Noble in 1999.

Above left: Bill Rose joined Noble in 1991 and later became Noble's vice president of Eastern Hemisphere operations.

Above right: Kurt Hoffman was president of Triton Engineering before becoming vice president of Noble's Western Hemisphere operations.

two years into his term as president. "I had worked so closely with Noble over the years and had been given the opportunity by Jim [Day] and the board of directors to have a substantial role in the company. Because Jim ran the management team very lean, because he outsourced the legal function, I was kind of a de facto part of the management team for many years, and I had the opportunity to see and participate in the transactions more than one would think an outside lawyer would have. So when I joined Noble, I was very knowledgeable about the company, its people, and what it stood for."[24]

One of Campbell's first directives was to develop credibility among Noble employees and investors by familiarizing himself with Noble's operations and finances. "I wasn't hired to come in and try to do things differently," Campbell said. "They wanted me to fit into the management team that had already been established and to try to perpetuate the successes that we've had."[25]

In December 1998, William C. "Kurt" Hoffman was appointed president of Triton Engineering Services. Hoffman had been with Triton since 1991, three years before Noble acquired it, rising to president of international operations before becoming president.[26]

In 1999, Bill Jennings, vice president of Western Hemisphere operations, chose to take early retirement, and Hoffman was promoted to vice president of Western Hemisphere operations.[27] (Noble's Western Hemisphere operations comprised rigs in the Gulf of Mexico; offshore Mexico, Brazil, Venezuela, and Canada; and Triton Engineering. Eastern Hemisphere operations, headed by Bill Rose, comprised drilling offshore West Africa, the Middle East, and India and in the North Sea.)

Glen D. Hale, who had been with Triton since 1993, succeeded Hoffman as Triton's president. After 34 years with Noble, Kenneth N. Delaney retired from his position as division manager of Gulf Coast Marine and was succeeded by Jimmy L. Puckett. CFO Byron Welliver, with 18 years of devoted service to Noble, also announced his early retirement. Other promotions included Bernie G. Wolford as division manager for Brazil and William C. Yester as division manager for the Middle East.[28]

The Pendulum Swings

In March 1999, OPEC jump-started a recovery when it agreed to cut production, and the resulting decreased supply prodded oil prices upward. Anticipating a tighter market, natural gas prices in the United States rose as well so that by the end of 1999 the price of oil and natural gas had swung the other direction, trading as high as $30. But, as Day indicated, "High oil prices are obviously not in the best interest of the U.S. economy or for the oil and gas sector over time. . . . As long as oil prices stay in the $19 to $20 range, drilling activity should continue to recover throughout the balance of the year."[29]

Whatever happened in the highly cyclical market, Noble Drilling had proven that it would fare well. Since the last major downturn in 1986, Noble had achieved geographic diversity, a focus on deepwater drilling, a large contract backlog, and a strong balance sheet. Because Noble was less concerned with establishing high dayrates and more

Opposite: The *Noble Jim Thompson* at work in the Gulf of Mexico after its EVA-4000™ conversion in 1999

concerned with earning its capital back during the initial term of contracts, it was better able to tolerate market down cycles. Furthermore, Noble had the stability that long-term contracts provided in case of market downturns yet was still able to reap the benefits of market upturns through its short-term contracts and diversity of rigs and services. It was clear that Noble's superior management and proven strategies had established the company as a leader in the offshore drilling industry.

Indeed, Noble's shares in December 1999 were up 94 percent, whereas the industry's shares had risen only 36 percent. Investor publication *TheStreet.com* explained why investors were so thrilled with Noble's stock:

> *Investors like the stock because of Noble's engineering prowess and disciplined capital management, which should drive outsized gains in earnings and cash flow. And Noble is often mentioned as a potential buyer in the drilling consolidation expected by analysts.*
>
> *The strength of Noble's drilling fleet is a major selling point. Nineteen of its 33 jackups, or shallow-water rigs, can drill in water at least 300 feet deep, which means they can command higher rates. And its extensive rig upgrade program is almost complete, doubling its deepwater capacity. That makes Noble one of the best-positioned players in the industry to take advantage of this year's rise in oil prices.[30]*

Upgrades Continue

Meanwhile, Noble had made more progress on its EVA-4000™ conversions. In June 1999, the *Noble Jim Thompson,* capable of drilling in 6,000 feet, was delivered to Shell Deepwater Development in the U.S. Gulf of Mexico for its three-year contract, and in August the *Noble Amos Runner,* rated at 6,600 feet, began a five-year contract under a rig-sharing agreement with Kerr-McGee, Murphy Oil, and Marathon Oil. In December, the *Noble Max Smith,* rated at 6,000 feet, began its five-year contract in the Gulf of Mexico with Amerada Hess. Not only did the *Noble Max Smith*'s conversion come in under budget, it also was finished in only 14 months—eight months less than Noble's first EVA-4000™ conversion, the *Noble Paul Romano.*

Finally, the *Noble Homer Ferrington,* which, like the *Ilion* and the *Noble Dave Beard,* was a rectangular Friede & Goldman 9500 Enhanced Pacesetter semisubmersible, was delivered to Mariner Energy in March 2000 after its upgrade rated it at 6,000 feet. During the upgrade, Noble replaced all of the rig's old drilling equipment with new equipment that brought the rig up to modern standards. Though it wasn't an EVA-4000™ conversion, the *Noble Homer Ferrington* had basically the same equipment as the EVA-4000™ semisubmersibles.[31]

Always thinking ahead, Noble's engineers began plans in 2000 for a Super EVA semisubmersible newbuild design. "The Super EVA is a brand-new design," explained Jitendra Prasad, who led the design team. "We wanted to have a triangular type of design, an inhouse design, that would be trademarked to Noble."[32]

To design the Super EVAs, the engineering team capitalized on lessons learned from the EVA-4000™ program to plan a triangular unit that would be larger, drill deeper, and have greater variable deck load than the existing EVA units. The Super EVA would also be dynamically positioned and would be designed to withstand harsh environments. "This will be an exciting new fifth-generation unit with unmatchable motion characteristics," said Leo Segerius, vice president, business development.[33]

The intent was not to build on speculation but to have designs already engineered if a need for newbuilds arose. "A drilling rig is not an asset that can withstand the bad times," explained Bob Campbell. "It goes from being an asset to a liability because if you can't work a drilling rig, you've got to stack it, and you've still got to pay crews and stacking costs. All of a sudden, not only are you not earning revenues with your asset, it's chewing up cash."[34]

As new rigs came off the shipyards in 2000 and 2001, the deepwater mar-

The *Noble Tom Jobe,* constructed in 1982, is one of many Noble rigs to have won an MMS safety award.

ket suffered from just the kind of overcapacity glut that Noble had been trying to avoid. By the summer of 2001, Leo Segerius said that dayrates in the deepwater market were at "a bit of a standstill" due to the overcapacity of sublets. "The sublets are made available by the oil companies that have an overcapacity of these rigs," said Segerius. He predicted a tighter market by the second or third quarter of 2002 and pointed out that deepwater would certainly continue to be a lucrative market for Noble. "It's an important business for us now and in the future," he said.[35]

Noble's engineers were also busy devising a new proprietary jackup design called the N9500 that would augment the company's opportunities in the jackup sector. The N9500 would be designed for both benign and harsh environments.

Staying Safe

As was its custom, Noble Drilling continued emphasizing safety, and in 1997 its efforts were rewarded for the fifth time when the *Noble Max Smith* received the district Safety Award for Excellence (SAFE). Previously the *Noble Paul Romano,* the *Noble Duke Hinds,* the *Noble Paul Wolff,* and the *Noble Tom Jobe* had won Mineral Management Service (MMS) SAFE awards. In 2000, the *Noble Eddie Paul* would win the Houma district SAFE award as well.

In 1998, Noble initiated a major "STEP change" offshore industry safety drive to add to the company's safety policies and procedures. In Noble's case, a STEP change represented its philosophy that Safety Training Enhances Performance. Dealing with change in order to keep pace with the competitive environment was the idea behind STEP change. Additionally, the program stressed that everyone had to share the same clear vision—that "safety is a value" and that Noble's motivated, skilled people had the capability to change.[36]

"Safety is something that is constantly being reinvented," said Joe Hurt, Noble's former manager of health, safety, and the environment. "It involves ensuring that everyone is going in the right direction and no one gets too comfortable regarding safety procedures."[37]

Then in June 1999, the company introduced the Noble Safety Leadership Workshop, led by Dr. Roy Rhodes. The workshop was a three-day training program for all of Noble's supervisory employees,

NOBLE DRILLING PARADIGMS

*E*VERY ORGANIZATION HAS BOTH WRITten and unwritten policies and procedures which—more often than not—become the driving force for all employees. Following are some that help differentiate Noble and make it unique.
                                          —*James C. Day*

EMPLOYEE CENTERED—People can and do make a difference. Teamwork is what makes us different from our competition. We grow our own and care about our own.

INTEGRITY—Our word is our bond. . . We do what we say, and we do not compromise what we cannot deliver.

FINANCIALLY FOCUSED—Employees at all levels are expected to accept responsibility for their respective financial performance. Our focus has been and will continue to be *"a dollar's worth of value for a dollar invested."*

FOCUSED ON OPERATIONS—An ever present priority is to continually seek improvements in all aspects of the organization.

QUICK TO CHANGE, SLOW TO CHANGE—Change has been a driving force in Noble. We will hold to traditional values, be well organized and focused; however, we can and will quickly seize opportunities through carefully considered plans.

INDEPENDENT OPERATIONS—Employees have independent responsibilities. Decisions made—from the lowest level to the highest level—drive and improve overall efficiency, both operationally and financially.

OPERATIONAL EGO—*"We are better"* is a positive expectancy throughout the organization. Benchmarking our operations against other drilling contractors keeps us focused and leaders in the industry.

MERGED FUNCTIONS: OPERATIONS AND MARKETING—Safe and efficient operations are the most effective marketing tool in our industry.

including those overseas. The workshop focused on achieving a new level of safety awareness and fine-tuning safety practices and was one more example of Noble's commitment to ongoing education and training.[38]

"In the process of doing the workshop, we tested every supervisor we have," said Rhodes. "Now, as anybody is coming up for promotion—whether we need drillers, rig managers, crane operators, or whoever—we've got the division managers looking at that data and trying to pick the best, the smartest, the most well-rounded individuals. There's a lot of nepotism in the old oil-field industry, and we want to make sure we make promotions based on competence and ability rather than on who you know."[39]

Furthermore, Noble began revising its *Safety Policy and Procedure Manual* in November 1999 following a company meeting in Rotterdam in which safety professionals from all over the company discussed what further steps Noble could take to keep pace with the rapid changes in regulations and the continued growth of the company.[40]

Part of Noble's stellar safety record was a direct result of teamwork by the rig crews, for only through a concentrated, coordinated effort could a rig operate for an entire year without a single lost-time incident (LTI). In 1999, the *Noble Johnnie Hoffman* reached five years without an LTI, and the *Noble Ronald Hoope* and *Noble Chuck Syring* celebrated four years without an LTI. Many other

rigs reached milestones of no LTIs in 1999: eight rigs celebrated three years, five rigs reached two years, and eleven rigs achieved one year without an LTI.[41] Even more impressively, for the first time in Noble's history, the entire organization went six months without a lost-time incident, from December 1999 to June 2000.[42]

Environmental Initiatives

The Safety Leadership Workshop also included a three-hour session to discuss environmental concerns. Noble had always paid close attention to minimizing the effects of its operations on the environment, and the workshop hammered home the idea that Noble was dedicated to being a responsible environmentalist. "During each session, we cover the basics of Noble's environmental policy," said Mike Cadigan, health, safety, environment, and quality manager. "In the last workshop, we challenged each rig to develop an environmental action plan that can be implemented on their rig, an initiative that would be geared at protecting the environment."[43]

The *Noble Lynda Bossler* (left) was the first jackup unit in the North Sea to win ISO 14001 certification. In 1999, the *Noble Johnnie Hoffman* jackup (right) reached an amazing five years without a lost-time incident.

As evidence of its devotion to the environment, in May 2000 the *Noble Lynda Bossler* jackup, located in the North Sea, received ISO 14001 certification from Det Norske Veritas (DNV) for adhering to the voluntary environmental management and protection standards developed by the International Standards Organization. The *Noble Lynda Bossler* was the first mobile offshore unit in the North Sea to receive such a certification.[44] "The Dutch and Danish governments have strict regulations," said Cees van Diemen, district manager for Netherlands-Denmark. "Our procedures, which are ISO 14001 certified, exceed those requirements. Our clients appreciate that very much since it is less costly for them to obtain drilling approvals then. We have created a niche."[45]

This effort for certification was spearheaded by Cees van Diemen and Gert-Jan Windhorst, Noble's HSE manager for European operations. Both individuals were subsequently involved with the certifications of the other rigs within the European fleet, including the *Noble George Sauvageau,* the *Noble Ronald Hoope,* the *Noble Piet van Ede,* the *Noble Byron Welliver,* and the *Noble Ton van Langeveld.* Noble's goal was to have all remaining rigs in the European fleet ISO 14001 certified by the

By 1999, both the *Noble Ronald Hoope* (above left) and the *Noble Chuck Syring* (above right) had operated for four consecutive years without a lost-time incident. The *Noble Ronald Hoope* can drill to 25,000 feet in water depths of 210 feet. The *Noble Chuck Syring* is capable of drilling to 20,000 feet in water depths of up to 250 feet.

end of 2001. As the demand for environmentally friendly operations grew worldwide, Noble was setting an example for all companies within the industry to follow.

The company was well on its way to meeting that goal. By the end of 2001, Noble expected to have three more rigs certified in Europe. Jimmy Puckett, division manager of Gulf Coast Marine operations, noted that his division was also working toward ISO 14001 certification, starting with a couple of rigs and then expanding the scope of certification just as Noble did in Europe. The Canadian division had one rig with ISO 9002 certification and was considering moving towards ISO 14001 certification. The company's Brazilian operations were also working on implementing the International Safety Management (ISM) code, a safety and

When You Never Your Standards, Recognizes You.

The Noble Lynda Bossler. Raising the standard for environmental focus and awareness. Congratulations from all of us at Noble.

The Noble Lynda Bossler is the first mobile drilling unit in the North Sea to meet the environmental standards developed by ISO 14001. The assessment and certification was performed by DNV (Det Norske Veritas), an independent accreditation company.

We at Noble are particularly proud of this recognition because it represents our *company-wide commitment to reducing the total environmental impact of our drilling operations. This international achievement carries with it an even greater responsibility as well, and one we are eager to accept: to always maintain the highest level of quality and integrity in everything we do throughout the Noble organization. From the people of Noble, that is our promise.*

Noble Drilling Corporation
13135 South Dairy Ashford, Suite 800
Sugar Land, Texas 77478
281.276.6100
www.noblecorp.com

Compromise
The World

Previous pages: Noble had bragging rights to owning and operating the first rig in the North Sea that met rigid environmental requirements for ISO 14001 certification. Though the certification was voluntary, the *Noble Lynda Bossler* exceeded the requirements, underscoring Noble's commitment to minimizing the environmental impact of drilling.

environmental standard administered by the International Maritime Organization.[46]

Still, Puckett said, "I do not think the industry knows everything we're doing to protect the environment. . . . We are involved in garbage management, reducing emissions, oil recycling, and minimizing plastic, paper, etc."[47]

Cadigan explained that the company had fleet-wide programs as well as "best practices being developed in pilot programs that will eventually spread to the entire fleet." The garbage management plan, for example, was a tool that tracked and recorded all wastes generated offshore. "By tracking and recording, we are identifying waste streams that can be segregated for recycling," said Cadigan. "Each of our divisions is working to identify new waste stream recycling capabilities."[48]

Noble already recycled scrap metal, paper, plastics, and oil. In addition, the company measured the nitrogen oxide emitted from rigs' engines. "This allows us to identify ways to run the engines more

efficiently and retrofit them with ECOTIP injectors that reduce our nitrogen oxide emissions, thus making them more friendly to the environment," Cadigan said.[49]

A Powerful Culture

Just as Noble Drilling had metamorphosed from a land-based drilling company to a deepwater drilling corporation with a large international presence, so too had the company's culture evolved into a more dynamic organization that was always looking to the future. Noble's board and management were willing—and able—to spend money to invest in improving the company, whether for safety, efficiency, or long-term strategy.

Another part of Noble Drilling's culture was to give credit where credit was due by appreciating the dedicated men and women who worked to make the company a success. "We have been asked why we have been successful when others in the drilling sector have had disastrous failures, and my response has been, quite simply, 'our people,' " wrote Jim Day in his 1999 letter to stockholders. "We can prove that our people make a difference. A recent analysis of all of the projects undertaken by the drilling services sector shows that Noble has outperformed the industry in its results. . . . Our results demonstrated we did not get caught in the hyperbole of the day, but remained focused on results and increasing shareholder value."[50]

"We really put a lot of responsibility on the people who manage our areas," said Kurt Hoffman. "We try to set the environment from the corporate office for them to manage under the Noble culture that we support. And they do one heck of a good job."[51]

John Rynd pointed out that Noble Drilling was a melting pot of diversity in terms of integrating people from Noble's various acquisitions into the organization. "That diversity of backgrounds lends itself to a good broad view of what's going on. There

The *Noble Homer Ferrington*'s upgrade, which furnished it with new equipment and made it capable of drilling in up to 6,000 feet, was completed in March 2000.

Noble formed a joint venture with Lime Rock Partners to acquire 50 percent ownership of the *Noble Julie Robertson,* an independent-leg cantilever jackup. After renovation to increase its leg length, the rig was capable of drilling in water depths of up to 390 feet.

are lots of different ideas that can be bounced off of each other," he said. "There are some Noble paradigms that we try to follow, but just because you didn't come up born and raised Noble doesn't mean you don't have opportunities."[52]

When Jon Murphy, manager of domestic marketing for the Gulf of Mexico, markets Noble's rigs, it's easy for him to tell potential customers why Noble stands out. "It's our culture," Murphy said. "We've taken the good points from all these companies we've acquired, and Jim [Day] has been able to mesh that to make a very solid company. We're on time and on budget because we've planned well and we execute well. Really it's the excellent performance of the men on the rigs that is selling them. Our reputation keeps growing every day, so it's an easy sell really."[53]

"Jim has empowered our people," said Dave Beard. "Once you gain his confidence, he gives you opportunities. I don't think any of us have ever had such opportunities or been given the chance to use our abilities as we have here. We empower our people with much more responsibility than any of our competitors do."[54]

That empowerment translated into a company-wide dedication to innovation. Noble employees were constantly seeking ways to improve operations, whether through engineering and design, safety and education, or quality assurance and preventative maintenance programs. The company's EVA-4000™ and extended-reach cantilever conversions were so innovative, in fact, that they helped catapult the company into the deepwater and ultra-deepwater drilling sectors. Noble had an enviable reputation for its safe and productive operations, thanks to its dedication to educating its employees. And the various software the company had developed earlier in the decade helped Noble to maximize its drilling rates and improve its efficiency. In addition, Noble's I.D.E.A.S.™ program provided more efficient rig operations, and its patented Noble Drill Smart System optimized drilling time.[55]

Disciplined Operations

The oil and natural gas markets moved steadily upward throughout 1999 and 2000, allowing Noble and the rest of the industry to grow in strength and status. "You could throw a dart now at the oil-service sector and make money," Day said at an investment conference in the spring of 2000. At the same time, however, he warned that "the ride up is going to be bumpy, not smooth."[56]

Though many were calling the upswing a "mega-market," Noble was careful to remain focused and disciplined should the market swing the other way, as it was wont to do. "One of the keys for Noble is our continued focus on efficient operations, irrespective of near-term market conditions," Day told employees. "As long as we maintain a conservative balance sheet and watch our operating costs, we will continue to outperform our competition."[57]

Byron Welliver retired as Noble's CFO in 1999 after 18 years of service. *(Photo courtesy Freeman Photography.)*

Byron Welliver, who retired as CFO in December 1999, noted that Noble's debt was kept low "because that was the way Noble did business. Noble organized its operations and made its spending decisions based on what it could do within current cash flow," he said. "The volatility of our business made the use of debt imprudent."[58]

Maintaining a conservative balance sheet meant emphasizing return on capital employed, and that meant more conservative requirements when making asset investments. In several cases, Noble formed joint ventures to acquire rigs, which allowed the company to acquire assets at less cost without adding new capacity to the market. Even when the acquired assets needed upgrading, Noble was easily able to get a higher return on capital employed over what the asset cost. "A rig is a big investment," said Steven Manz, vice president of strategic planning. "By co-owning one, we put only part of the cost on our balance sheet."[59]

In January 2000, Noble formed a 50-50 joint venture with Lime Rock Partners to acquire the *Ocean Scotian*, a North Sea harsh-environment jackup that the company renamed the *Noble Julie Robertson*. "At the time, Lime Rock was a little private-equity group based in Connecticut," said Manz. "The group was looking for investment opportunities, and they stumbled across the *Ocean Scotian* in the North Sea. They hustled and got a contract to buy the rig from Diamond Offshore, but they were financial investors. They had nobody there who knew anything about renting or operating a rig."[60]

Lime Rock brought the deal to Noble. "They felt very comfortable that Noble was a conservative company and well run," said Manz. "Historically, we showed better performance in terms of utilization and safety and customer reputation than some of our competitive groups in the North Sea, and they felt Noble would be the best steward for managing their half of the investment."[61]

Noble managed the upgrade, marketing, and operation of the rig and sent Lime Rock financial summaries every month. After being upgraded in the Netherlands to conform to new North Sea regulations, the *Noble Julie Robertson* became available for service in mid-2000.[62]

In June 2000, Charles Yester, Middle East division manager, was instrumental in forming another 50-50 joint venture for Noble, this time with Crosco Integrated Drilling & Welling Services (a subsidiary of Croatia's INA-Industrija nafte d.d. Zagreb), to jointly own and operate the *PANON*, a 300-foot jackup rig located in the Mediterranean. As with the *Noble Julie Robertson*, Noble was in charge of managing, upgrading, and marketing the rig. Crosco provided key operations and technical personnel. The rig was mobilized to the Arabian Gulf, where it began its conversion from a slot configuration to a cantilevered jackup.[63]

Noble also continued trimming away excess operations. By the summer of 2000, the company had finished consolidating its Gulf Coast Marine operations from Lafayette to Houston. Furthermore, the company had begun researching ways to cut the total cost of its supplies through an e-procurement arrangement. "We're looking at how we can cut out the need for purchase orders and invoices and just directly acquire the consumables that we need without all the intermediate steps," said Roger Lewis.[64] As vice president—special projects, Lewis was also looking at how Noble could provide greater value to its customers while reducing costs by working with another major oil-field service provider.

In October, Triton Engineering Services decided to withdraw from its turnkey drilling contracts, which produced lower margins at a higher risk, to focus on well-site management, project management, and technical services. "Our change in focus has been under consideration for several years and was precipitated by the extremely tight rig market, which can ultimately impact rig performance and turnkey results," said Triton's president, Glen Hale. "Given the strong overall market, we believe there are ample opportunities to diversify our operation and improve our financial performance."[65]

Moreover, Noble was adding value by eliminating redundancies through SAP (Systems Applications and Procedures) software. Starting in the summer of 2000, Noble began implementing information technology that would automatically update the systems on its rigs. Rather than spending $2 to $3 a minute to transmit data back and forth from rigs to divisional offices via the old satellite systems, the new system allowed rigs to use the Internet to download and upload real-time informa-

Noble Drilling moved its offices to the Houston suburb of Sugar Land, Texas, in 2000. *(Photo by Joan Thompson.)*

tion. Aside from being far less expensive, the Internet was faster, more accurate, and more reliable.

"In the next couple of years, we're really going to focus on communications with our rigs," said Tom O'Rourke, director of administration. "In a perfect world, those rigs should become just like our divisional offices, where they have the phone service, the electronic business services, and everything else. Instead of going from the rig to the divisional office and from the divisional office to the corporate office, the information will go from the rig to one black [computer] box."[66]

Fortified for the Future

To remain consistent with the company's continuous focus on overhead expenses, Noble moved its headquarters to the Houston suburb of Sugar Land in the early summer of 2000. Meantime, the company gained a new leader for its finances in September, when Mark A. Jackson joined Noble as senior vice president and chief financial officer. Jackson had 22 years of experience in finance and accounting.[67]

By the third quarter of 2000, Noble's net income had increased a whopping 78 percent from the previous year. Though the company's operations had improved worldwide, the biggest improvement came from the increased activity in the Gulf of Mexico, where five of Noble's EVA-4000™ rigs were drilling. The *Noble Paul Wolff*, working offshore Brazil, and the *Noble Homer Ferrington*, working for Mariner Energy, also contributed substantially to Noble's earnings.[68]

By that time, Noble Drilling's fleet consisted of 49 offshore units, which included nine semisubmersibles, three dynamically positioned drillships, 34 independent-leg cantilever jackups, and three submersibles. The company also provided labor contract drilling services, well-site and project management services, and engineering services and had plans to expand its services even further.

"The industry is changing, and we need to be in a position to be more than just a drilling contractor that leases equipment for a dayrate," said Campbell. "We're going to have to participate in the technological revolution and increase our ability to utilize intellectual capital, not just iron, and provide services. In this day and age, you can't stand pat and just rely on your core competencies. You've got to be nimble. You've got to be able to make decisions to grow your business."[69]

Whereas a few years earlier the drilling sector had suffered from too many rigs and not enough contracts, by the fall of 2000 the tables had turned. Day, in fact, predicted a shortage of rigs in the coming year. "We've been one of the most active consolidators in our sector," he said. "We've acquired seven companies since 1985. And we have attempted to further consolidate recently through discussions with some of our competitors, but nothing has proved successful at this point. I think further consolidation does make sense, if it's done appropriately where it's accretive to shareholders."[70]

Ronald Hoope, manager of commercial affairs for Noble's Eastern Hemisphere operations, expected the current market's up cycle to last until 2004 or 2005. "It's all about the cycles," he said. "The Gulf of Mexico reaches the up cycle first, and then typically nine months later, the North Sea follows.

Investors and analysts are quick to attribute much of Noble's success to its management and board of directors, whose vision, instincts, and keen business sense have positioned the company as a leading provider for the worldwide oil and gas industry.

Thereafter, West Africa, the Middle East, and then last, Southeast Asia."[71]

Bernie Wolford, division manager for Noble's Brazilian operations, expected that the drilling activity offshore Brazil would also increase over the next few years. "Brazil has recently opened sizable unexplored areas for leasing by international oil companies," he said in July 2001. "This will lead to more exploratory drilling, and if significant reserves are found, major development programs."[72]

Wolford also noted that Petrobras, Brazil's national oil company, was "slowly going public," which meant it would become more profit motivated. This was good news for companies like Noble Drilling. Petrobras revealed a five-year plan to increase production from 1.4 million barrels per day to 2 million barrels to meet the current rate of consumption. "Petrobras is more or less recognized as the deepwater leader because the fields offshore Brazil are among the deepest in the world," said Wolford. "It has a lot of experience in very ultra-deepwater and is, accordingly, exploring more and using advanced development techniques to achieve its goals."[73]

Noble's future in the North Sea also looked bright. Cees van Diemen expected the busy jackup activity in the southern North Sea to continue and predicted increased semisubmersible activity in Norway.[74]

But Ronald Hoope also noted that there were some weak spots in the market, such as the summer

Robert D. Campbell
President and Director

Michael A. Cawley
Director

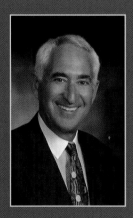
Lawrence J. Chazen
Director

Luke R. Corbett
Director

Marc E. Leland
Director

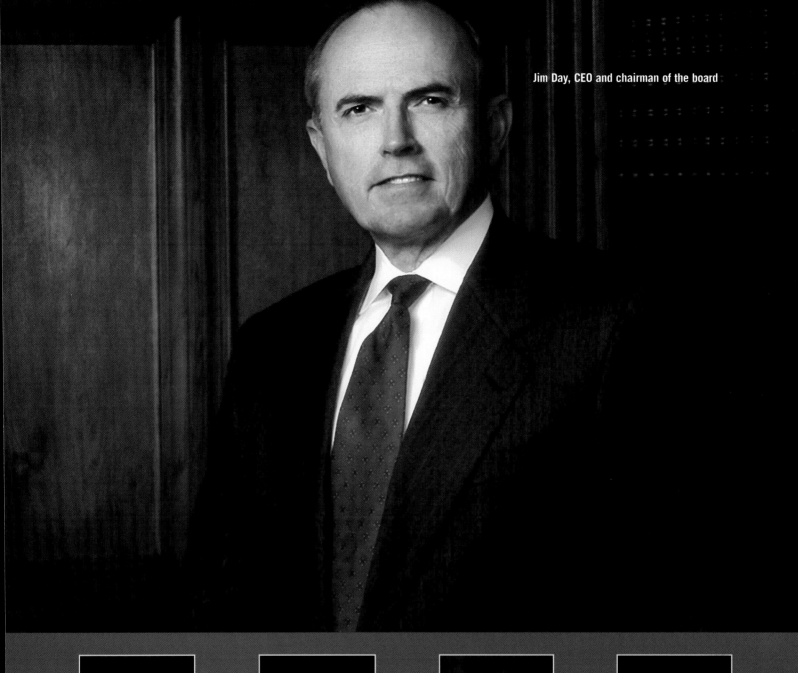

Jim Day, CEO and chairman of the board

Jack E. Little
Director

William A. Sears
Director

Tommy C. Craighead
Director Emeritus

John F. Snodgrass
Director Emeritus

2001 market for semisubmersibles and drill-ships. "One of the longer-term weak spots will occur if we, as contractors, do not have discipline and overbuild the market with newbuilds," he said. "Our customers like newbuilds, but if we start over-building the industry, then we have too many rigs, the rate goes down, and the market collapses." Hoope also pointed out the danger of oversupply-ing a certain region, which would lower the dayrates that contractors could charge.[75]

The cycles, of course, were dependent on the price of oil, and Hoope felt confident that OPEC "finally has its act together. . . . OPEC is flowing more oil into the market when the oil price is too high, and shutting it down when the oil price is too low. In previous cycles that was always OPEC's intention, but this time they are really doing it."[76]

Further signaling to the world that Noble Drilling was fortified for the future, despite the uncertainty of the market, on December 19, 2000, Standard & Poor's announced it would be adding Noble Drilling to its prestigious S&P 500 index. The selection was based on Noble's size in the industry and its stellar performance over time.

Throughout, company officers were proud of having the long-range vision to move Noble from a primarily domestic, land-based drilling contractor to an oil-service company focused on international offshore and deepwater drilling. Indeed, Noble had come a long way since it left its parent's nest in 1985, but though it had transformed itself into a new kind of company in the short span of 15 years, the change had occurred so gradually and con-stantly as to be nearly seamless.

Noble's management was proud of keeping a lean staff and a clean balance sheet. "Although we went through some pretty tight times when we were initially spun off from Noble Affiliates, management and the board have just done a fabulous job of keep-ing Noble's balance sheet in order, and that's some-thing that very few contractors had," said Lewis.[77]

As the company prepared to celebrate its 80th anniversary, Jimmy Puckett reflected on its out-standing growth since it became a public company: "Our stock price has risen from approximately $3.50 a share to a 52-week high of $54, a 1,443 percent increase. Revenues have grown from $35.8 million to $882.6 million, an increase of 2,363 percent. We reported a $43.95 million loss when

we first went public, and now our net income is $165.55 million. Our offshore fleet has grown from two deepwater units to 49 premium assets, and I know this is just the beginning."

Julie Robertson, senior vice president and cor-porate secretary, said, "During the downturns, we were able to make the most of our clean balance sheet and make good things happen in bad times. If management hadn't done that, if we had sat on our hands during the bad times like a lot of com-petitors did, we would have been swallowed up. Jim is a leader in the truest sense of the word—not just for Noble, but for the entire drilling industry."[78]

Noble owed much to its board of directors, made up of some of America's best minds, who all lent a unique slant to Noble's operations. Rather than simply rubber stamping management, their great depth of expertise contributed substantially to the company's focus and direction. In the summer of 2001, Noble Drilling's board was made up of eight members: Robert D. Campbell, the company president, joined the board in early 1999. Michael A. Cawley, president, CEO, and trustee of the Samuel Roberts Noble Foundation, became a member in 1985. Lawrence J. Chazen, president of Lawrence J. Chazen, Inc., joined in 1994. James C. Day, chairman and CEO, boasted the longest tenure, having joined in 1983. Marc E. Leland, president of Marc E. Leland & Associates, joined in 1994. Jack E. Little, retired vice president and chief executive officer of Shell Oil Company, joined in late 1999. William A. Sears, retired direc-tor of operations at British Petroleum Exploration, joined in 1998. Finally, John F. Snodgrass, president emeritus and a trustee of the Noble Foundation, served as director emeritus. Tommy C. Craighead, president of T. C. Craighead Interests, retired from the board in April 2001, after serving 13 years. Adding to an experienced board, Luke R. Corbett, chairman and CEO of Kerr-McGee Corporation, joined as a director in October 2001.

Day described Noble Drilling as a work in progress. "We are a very focused company," he said, "focused on understanding our finances and opti-mizing shareholder returns and in providing the best operating results for clients and an environ-ment for employees that provides opportunities and is safe. We've had some very difficult times, and I am very proud of the people who helped manage through that period. It would be nice to sit back and say that the market is going to be so good that we don't have to worry about any more bad times, but we know that things can change rather quickly. We're going to take advantage of the market, remain focused, keep a clean balance sheet, and recruit and retain the best people possible. There are going to be more opportunities. The company is going to get bigger either through new construction efforts, such as the *Noble Clyde Boudreaux* semisubmersible which is being upgraded to operate in 10,000 feet of water, or through additional acquisitions. The path this talented management team has blazed has been challenging, but very gratifying, and in my mind, even after almost a quarter of a century running this race, the best is yet to come."[79]

NOTES TO SOURCES

Chapter One

1. Odie Faulk, Laura E. Faulk, and Sally M. Gray, *Imagination and Ability: The Life of Lloyd Noble* (Western Heritage Books, 1995), 25.
2. Daniel Yergin, *The Prize: The Epic Quest for Oil, Money & Power* (New York: Simon and Schuster, 1992), 179.
3. Noble Drilling 1995 Annual Report (75th Anniversary edition).
4. Faulk, Faulk, and Gray, *Imagination and Ability*, 56.
5. Ibid., 58–59.
6. Ibid., 64.
7. Ibid., 58.
8. Noble Drilling 1985 Annual Report.
9. Art Olson, interviewed by Glenn McGee, transcript, 27 April 1976, Noble Affiliates archives.
10. Faulk, Faulk, and Gray, *Imagination and Ability*, 56.
11. Ibid., 74.
12. Ibid., 80.
13. Ibid., 109.
14. Ibid., 110.
15. Ed Holt, interviewed by Sally Gray and Bob Donahue, tape recording, 22 April 1999, Samuel Roberts Noble Foundation.
16. "Rotary Drills Two Wells in Short Space of 30 Days," *Wichita Beacon*, 3 October 1929.
17. Ibid.

Chapter Two

1. Faulk, Faulk, and Gray, *Imagination and Ability*, 115.

2. Olson, interview.
3. Ibid.
4. Noble Affiliates 1979 Annual Report, 5.
5. Faulk, Faulk, and Gray, *Imagination and Ability*, 111.
6. Kenny Franks, *The Oklahoma Petroleum Industry* (Norman: University of Oklahoma Press, n.d.), 138.
7. Ibid., 127.
8. Noble Drilling 1995 Annual Report.
9. *International Directory of Company Histories*, volume II (St. James Press).
10. Roger Olien and Diana Davids Olien, *Wildcatters: Texas Independent Oilmen* (Texas Monthly Press, 1984), 43.
11. Yergin, *Prize*, 250–251.
12. Faulk, Faulk, and Gray, *Imagination and Ability*, 143–145.
13. Ibid., 145.

Chapter Three

1. Franks, *Oklahoma Petroleum Industry*, 186.
2. Faulk, Faulk, and Gray, *Imagination and Ability*, 216.
3. "World's Biggest Oil Campaign Gets Underway," *Tulsa Tribune*, 5 February 1943.
4. Speech at banquet for 25th anniversary of Noble Drilling, 1946.
5. Guy H. Woodward and Grace Steele Woodward, *The Secret of Sherwood Forest* (Norman: University of Oklahoma Press, 1973), 13.
6. Ibid., 14.

7. Noble Drilling 1995 Annual Report.
8. Boulton B. Miller, "Oil Patch Warriors," *I, Witness to History* (Wesley Retirement Communities, 1996), 1–17.
9. Woodward and Woodward, *Secret of Sherwood Forest*, 73.
10. Faulk, Faulk, and Gray, *Imagination and Ability*, 200.
11. Woodward and Woodward, *Secret of Sherwood Forest*, 103.
12. Faulk, Faulk, and Gray, *Imagination and Ability*, 203.
13. Woodward and Woodward, *Secret of Sherwood Forest*, 122.
14. Faulk, Faulk, and Gray, *Imagination and Ability*, 204–205.
15. Lewis Dugger, interview by the author, tape recording, 12 November 2000, Write Stuff Enterprises.
16. Woodward and Woodward, *Secret of Sherwood Forest*, 210.
17. Faulk, Faulk, and Gray, *Imagination and Ability*, 220.
18. Glenn McGee, "Horns and Wings: The Legend and the Legacy of Lloyd Noble," 1981, 48–49.
19. Faulk, Faulk, and Gray, *Imagination and Ability*, 222–224.
20. Noble Drilling 1995 Annual Report.

Chapter Four

1. Franks, *Oklahoma Petroleum Industry*, 191.
2. Ibid.
3. Olien and Olien, *Wildcatters: Texas Independent Oilmen*, 86.
4. Lloyd Noble speech, transcript, 22 October 1945, first

meeting of trustees of Samuel
Roberts Noble Foundation.
5. Ibid.
6. Samuel Roberts Noble
Foundation publication, 1955.
7. Faulk, Faulk, and Gray,
Imagination and Ability, 235–236.
8. Noble Drilling
1995 Annual Report.
9. Faulk, Faulk, and Gray,
Imagination and Ability, 235–236.
10. Ibid., 236.
11. Irene Nolan,
"Looking Back: The
Story of Esso No. 1,"
Island Breeze,
July 1999, 18.
12. Neil Williams, "Esso 1
State—Most Easterly Test
Modern Exploration," *Oil and
Gas Journal,* n.d., 116.
13. Nolan, "Looking Back," 19.
14. Yergin, *Prize,* 358.
15. Nolan, "Looking Back," 19.
16. Ibid., 18.
17. Ibid., 19.
18. Ben Dixon MacNeill,
"Standard Will Resume Oil
Explorations off Coast in Three
Weeks," *(North Carolina)
Daily Advance,* 18 October 1946.
19. "New Carolina Test Planned;
Maryland Drilling Starts,"
Oil and Gas Journal,
26 October 1946, 91.
20. Ibid.
21. Yergin, *Prize,* 393.
22. Ibid., 391–393.
23. Ibid., 379.
24. Franks, *Oklahoma Petroleum
Industry,* 192.
25. Yergin, *Prize,* 410.
26. Kenny A. Franks and
Paul F. Lambert,
*Early Louisiana and Arkansas
Oil: A Photographic History,
1901–1946* (College Station:

Texas A&M University
Press, 1982), 211–212.
27. Noble Drilling
1995 Annual Report.
28. Ibid.
29. Ibid.
30. Ibid.
31. Faulk, Faulk, and Gray,
Imagination and Ability, 243.
32. McGee, "Horns and
Wings," 284.
33. Minutes of Special
Meeting of Board of Directors
of Noble Drilling Corporation,
Book No. 3, 1 April 1948.
34. Neil Williams, "More Than
675 Drilling Rigs, Third of
Nation's Total, Running in Gulf
Coast Area," *Oil and Gas
Journal,* 24 June 1948, 194.
35. "Running High: Noble
Drilling Corp., Tulsa," *Oil and
Gas Journal,* 24 June 1948, 328.
36. Faulk, Faulk, and Gray,
Imagination and Ability, 270.
37. "Lloyd Noble, Oilman Dies
on Texas Visit," *Dallas Morning
News,* 15 February, 1950.
38. McGee, "Horns and Wings,"
91; Faulk, Faulk, and Gray,
Imagination and Ability, 269.
39. Olson, interview.
40. "Prophecy of Death? Did
Noble Know Time Was Up?"
Daily Oklahoman,
15 February 1950.
41. "Lloyd Noble, Oilman Dies."
42. Faulk, Faulk, and Gray,
Imagination and Ability, 272–273.
43. Roy P. Stewart, "Church
Overflows at Lloyd Noble Rites,"
Daily Oklahoman,
19 February 1950.
44. McGee, "Horns and Wings,"
91; Faulk, Faulk, and Gray,
Imagination and Ability, 268.
45. *Noble Link,* spring 1982, 17.

Chapter Four Sidebar

1. Holt, interview.
2. Faulk, Faulk, and Gray,
Imagination and Ability, 253.
3. Ibid., 281.
4. *Sunday Oklahoman,*
18 October 1998, 1.
5. Noble Foundation
1999 Annual Report.
6. John March, interviewed by
Bob Donahue and Sally Gray,
videotape, 16 September 1999,
Samuel Roberts Noble
Foundation.

Chapter Five

1. McGee, "Horns and Wings," 46.
2. Dugger, interview.
3. Holt, interview.
4. Eugene Rosser,
interviewed by Glenn McGee,
tape recording, 7 May 1976,
Samuel Roberts Noble
Foundation.
5. Noble Affiliates
1979 Annual Report, 5.
6. John L. Kennedy,
*Fundamentals of Drilling—
Technology and Economics*
(Tulsa: PennWell Books,
1983), 20.
7. Ibid., 17.
8. Noble Drilling
1985 Annual Report.
9. Noble Affiliates
1979 Annual Report, 5.
10. Ibid.
11. Noble Drilling
1995 Annual Report.
12. Michael P. Malone, Richard
B. Roeder, and William L. Lang,
*Montana: A History of Two
Centuries* (Seattle: University of
Washington Press, 1991),
335–336.

13. Robert Gramling, *Oil on the Edge: Offshore Development, Conflict, Gridlock* (Albany: State University of New York Press, 1996), 69.

14. William P. Sterne, "Novel Offshore Rig Drills Six Holes from Fixed Derrick," *Oil and Gas Journal,* 11 January 1954, 59.

15. William P. Sterne, "Cheaper by the Half Dozen," *Oil and Gas Journal,* 18 January 1954, 83.

16. Ibid., 85.

17. "Noble Flanges Up One Well, Spuds in Next . . . in One Tour— 8 to 12 Hours," *Oil and Gas Journal,* 18 January 1954, 90.

18. Faulk, Faulk, and Gray, *Imagination and Ability,* 235–236.

19. Noble Drilling 1995 Annual Report.

20. Faulk, Faulk, and Gray, *Imagination and Ability,* 236.

21. Noble Affiliates 1979 Annual Report, 6.

22. Willard Haselbush, "Profile of a Business: Walker Co. Set for Oil Boom," *Denver Post,* 19 January 1964, D1.

23. Ibid.

24. Yergin, *Prize,* 539.

25. Ibid., 523.

26. "By George, He Did It," *Noble Link,* winter 1980, 6.

27. Holt, interview.

28. "Sam Noble," *Noble Link,* 1978, inside cover.

29. Ibid.

30. Noble Drilling 1995 Annual Report.

31. Ibid.

32. Noble Drilling, company brochure, circa 1971.

33. Charles Copeland, interviewed by Anthony L. Wall, tape recording, 3 August 2000, Write Stuff Enterprises.

34. March, interview.

Chapter Six

1. Sam Noble, farewell letter as CEO, Noble Affiliates 1979 Annual Report.

2. James Flanigan, "Helmerich & Payne Versus Parker Drilling," *Forbes,* 54.

3. Noble Drilling, company brochure, circa 1971.

4. Mike Cawley, interviewed by Anthony L. Wall, tape recording, 7 June 2000, Write Stuff Enterprises.

5. Noble Affiliates 1972 Annual Report.

6. Ibid.

7. Sam Noble farewell letter.

8. Yergin, *Prize,* 588.

9. Noble Affiliates, 1972 Annual Report.

10. Barry K. Worthington, "Energy," *The United States: A Handbook* (New York: Facts on File, 1992), 1401.

11. "Ecuadorean Petroleum Developments," *Latin America Economic Report,* LAER II; 30, 120.

12. Noble Affiliates 1975 Annual Report.

13. Noble Affiliates 1976 Annual Report.

14. Noble Affiliates 1977 Annual Report.

15. Ibid.

16. Ann C. Brown, "Give me a B! Give me a U! Give me a Y!," *Forbes,* 20 February 1978.

17. James Day, interviewed by the author and Anthony L. Wall, tape recording, 8 June 2000, Write Stuff Enterprises.

18. Jim West, "U.S. Independents Holding Their 80% Share of Drilling," *Oil & Gas Journal,* 23 October 1978, 85.

19. Ibid.

20. Ibid.

21. "Investors will be playing it cautious," *Business Week,* Industrial Edition, 1978, 66.

22. Noble Affiliates 1979 Annual Report.

23. Noble Affiliates 1972 Annual Report.

Chapter Seven

1. PR Newswire, Ardmore, Oklahoma, 8 April 1980.

2. Noble Affiliates 1980 Annual Report, 2.

3. "A Free-Market Infusion for Synfuels Corp.," *Business Week,* 13 April 1981.

4. "Reagan Taps Noble and Schroeder to a Scaled-Down Synfuels Corp.," *Coal,* May 1981.

5. Noble Affiliates 1980 Annual Report, 7.

6. Ibid.

7. Ibid.

8. Noble Affiliates 1981 Annual Report, 2.

9. PR Newswire, Ardmore, Oklahoma, 7 December 1981.

10. "Drilling-Production," *Oil & Gas Journal,* 19 January 1981.

11. PR Newswire, Ardmore, Oklahoma, 29 December 1981.

12. Ibid.

13. Fred Adlam, "Noble Reengineers Second Jackup Based on Drilling Experience

with First," *Oil & Gas Journal,*
21 February 1983.
14. PR Newswire, Ardmore,
Oklahoma, 7 December 1981.
15. "Rig Expansion Ends,"
Drilling News, published by
Noble Affiliates, January 1983.
16. "Services/Suppliers,"
Oil & Gas Journal,
11 August 1980.
17. Noble Affiliates
1981 Annual Report, 3.
18. "Personals," *Oil & Gas
Journal,* 19 April 1982.
19. "Services/Suppliers,"
Oil & Gas Journal,
20 September 1982.
20. Susan Lee, "The Death
of Commodities?" *Forbes,*
28 January 1985.
21. Noble Affiliates
1982 Annual Report, 2.
22. Noble Affiliates
1983 Annual Report, 2–3.
23. Noble Affiliates
1984 Annual Report, 14.
24. Marcia A. Parker, "Noble's
Butler Sees Recession as Best
Time to Boost Reserves,"
Oil & Gas Journal,
4 July 1983.
25. "In Good Repair," *Noble Link,*
published by Noble Affiliates,
spring 1983.
26. Noble Affiliates
1983 Annual Report, 9.
27. Ibid., 10.
28. "Shallow Rig Purchased,"
Noble newsletter, August 1984.
29. Roy Rhodes, interviewed
by Anthony L. Wall, tape
recording, 8 June 2000,
Write Stuff Enterprises.
30. "Good Help Comes Through
Good Training," *Drilling News,*
published by Noble Affiliates,
January 1983.

31. Noble Affiliates
1981 Annual Report, 5.
32. Noble Affiliates
1984 Annual Report, 15.
33. Southwest Newswire,
Ardmore, Oklahoma, 19
September 1985.
34. Noble Affiliates Notice of
Annual Meeting of Shareholders,
25 March 1985, 10.
35. PR Newswire, Ardmore,
Oklahoma, 24 September 1985.
36. Robert Campbell,
interviewed by the author,
tape recording, 6 June 2000,
Write Stuff Enterprises.
37. "Our Mettle Will Be Tested,"
Noble Link, Summer 1985, 12.

Chapter Eight

1. Noble Drilling
1985 Annual Report, 2.
2. Noble Drilling
1986 Annual Report, 2.
3. Susan Ellerbach, "Tulsan
Eyes U.S. Drilling Industry,"
Tulsa World, 9 October 1988.
4. Day, interview.
5. Bruce Curtis,
"Noble Targets Global
Market for Growth,"
Tulsa Business Chronicle,
29 August 1988.
6. Noble Drilling
1992 Annual Report, 3.
7. Day, interview.
8. Ibid.
9. Curtis, "Noble Targets
Global Market."
10. Noble Drilling
1986 Annual Report, 3.
11. Lynda Bossler, interviewed
by Anthony L. Wall,
tape recording,
18 April 2000,
Write Stuff Enterprises.

12. Shaun Schafer, "Former
Office of Drilling Firm Latest
Downtown Site to Sell,"
Tulsa World, 25 February 1998.
13. Noble Drilling
1987 Annual Report, 2.
14. Day, interview.
15. Ibid.
16. Curtis, "Noble Targets
Global Market."
17. Day, interview.
18. Ibid.
19. Matt Simmons, interviewed
by Anthony L. Wall,
tape recording, 17 August 2000,
Write Stuff Enterprises.
20. Ibid.
21. Nick Swyka, interviewed
by Anthony L. Wall,
tape recording,
1 August 2000,
Write Stuff Enterprises.
22. "Noble Drilling Corp.
Expands Fleet of Land,
Marine Rigs,"
Oil & Gas Journal,
8 February 1988.
23. Swyka, interview.
24. Curtis, "Noble Targets
Global Market."
25. "Noble Drilling to Buy
Bawden Drilling; Seeks Reentry
into International Market,"
Platt's Oilgram News,
8 August 1988.
26. Copeland, interview.
27. Alan Hay, interviewed
by Anthony L. Wall,
tape recording,
8 June 2000,
Write Stuff Enterprises.
28. "Noble Drilling Announces
1988 Results," PR Newswire,
Tulsa, Oklahoma,
26 January 1989.
29. "Results of Noble Drilling
Shareholders' Meeting," PR

Newswire, Tulsa, Oklahoma, 27 April 1989.

30. Noble Drilling 1989 Annual Report, 2.

31. Teresa McUsic, "Noble Drilling Announces Move to Houston," *Tulsa World,* 31 May 1989.

32. Copeland, interview.

33. Bill Jennings, interviewed by Anthony L. Wall, tape recording, August 2000, Write Stuff Enterprises.

34. Simmons, interview.

Chapter Nine

1. Sam Fletcher, "Activity and Hopes Rise for Offshore Sector," *Oil Daily,* 7 May 1990.

2. Ibid.

3. Transcript of CBS News' *Sunday Morning,* 16 September 1990, anchored by Charles Kuralt.

4. Ibid.

5. *Journal of Commerce,* 3 August 1994.

6. Day, interview.

7. Noble Drilling 1991 Annual Report, 2.

8. Bill Rose, interviewed by Anthony L. Wall, tape recording, 4 August 2000, Write Stuff Enterprises.

9. Byron Welliver, interviewed by Melody Maysonet, 10 July 2001, transcript, Write Stuff Enterprises.

10. Noble Drilling 1990 Annual Report, 11.

11. Roger Lewis, interviewed by the author, tape recording, 18 April 2000, Write Stuff Enterprises.

12. Simmons, interview.

13. Ibid.

14. Noble Drilling 1992 Annual Report, 7.

15. Jay Courage, interviewed by Anthony L. Wall, tape recording, 8 September 2000, Write Stuff Enterprises.

16. Noble Drilling 1993 Annual Report, 8.

17. Ibid.

18. Ibid., 10.

19. Stacy D. Johnson, "Noble Remembered as Man Full of Generosity, Integrity," *Daily Oklahoman,* 24 September 1992.

20. Day, interview.

21. "Noble Drilling Corp.," *Inside F.E.R.C.'s Gas Market Report,* 14 February 1992.

22. "Noble Cuts Back," *Platt's Oilgram News,* 5 February 1992.

23. Mary Jo Nelson, "Drilling Firm Ends State Operations," *Daily Oklahoman,* 5 February 1992.

24. Noble Drilling 1990 Annual Report, 6–7.

25. Noble Drilling 1992 Annual Report, 10.

26. Noble Drilling 1993 Annual Report, 10.

27. *Noble Link,* fall 1992, 10.

28. Jennings, interview.

29. Noble Drilling 1992 Annual Report, 9.

30. Ibid., 13.

31. Noble Drilling 1993 Annual Report, 12.

32. "Noble Drilling Expands Operations into Mexico," PR Newswire, Houston, Texas, 22 January 1993.

33. Noble Drilling 1990 Annual Report, 5.

34. Larry Perras, interview by Melody Maysonet, tape recording, 21 December 2000, Write Stuff Enterprises.

35. Noble Drilling 1989 Annual Report, 5.

36. Noble Drilling 1991 Annual Report, 2.

37. Noble Drilling 1993 Annual Report, 12.

38. Hay, interview.

39. *Noble Link,* fall 1992, 4.

40. Noble Drilling 1989 Annual Report, 6–7.

41. Day, interview.

42. Mark Burns, interviewed by Anthony L. Wall, tape recording, 4 August 2000, Write Stuff Enterprises.

43. Noble Drilling 1992 Annual Report, 12.

44. Ibid.

45. Ibid.

46. Ibid., 9.

47. Noble Drilling 1993 Annual Report, 12–13.

48. Ibid.

49. Noble Drilling 1991 Annual Report, 7–8.

50. Ibid., 8.

51. Noble Drilling 1992 Annual Report, 8.

52. Ibid., 5.

53. "Offshore Logistics and Noble Drilling Announce Joint Interest in Production Services Business," PR Newswire, Houston, Texas, 17 July 1992.

54. Michael Crowden, "Grasso, Noble Form Partnership," *Offshore,* July 1993.

55. "Grasso Corporation Announces Signing of Definitive Agreement with Noble Drilling Corporation and Offshore

Logistics, Inc.," Southwest
Newswire, Houston, Texas,
9 June 1993.
56. Noble Drilling
1993 Annual Report, 3.
57. Welliver, interview.
58. Noble Drilling
1993 Annual Report, 1.

Chapter Ten

1. Noble Drilling
1994 Annual Report, 1.
2. Ibid., 2.
3. Ibid.
4. Ibid., 4.
5. Day, interview.
6. Larry Richardson, interviewed
by Anthony L. Wall,
tape recording,
21 July 2000,
Write Stuff Enterprises.
7. Kurt Hoffman, interviewed
by the author, tape recording,
19 December 2000,
Write Stuff Enterprises.
8. Richardson, interview.
9. "Noble Drilling Corporation
Announces Completion of Chiles
Offshore Corporation Merger,"
PR Newswire, Houston, Texas
16 September 1994.
10. Firas Barazi, "Merger of
Noble, Chiles Offshore to
Create Largest Drilling
Contractor in Gulf of Mexico,"
Oil Daily, 15 June 1994.
11. "Noble Drilling Services Inc.
Names New Officers," Southwest
Newswire, Houston, Texas,
16 September 1994.
12. Danny Adkins, interviewed
by the author, tape recording,
18 April 2000,
Write Stuff Enterprises.
13. Jennings, interview.
14. Day, interview.

15. "West Africa: Rising Demand
for Rigs," Africa Energy & Mining,
18 October 1995.
16. "Three Houston Contractors
Sign Rig Transactions,"
Oil & Gas Journal, 17 July 1995.
17. Dave Beard, interviewed
by Anthony L. Wall,
tape recording,
18 April 2000,
Write Stuff Enterprises.
18. Jennings, interview.
19. Ibid.
20. "New IDEAS to Improve
Rig Performance, Safety,"
Noble Link, spring 1995.
21. "New Frontiers,"
Noble Link, winter 1998, 4.
22. "Noble Offshore Awarded
Hibernia Contract,"
Oil Daily, 5 August 1994.
23. Hoffman, interview.
24. Ibid.
25. "Noble Drills Deepest Well
in Western Newfoundland,"
Noble Link, fall 1984, 6.
26. "Noble Named 'Approved'
Drilling Contractor by Amoco,"
Noble Link, summer 1994, 5.
27. Rhodes, interview.
28. Adkins, interview.
29. Day, interview.
30. Noble Drilling
1996 Annual Report, 4.
31. James C. Day's testimony
before the Oversight and
Investigations Subcommittee
and the Energy and Mineral
Resources Subcommittee,
23 June 1994.
32. Agic Salpukas, "Offshore
Drilling Now Seems Potential
Investment Territory," New York
Times, 30 June 1994.
33. "EVA-4000: New Life
for Noble Rigs,"
Noble Link, summer 1998, 2.

34. Jitendra Prasad, interviewed
by the author,
tape recording,
10 November 2000,
Write Stuff Enterprises.
35. Ray Tyson, "Noble
Drilling to Shift Whole Fleet
to Deepwater Units,"
Platt's Oilgram News,
20 September 1996.
36. Rick Hogan, "Noble Signs
4-Year Contract with Shell Oil,
Plans to Convert Rig to Drill
in Deep Water," Oil Daily,
27 December 1996.
37. Ibid.
38. Beard, interview.
39. Welliver, interview.
40. John Rynd, interviewed
by Anthony L. Wall,
tape recording,
18 April 2000,
Write Stuff Enterprises.
41. Jennings, interview.
42. Adkins, interview.
43. Jennings, interview.
44. Day, interview.
45. "EVA-4000: New Life," 3.
46. Noble Drilling
1997 Annual Report, 12.
47. "Noble Drilling Corporation
Makes Announcement," PR
Newswire, Houston, Texas,
26 April 1996.
48. Jennings, interview.
49. Rose, interview.
50. Nelson Antosh, "Noble
Agrees to Buy Unit of Dutch
Firm; Deal Would Increase Its
Size by 25 Percent," Houston
Chronicle, 15 March 1996.
51. Rynd, interview.
52. Noble Drilling
1996 Annual Report, 1.
53. "Moody's and S&P
Raise Assessments of Noble
Drilling's Senior Notes,"

Petroleum Finance Week, 17 June 1996.
54. "S&P Puts Noble Drilling on Its Watch List Following Agreement to Buy Neddrill," *Petroleum Finance Week,* 6 May 1996.
55. "Noble Drilling Announces Letter of Intent for First EVA Conversion and Rig Acquisition," PR Newswire, Houston, Texas, 23 December 1996.
56. "Drilling Contractor Pursues Deeper Ambitions Following Merger," *Offshore,* August 1997.
57. "Nabors Industries Announces Acquisition of Land Drilling Rigs from Noble Drilling Corporation," Business Wire, Houston, Texas, 16 December 1996.
58. Lewis, interview.
59. Adkins, interview.
60. Lewis, interview.
61. Noble Drilling 1996 Annual Report, 1–2.
62. Ibid., 5.
63. William Furlow, "Drillers Can't Wait for Wall Street," *Offshore,* June 1997.
64. Welliver, interview.
65. Noble Drilling 1997 Annual Report, 5, 7.
66. "Noble, Petrobras Sign Deal," *Oil Daily,* 31 March 1997.
67. Noble Drilling 1997 Annual Report, 9.
68. Ibid., 7.
69. Ibid.
70. "Drilling Feats Rewrite World Record Book," *Noble Link,* winter 1998, 2.
71. Hillary Durgin, "Pride Petroleum to Buy Jack-up Rigs from Noble," *Houston Chronicle,* 20 February 1997.

72. Courage, interview.
73. Noble Drilling 1997 Annual Report, 1.
74. Ibid., 12.
75. Day, interview.
76. "Fortunes Are Cyclical, Noble Drilling Corp. Reminds Investors," *Calgary Herald* (Canada), 2 September 1997.

Chapter Eleven

1. Noble Drilling 1998 Annual Report, 12.
2. Ibid., 2.
3. "Noble Drilling Corp. Rtgs Raised," Business Wire, New York, 22 April 1998.
4. "Fortune Ranks America's 100 Fastest-Growing Companies," PR Newswire, New York, 8 September 1998.
5. Michael Davis, "Lower Oil Prices Force New Batch of Major Layoffs," *Houston Chronicle,* 23 October 1998.
6. "A Message from the President," *Noble Link,* summer 1998, 1.
7. "Noble Drilling Corporation Announces Promotions and Retirements," PR Newswire, Houston, Texas, 30 December 1999.
8. "Noble Seeks Acquisition," *Tulsa World,* 27 December 1998.
9. Noble Drilling 1998 Annual Report, 8.
10. Ibid., 7.
11. Ibid., 8.
12. Ibid.
13. Ibid.
14. Mavis Scanlon, "Thrifty Fleet Overhaul Is Thrilling Investors in Noble Drilling," TheStreet.com, 8 December 1999.

15. PR Newswire, Houston, Texas, 2 October 1998.
16. "First EVA-4000 Conversions Leave the Shipyard," *Noble Link,* spring 1999, 4.
17. Noble Drilling 1998 Annual Report, 7.
18. Noble Drilling 1999 Annual Report, 6.
19. Hans Deul, interviewed by Anthony L. Wall, tape recording, 18 April 2000, Write Stuff Enterprises.
20. Jerry Greenberg, "Noble Drilling Preparing Alloy Riser for Ultra-deepwater Unit," *Offshore,* January 2000.
21. Adkins, interview.
22. Greenberg, "Noble Drilling Preparing Alloy Riser."
23. "First EVA-4000 Conversions Leave," 5.
24. Campbell, interview.
25. Ibid.
26. "Noble Drilling Corporation Announces Promotion," PR Newswire, Houston, Texas, 3 December 1998.
27. Noble Drilling 1999 Annual Report, 3.
28. "Noble Drilling Corporation Announces Promotions and Retirements," PR Newswire, Houston, Texas, 30 December 1999.
29. Noble Drilling 1999 Annual Report, 2.
30. Scanlon, "Thrifty Fleet Overhaul Is Thrilling."
31. "The Noble Paul Wolff: Deepwater Success Story," *Noble Link,* spring 2000, 9.
32. Prasad, interview.
33. Leo Segerius, interviewed by Melody Maysonet, transcript, 10 July 2001, Write Stuff Enterprises.

34. Campbell, interview.
35. Segerius, interview.
36. "Organizational Development," *Noble Link,* spring 2000, 2.
37. "Noble Employee Makes Safety Top Priority," *Noble Link,* spring 2000, 11.
38. Noble Drilling 1999 Annual Report, 7.
39. Rhodes, interview.
40. "Safety Leadership Conference Attendees Revise, Update Procedure Manual," *Noble Link,* spring 2000, 3.
41. Noble Drilling 1999 Annual Report, 7.
42. Rhodes, interview.
43. Mike Cadigan, interviewed by Melody Maysonet, transcript, 10 July 2001, Write Stuff Enterprises.
44. "Noble Drilling North Sea Jackup Receives ISO 14001 Certification from DNV," PR Newswire, Houston, Texas, 30 May 2000.
45. Cees van Diemen, interviewed by Melody Maysonet, transcript, 17 July 2001, Write Stuff Enterprises.
46. Cadigan, interview.
47. Jimmy Puckett, interviewed by Melody Maysonet, transcript, 10 July 2001, Write Stuff Enterprises.
48. Cadigan, interview.

49. Ibid.
50. Noble Drilling 1999 Annual Report, 2.
51. Hoffman, interview.
52. Rynd, interview.
53. Jon Murphy, interviewed by Anthony L. Wall, tape recording, 21 July 2000, Write Stuff Enterprises.
54. Beard, interview.
55. Noble Drilling 1999 Annual Report, 5.
56. "Service Companies Downplay Financials, Focus on Technology," *Oil & Gas Investor,* May 2000.
57. "A Message from the Chairman," *Noble Link,* winter 2000, 1.
58. Welliver, interview.
59. Steven Manz, interviewed by Melody Maysonet, tape recording, 3 July 2001, Write Stuff Enterprises.
60. Ibid.
61. Ibid.
62. Noble Drilling 1999 Annual Report, 7.
63. "Noble Drilling Announces Formation of Joint Venture with CROSCO," PR Newswire, Houston, Texas, 14 June 2000.
64. Lewis, interview.
65. "Triton Engineering to Focus on Revised Business Model," Sugar Land, Texas, 26 October 2000.

66. Tom O'Rourke, interviewed by Anthony L. Wall, tape recording, 8 June 2000, Write Stuff Enterprises.
67. "Noble Drilling Corporation Announces New Chief Financial Officer," PR Newswire, Sugar Land, Texas, 1 September 2000.
68. "Noble Drilling Reports Second Quarter 2000 Results," PR Newswire, Sugar Land, Texas, 27 July 2000.
69. Campbell, interview.
70. "The Wall Street Transcript Publishes Interview with Noble Drilling CEO James Day," Business Wire, New York, 21 September 2000.
71. Ronald Hoope, interviewed by Melody Maysonet, tape recording, 10 July 2001, Write Stuff Enterprises.
72. Bernie Wolford, interviewed by Melody Maysonet, tape recording, 17 July 2001, Write Stuff Enterprises.
73. Ibid.
74. Van Diemen, interview.
75. Hoope, interview.
76. Ibid.
77. Lewis, interview.
78. Julie Robertson, interviewed by Anthony L. Wall, tape recording, 8 June 2000, Write Stuff Enterprises.
79. Day, interview.

INDEX